Twilight
on the
Thunderbird

A Memoir of Quileute Indian Life

by

Howard Hansen
'cKulell'
"Sea Gull"

ISBN: 978-1-60944-071-8

Printed at Third Place Press, Lake Forest Park, on the Espresso Book Machine v.2.2.
thirdplacepress.com

This memoir has been in process since 1958. It has caused frustration, dejection, hope, doubt; and now at last, those time-eaters are done.

Possibly no one can know the rocks in the paths of one such as I but for who has lived it.
Joanne has lived for over forty years waiting for this work. For forty years in hope and patience and now, Joey, here's what you waited for.

It's dedicated to you.

Contents

Introduction

by Brian Herbert

Howard Hansen is one of the most interesting people you could ever possibly meet. Born a Quileute Indian at La Push on the northwest coast of Washington State, his tribal name is *cKulell*, which means "Seagull." He is an elder in the tribe, and once said to me, "Brian, I spend more time in the spirit world than in this one." He went on to tell me that when he was a boy, the elders of the tribe noticed that he was especially gifted in the spirit realm, and that he was far more cerebral than other young Quileutes. For this reason, the old men and women took him under their wing, and taught him special things.

Howie is my godfather, and has spoken to me often of the elders of his tribe who watched over him when he was a boy in the 1930s, including one named *Se-ic-tiss*, an elderly man who was known for his skill at carving the emblem of the tribe in wood, a thunderbird carrying a whale in its claws. *Se-ic-tiss* had been born in 1857, before whites ever went to La Push—a settlement so isolated that it did not receive word of the assassination of Abraham Lincoln until ten years after it happened. By the 1930s La Push was still isolated, and anyone wanting to get in or out either rode a canoe between the native village and Neah Bay or took a dirt road that had been built around 1920, so narrow that two small Model T Fords could only pass one another with difficulty on it.

In his youth, Howie said there was a solid forest of old growth trees that stretched from La Push to Forks on the Olympic Peninsula —fourteen miles of verdant primeval trees, thousands of years old. He recalled one place on the way that was a dip extending for half a mile, and on both sides Sitka spruce trees stood so tall that they obliterated the sky and formed a dark tunnel, with light at each end. Now all of that is gone, destroyed by timber companies and developers.

When my father, the famed author Frank Herbert, met Howie in the 1940's, the young Indian had recently left the reservation, and had been adopted by a Danish fisherman in Seattle. Soon after meeting, the two young men were talking about vagabonding around the world. Frank Herbert and Howie Hansen were explorers and adventurers at heart, men who were intensely curious about innumerable subjects. (I have written of their interesting relationship in *DREAMER OF DUNE*, the biography of Frank Herbert.)

In 1958, Howie told Frank Herbert about the lost forestlands near La Push, and he lamented about the Quileute way of life that was also vanishing. Howie said the entire world was dying, because it was being misused by western civilizations that plundered resources from the planet and did not give back to it.

"White men are eating the earth," Howie said. "They're gonna turn this whole planet into a wasteland, just like North Africa." Frank Herbert agreed, and responded that earth could eventually become so decimated that it would be a "big dune." His incredibly popular, best-selling novel *DUNE* (1965) describes exactly that—a planet covered with sand. The legendary novel, which is the most admired book in science fiction, contains many important intellectual layers. One of them is the powerful environmental-protection message, and Frank Herbert based that in part upon discussions he had with his best friend, Howard Hansen.

For much of his life, Howie has assembled the lore and language of his native people, supplementing his own copious writings (more than a million words) with tape recordings and his own drawings of the personalities he knew in the tribe, and depictions of the serene coastal village where they lived, La Push. He is a terrific artist, and for years he has been an art instructor in Seattle.

Some of Howie's written documentation has involved the language of the Quileute, which has many complex sounds, such as one that requires putting the tongue up against the back of the teeth and blowing, like trying to say "L" in English. Anthropologists say the Quileute language is thousands of years old, going back farther than any native tongue in the Pacific Northwest. It was in that remarkable mode of communication that stories and lessons were passed on orally for thousands of years, an unwritten tradition going from tribal member to tribal member—a practice that is fading away with the passage of time.

Now, with the Quileute nation assimilating into western culture, and the traditional ways of *cKulell*'s people vanishing (including their language), Howie feels an urgency to tell the story of his people, so that it will not be lost to the young men and women of his tribe.

Here is a portion of that immense chronicle, written by an elder who knows his subject well. . . .

PREFACE

At Ocean, near Ozette *Old Village* site is a place known as Cape Alava. This is the farthest West point of land of the contiguous United States. About eighteen and a half miles southerly of Cape Alava lies La Push, reserved for *Quileute* Indians, beside a once strong running riffle-filled river named *Quillayute*. This river's near five-mile length gives an *'est'* to Washington State: short*est* navigable river...perhaps the shortest navigable river in North America between Canada and Mexico. Oregon has the shortest river but it's not navigable.

Another '-est' for this area is 'raini*est*'. Few places in the United States are wetter. Along Olympic Mountains' Western slope such abundant rain falls it feeds one of the world's odd floral growths: Temporate Rain Forest. This Rain Forest shares rain with Vancouver and Queen Charlotte Islands, as well as coastal British Columbia. It isn't the tropical rain forest; this Rain Forest is unique. In Washington State it's the Olympic Peninsula Rain Forest and no other. Coast is wet and chill from *cKlumbyuh* (Columbia River) 'to the poles'. (Note: I know of no 'the' to Quileute language, Ocean is *Ocean*, Lake is *Lake*, People are *People*). Sixteen miles South-Easterly of Quillayute is *Hoh* River; rain-fall is regular; predictable; as at Ketchikan, in South-east Alaska, measured in feet, not inches. Annually, over ten feet of rain isn't unusual. Under ten feet is. Adding to the peculiarity of Olympic Peninsula, past Port Angeles, East-north-easterly of La Push is the city of Sequim, said to have less rain per year than any place on the Pacific Coast of the United States. Except the deserts of Southern California 'they' say.

And it's wild. Explorers who traveled South American jungles reported the vegetation of *this* rain forest as nearly impenetrable. Early in the twentieth century it was of mostly uncharted and unexplored areas. The Olympic Mountains weren't really *explored* until the late 1870s.

The Northwest coast of Washington State is strange, filled with natural oddity. Intrigue. *It is 'spirited'.*

The constant supply of water falling against the Olympics and draining sea-ward made the Quillayute (above high-tide's reach) a tough river. Despite its short length. Until the 1960's. Until then it had all the seasonal violence of a typical Northwest river. Two other rivers, *Sol Duc,* meaning 'clear or sparkling waters' and Bogachiel, meaning 'muddy (water)', join to form the moderately meandering Quillayute, (meaning?—lost). Near Quillayute's mouth, Dicky River, which drains Dicky Lake, adds to the volume. Watershed from the Northwestern part of the Olympic Mountains pours down Sol Duc and Bogachiel (aided by its tributary, *cKlawah*: 'between the rivers'), to drain a vast area of that segment of the mountains: Several heavy streams combined to create what was once a potent little river: Quillayute. Quillayute emptied at Rialto Beach until Northwesterly seas sanded up the mouth (about 1921 we were told). Then River over-flowed; a sand-bar which had held a lagoon in place broke away (where River empties today), on the South-Eastside of *Ahkalut*: ('top of the rock' or island, now called 'James Island' or J.I.), and a new river-mouth was formed. Quillayute was powerful because it had giants backing it. But powerful and tempermental as it was it hadn't been able to drive away its people. In this wild, forgotten corner of North America lived and live the Quileute Indians. Like their river they've been there 'forever'.

The Quileute are considered by some anthropologists to be the original Northwest natives. They, and Chemacum people whom Sealth and his people massacred.

Quileute and Chemacum spoke the same language and it has no relationship to any other, linguists tell us.

'Since the beginning of time' the shadow of *Ahkalut* has fallen on Quileute People (*Po-oke*), at Quillayute River: *Taboke*: 'just this one, *no other river*', Elders said. The drainage system forming Quillayute has been the home of *Po-oke* since the dawn of their knowledge about themselves. They roamed this area hunting, foraging; living; their huge Cedar-plank '*dtick ah tical* ('smoke-houses' ['long-houses' *Hoquat* called them]) dotting the land. Along the several rivers was their laughter and sorrow; the general activities of concentrated life and habitation. They didn't just *live*, they were nearly self-reliant. As with all, their laughter and sorrow were constant. Plain people. In semi-isolation they lived simply, picking varieties of berries; digging Camas bulbs; Clam digging; gathering Mussels; dip-netting Smelt (both Surf and River); trapping returning Salmon in weirs; taking Elk in season. In short supplying the larder for Winter. Camas; Whale; Seal and other foods were traded for what we couldn't supply locally. Quileute people were plentifully endowed with the necessities for living in comparative independence…but as do all, they knew periods of intense need.

It should be said that '*what is*', for us, out there, is still as in 'those days', River is still River, a condition of Great Spirit creation we call by its name, with capital as in any other created thing with first name: Island is Island, Beach is Beach…creations of Great Spirit, thus the recognition of its uniqueness, therefore name of importance.

This will all be presented in that manner, Beach has Beach Spirit or it would be some-thing else; River; Ocean, have individual Spirits to *Po-oke* mind. And therefore named as is one's *Chutsk* (baby), or Horse; or *Byack* (Raven). In our minds what exists is from Divinity; God; Great Spirit, …it has 'Spirit' therefore. Rock Spirit, Tree Spirit…it means that the 'Spirit' is the principle, the design for whatever the element of Great Spirit's design creates.

Their activities were in the 'shadow' of beloved Ahkalut. Ahkalut symbolized home and protection and pride. It has watched them since their arrival, known their history as no other thing but River. It keeps Quileute secrets well, Ahkalut, a steady, sturdy, unmoving bastion knowing *Po-oke* as even they do not.

From the top of the island, from Ahkalut, from many smoke-houses, pale blue driftwood smoke wafted skyward through open-plank vents of the roofs and out into the dark, overcast, rainy skies, sentinels of smoke calling home the whalers and seal-hunters from far at sea. 'Smoking Island' those sea-venturers called it. In any history of Sea-farers, only the stalwart went seeking Seal and Whale. These primitive people' developed sea-hunters as daring as any—faring far seaward for their prey. Hunting from 'simple' dug-out Cedar canoes… "*cKeynoo*'. '*Ahkalut* shadow' grows cooler and more dim as years pass, soon the 'shadow' of Ahkalut will be gone. The day they waken no longer using the Quileute name, can't remember it, it will be a different island: James Island, and the shadows will fall only on a forgotten past, the past of the tribe of *Po-oke* who are no more. History is like that. And the Quileute, without an alphabet, had legend carriers who carried their knowledge of tribal history before the imposition of 'superior knowledge' by the gun-toters.

"Because their history was vocal, one family might carry certain legends and others were entrusted with what was theirs to preserve. When they who were last trained in the family's responsibility, (to keep part of tribal history), have gone, when they have no one to whom they can pass it, their history is lost." I wrote that in 1958. Prophetic: now most of it is lost.

Legend was law; history; education; moral code. The natural questions Peoples ask and their inabilities to answer them satisfactorily in any other way no doubt gave rise to Legends. Ultimately, *Po-oke* answers to natural phenomena were in legend form. How did Animals develop? Why does Wind 'always' blow from West at one place on Coast? From whence came Rivers; Lakes; Storms? The answers to these and other questions were not fables nor tales. They were the history in legend form of all that was. The existence of the Universe was told and accepted through and by Legend.

This is Quileute history as seen and remembered by me. It's history by word-of-mouth and memory. There is no research: no scientific investigation. Living; listening to Elders; these the basis for my effort.

Recording their gone-away-world as they had memory of it and of what I lived for my early years is not an attempt to re-do nor to compose a history for them. It isn't an attempt to make it fit into previously deduced and neat niches. This compilation is as they passed it down, generation to generation. It is their history, not mine, except as *I* was told, as I lived it and heard it told.

Finally, in a sense they were pleased about in 1958 (but for one man and his family), they were unanimous in favor of having an 'insider' report how they had lived in their personal, now gone, way of Life. This is not a 'scientific history' of Quileute People, *Po-oke*. It is the record of my first fourteen years as a La Push boy-child seeking for knowledge of Spirit; Power; Medicine; Great Spirit/God influences.

This is their gift, from their past, to their future, left in books alone. And in many cases is the passing of Legend and Song ownership to the world of the book and tape recorder. They were proud of the gift to themselves by 'the Spirit World' of Songs of Under-standing and Education for one another. It is 'gift' to all, that these proud possessions of the Tribe (through individuals) are committed to tape and paper, given to us.

In 'those days' songs and legends couldn't be repeated without permission of the *current* owner. Only one person could use a particular Song. In those days who was 'gifted' songs was now 'possessor' and able to repeat them. In 1958 these many were given to me to pass, to continue. Without our use and passing all Quileute existence goes.

So too only one person could relate a particular Legend. Legends were *gifted*. Unless one specifically authorized the use of specific legends they were, under penalty of '*spiritual reprisal*', not to be taken by any. Because 'power', i.e. Knowledge, is in Songs; Drumming; Dancing; Legends; full *'power'* alone remains where it isn't diminished by dilution. Thus one 'owner'; one 'user'. Singing, drumming, dancing, these were how *we* prayed.

The eldest Daughter or Son was the traditional heir to Songs and Legends of a family and no other could use them, even brothers and sisters of that heir. The Songs and/or Legends of Mother or Father couldn't be used until given to the heir by them But from the *ceremonial day of gifting* the *parent* may no longer use them. Without permission. They have become an integrated part of the soul of the person to whom they now belong. To Quileute as to others of similar cultures, all things have 'soul'. Even the breath.

They, the Elders, realized (from the evident indifference displayed by more recent generations) that Songs they have recorded (for me for us) and these Legends which are 'entaped' will soon be lost. For this reason they pass them on 'to be in print'.

To recall seventy-years or more after what an Elder seventy-years age-wise, *then* re-counted about 'the old days' isn't extremely difficult for me; it was still 'the old days' when I left and I recall nothing of La Push since then, such as 'modern' times. I'm as remote as their ancestors, but for 'near-ancient' ones, such as I, and Porky Payne...Kenneth. But what I have is not mine...it's property of *Po-oke*: Quileute People.

Compiling these Legends and Songs in an autobiography is fascinating. To Life again (in my mind) are the wonderful, colorful, playful, funny people of *Then*, of 'that was La Push': *La Push was like that*. That's what I want to convey.

Historically it is impossible to find 'the beginning of being here' and Time. Western Time and Native Time are not same in any way.

Western Time segments mechanically; Native Time is *right now.* (Different too are directions per *compass:* North, East, South, West, western style. But Native directions are *Sunrise* way, *Sunset* way, *Cold* way (North), *Warm* way (South), Center…(where we are), and Up and Down. Thus time and direction are totally relative to conditions each of us is experiencing.

In this work, where 'Legend relating' is from 1958 recordings, the linguistic, the grammatical presentation is adhered to. Many of them were recorded by Uncle Yum. Boyhood 'mental recordings and the verbal presentations' are as close as memory allows. Not too difficult to recall inasmuch as it was 'our way'. There is no formal 'most contributory person'. Any *Po-oke* can be singled out by me as most contributory, meaning that whatever that person gave was imperative to my recollections of *Po-oke* and La Push. None were not important; none were more important. But I have to mention the marvelous gift of time and self of Uncle 'Yum', William E. 'Little Bill' Penn. (Uncle Yum crossed The River in the early 1960's).

He owned many songs not originally his family's property. They were passed to him as Elders lay dying…knowing his power and knowing their Spirit gifts would be protected. He was recognized as one of the most powerful thinkers of his tribe; being recognized as far away as Washington D.C. as a tremendous aid to *Po-oke* and other local natives.

Coastal Tribes knew him, his value. When President F. D. Roosevelt made a touring car trip around Olympic Peninsula in the later '30s, the combined Indian tribes appointed Uncle Yum the official Indian escort to ride beside the president, to tell of difficulties the Natives were having. This is but one of the honors Native People had bestowed upon him. The great value to the young of my day, out there, of people such as Uncle Yum, was 'The Uncle' (*Chi-ila*) status they brought…or AUNT! (*cKai-is*). Guidance for the benefit of the Tribe and the benefit of 'the guided'.

Of 'legends recording' by Uncle Yum he said, "There are few of us who could do this. Many Indians could speak fluent English but few could translate freely from Indian to English or vice-versa. When you been trained to think quick as in Quileute tongue, it's a hard job. Translating. English takes too much time to tell. A few words in Quileute tell the same story faster."

"Mr. Roosevelt had me to Washin'ton D.C. to Congress and I talked. First in Quileute. Then I said it in English. It made 'em mad, what I said, I guess, they stood up and hollered, clapped their hands, hollerin'!" Then he laughed. "Fun trip."

I laughed too and said, "That was a standing ovation they gave you Uncle Yum!"

"Ay-y. That's what they said. Scared me though so I come home fast. Suppose they run after you and catch you, that many." He smiled at a random thought about 'that day' during 'those days', and I examined his beautiful Indian face, and head…I looked lovingly at an adored Elder from my childhood, who had tried to guide me to 'his ways' of seeing Life. As I laughed I said, "You coulda come back every day talkin' *Po-oke* they'd never understand an' you'd get free lunch everyday."

"Let's go then," he said. But in an instant his 'presence' was diverted as he pondered. "In the history of our relations with Whites, probably no more than twenty, thirty Indians been capable to translate *Ha-atch*…good. I think less than half a dozen whites were able to do it. We think different than they do." Our God is Great Spirit, Great Mystery. They love *Gold* as God: 'What can I do to get more?' It buy them everything but Peace. Where do you see happy face on the people over there (anywhere)?. Yet the poor condition of Life we live, most *Po-oke* in Village smiles, laughs, jokes, like Black People. Our purpose in Life was to help each other. They (non-*Po-oke*) try to own all the money so they can benefit from everyone else. We think different. The person who keeps working for self gets avoided here, don't need 'em.

"To try to convert Quileute into English or other way is near impossible. You got to be able to think two ways absolute opposite at base and understand 'em both."

Uncle Yum may not be most important contributor because each was as important to what I learned as any other. They dedicated themselves to instructing in Truth. From some I heard and saw more than from others but the importance was equal. I loved and do love them all. They were my People. Now mostly unknown by me, the Young, the Adults, the Elders are still *Po-oke* in Spirit; still trying to Live Life without offense to any; still trying to Live without interference; still my people.

Obviously, without knowledge through use of language the thinking isn't possible. No more can we think in Latin than in ancient

Egyptian. The colloquialisms and vernacular and the swearing is lost to the descendents. An example of the difference between Quileute and English American: In English, 'Please come into our home as our guest. Our family is your servant. We will take great pleasure in attending your needs. You will be safe and protected while you remain with us. Please honor us with your presence.' Quileute would say '*cKola ahlash*'. The same meaning would be involved. Who thinks that way today? Play acting 'elders' with more knowledge of football and its players than of *Hoo-Day Hoo-Day* girls?

Impressed as I am with the history of the ancient Egyptians there is no manner on Earth by which I could behave or think in their ways. Even to Live in Egypt now peopled by 'inheritors', not even descendents, it would be impossible for me to become 'Egyptian'. When the Living Life Style has passed it will not be reclaimed. For who was denied the way of *Po-oke* life for three generations tell me how the return will be possible. All one can do is to recall what one can of what one experienced and compare it to the effort to re-birth via snippets and anthropological recordings, incomplete as they may be.

This is not a 'scientific history' of Quileute People, *Po-oke*, it is the record of my first fourteen years as a Child seeking for knowledge of Spirit; Power; Medicine; Great Spirit/God influences.

There is a glossary of conceptualized words…it's impossible for letters of the alphabet to depict 'hiss-like' sounds, clicking at the back of the teeth, and on and on. There are sounds never heard outside Quileute conversation as in those days of almost a century ago. There must be as many *Po-oke* sounds to make words as are in English, with few similarities. An example is *cKwyeh-Tee*, likely the same rascally character as Coyote to other Amerians. Oddly similar sound to the names. *cKwyeh-Tee* and Coyote (Coyote said 'Kyo-tee') I think Oddly similar behavior characteristics.

cKwyeh-Tee as 'heard word' begins with a popping at the top-back of the tongue, similar to trying to dispel a fish-bone at the throat/tongue saying the 'CK' of 'stu*ck*' or 'tru*ck*' at the 'popping' out of the breath. The rest is easy.

ACKNOWLEDGEMENTS

The first thing I recall of 80 years, or thereabouts, is of approaches to me by others, parents are a huge part of that certainly, but the first impression I have of 'other' influences on my Life has to be 'Old Man,' 'Doctor Lester': Lester Payne. He and Lavan Coe were brothers and men of awesome Spiritual Power. (Often I wonder if 'Dr.' Lester Payne was related to Tommy Payne, also 'BIG Power' at La Push. Little Bill Penn put a funnel to my head and never stopped pouring information about *Po-oke*.

It began as I was looking at a shrub in our front yard, unaware of the other people nearby. I started at the question by Dr. Lester.

"What you doin' *sitsqua* (little boy)," he asked me.

"Findin' out what it feels like to be green," I answered.

He was elated. "He's one of them," he shouted, "I pick HIM!"

A lively discussion followed, Mama telling him he was a crazy old man and to forget about

'That *Spirit* stuff,' and 'he don't need it!'

"You know our ways," he said. "I pick him."

That began an ongoing journey. It started a Life based on Quileute Indian teachings. From then on, I was taken to Lodge meetings of *Tss'y'uck* (fishermen/whalers/seal hunters); of *Tloquali* (wolf mask, black face society); *Tsaywhutleok* society (hunters on land—Elk hunters, Deer, Bear, Grouse, etc.), where I learned Quileute mythology and legend, learned to drum and sing Spirit songs of *power*, to analyze Life.

In lodge I heard and saw men behave differently (than outside, in village life). Grant Eastman's dance (he could hurl a harpoon through a swimming seal); Joe Pullen, last Quileute to take a whale (his drumming and singing). And the man who was famous for Elk hunting power, Stanley Grey. Morton Peck was *Tsyuck*, said to hear the thoughts of fish; of ocean dwellers.

They talked about the 'world of the mind,' unseen but known to them. Stanley Grey told me about 'Etherea' and how to get there.

Se-ic-Tiss Ward was called *Lawotsakil* (Wolf). He became a dedicated cedar carver, who carved a Quileute icon (of Whale and Thunderbird in the 1930s), *Se-ic-Tiss* was said to have been born in 1857 or 1858. He laughed when he told about the 'Great White Chief' who was shot (Lincoln). He laughed because the news didn't get to La Push until he was about 18, ten years later.

There are *Hoquats* (Whites) who were blessings. John Hansen, a Danish boat-builder who took me to live with him and his son Jack in Ballard, without other family, when I was 14. This man, 'Dad,' is likely to have been the most influential person away from La Push whom I have known. Certainly his sense of justice, his honor, his boat-building ability, his personal character of 'fair-play' brings no equal to mind (Try taking an unruly La Push native kid into your home and still be concerned and protective).

Wayne Richwine was certainly a blessing.

Other influential people who kept me from prison, inadvertently, without knowing it are too numerous to recall, but certainly the ancestors of today's population of La Push are not forgotten. In some order of recalling them, the adult's of the 1920s, 30s, and 40s La Push rush in, they who constituted the civilization of a people emerging from a different way of Life. They were my guides. They were my heroes. To them I give limitless loyalty. Blessed who knew them.

Quileute Reservation was our nation. We were overwhelmed by 1942 or 1943, and the ceremonies of thousands of years were forgotten. They talked about it but Lodge practices were done. In a group, helping one another with food and shelter, we were invincible. Overseen, we lost.

I have to thank Frank '*Dune*' and Bev Herbert, and their son Brian, my godson, and his family for encouraging this autobiography: (*To record the lost ways of a once independent people who weren't war-like enough.* ~Frank) It's impossible to thank all who aided me along THE TRAIL. Who trusted and thanked *me* (!!!!) for whatever I might have contributed to their Lives, are dear to my heart. Commercial fisherwomen and men in Alaska gave much of friendship and acceptance. Having imposed on Dr. J. (James Thomas, PhD) for advice, I have a deep appreciation for it. His readiness to involve in this work amazes me. Having read his insightful book *The Shaman in the Disco and Other Dreams of Masculinity*, several times, I find his advice more beneficial than had I not seen his recorded thoughts and gained insight into his seeking mind.

'Little Bill' Penn made me into a spiritual son. His advice and information about the People knew no tiring, the same with 'Big Bill' Penn. Others who trusted me and helped guide my direction, my goals, were Tyler Hobucket; Chester Johnson; Dema and Billy Hudson; Mark Williams; Carrie Grey (Stanley's wife); Charley Howeattle and Mary; Freddy Woodruff and Sarah and family: Russ, Sonny, Nola; Russ and Stephanie's family; Sonny's and Jill's family; the Payne family; Jacksons; Sailto; Joe and Cecile Pullen; the Masons; the Wards. In this line of thanks, whether remarked or not some may be overlooked. Not by lack of importance, but by my lack of youthful remembrance. Susie Morganroth was kind. The Clevelands; Hank Taylor; Rosy and Roy Black and their family (Vern, my age); these are some of those to be remembered. (Rosy Black was Tommy Payne and Elsa's daughter, as was Walter their son); the Bright family; these are some of 'them.' I can think of a few with whom I've been out of step. The rest of my associates, co-workers and/or employers have been enormously beneficial and important to me. Many have heard of this project and wondered about it and the progress, if any, over the years since 1958. Many thanks to *Kwash Kwash* (Jay) Powell and Vickie, and deep thanks to Barbara Brotherton of the Seattle Art Museum. No limit exists for whom to thanks. Additionally, Ingrid Welti and her son Russ are huge in this work. Peggy Obrien Murphy is priceless for who and what she is. Her husband Seamus is thanked for his patience. And not forgotten is Vlad Verano of Third Place Press in Lake Forest Park. No parallel in helpfulness, patience personified. Thanks Vlad.

Liatskal-acks (Thank you) to the Great Spirit for it all.

cKulell.

TWILIGHT ON THE THUNDERBIRD

BELL, DRUMS
and SHAKER CHURCH

Looking back, over the decades of my Life, I recognize a 'base', a fundamental sensation not lost over the years. I 'see', at home in our small Ocean Coastal Village, two things 'focusing' us: a Bell as 'messenger' (at its end by my Birth); and Village drumming.

Attention demanding, sometimes ominous, a message spread throughout Village at the deep, almost sad, throb of Shaker Church Bell. Bells sing with different voices no matter where, yet bells heard in years of world roaming have not affected me as did Shaker Church Bell. Coast Guards had a bell below the look-out tower which would be rung according to the language of ship's bells, one ring added each half hour to total eight, then renew. That bell was like a ticking clock, heard and understood, though unconsciously.

One buoy anchored out from James Island, *Ahkalut*...the 'Whistler'...had a bell, most commanding on nights of no wind and big seas. Another buoy was 'the Skunk', painted black and white. It 'moaned'. I loved to lay on dry Beach-sand at night listening to 'Whistler's' 'bong', 'Skunk' moaning: the music of buoys playing as backdrop for Surf; Star-shine; shooting stars; the Milky Way. Now, *today*, 'street' arc-lights render star viewing impossible against a sky no longer black; auto traffic blunts the buoys' songs. The mystique of night-time's *cKwahleh* Beach is gone. (*cKwahleh* is Quileute for Ocean). Few views of Milky Way are had.

(Because of its importance to Tribal Life I want to explain about Shaker Church and its importance to our Lives. Shakers were not Christian nor accepted *by any Christian community*. We used certain impressive-to-us elements of Christian dogma, the sign of the cross from Catholicism; singing praises to the Great Spirit as Protestant-ism displays; pantheism as expressed in some Oriental [and other] beliefs; we were none of these but included what seemed appropriate to thanking God/Great Spirit for what it gave) from all.

Commercial Salmons-fisher-boats from 'over there' (other places) had mandatory fog-bells. Ashore, we could hear them on calm, foggy days, muted by the thick air. Ordinary bells. Each saying one thing, "Here I am, in Fog!" Speaking its own in-built message. By the tone we knew the bell, knowing the bell we knew why it spoke. Impressive bell voices to me were bells (just aft of the stem on the bows of merchant ships) which were rung by the bow-lookout. Bells have voices which seem to remain same.

But not *Church Bell*. *Bell* had different voices; different respons-es. When Bell spoke to Village at night it was for Church or prede-termined function. In day-time, apprehension gripped the hearts of young and old alike. It might be saying Death visited; it might call for funeral; to call us together about Baby/Child missing; or fire call, whatever. No single condition of day-time Village Life attracted such total and immediate attention as first clang of Bell. From whatever 'corner' of Village, the second clang was accompanied by the pounding of running feet as Children and Dogs raced to Church to learn 'cause' then to race back toward 'plodding' Adults to report.

Bell could be dirgeful; soft; harsh; demanding. It was messenger for La Push.

Bell rang early on Sunday, 7 December, 1941. (Hearing the news I knew, instinctively, that our world had been sunk with the *Arizona*. And it had been. War-time kills most of human gain. But 'winners' make buckets of money).

Bell-voice wasn't loud, but carried. People said they could hear it as far as Hobbies Mitt farm (Harvey Smith farm). Really, more 'feel' it. I don't know if Maxfield, farming over a mile away, ever heard it. That would depend on wind of course. The peal wasn't a shrill high pitched ringing nor a deep, Asian-temple bronze window-shatterer. With many voices, Bell was speaking directly to the hearer, giving information as watch-Dog speaks to owner.

Strangely, I think of the beverage 'green-tea' as way of describ-ing Bell's voice. Too weak, green tea is as I imagine grass in water to taste: vapid. Too strong and it's astringent in the mouth. Sometimes tea made strong enough to taste its essence, soothing, warm, refreshing, might have soaked 'the trifle-too-long' with sharp astringency detectable. Perfect, for me, is that green tea which flows sweet, clean. A refreshing brew where the taste sensations continue. Bell was like that. Bell was mellow, without harshness. I loved Bell. There was Church; there was Surf; there was Bell. We were they who were blessed, having this kind of Spiritual protection.

Bell disappeared between demolition of Old Church and construction of new, and, but for a short passage of its voice which I recorded in 1958, I know of no other recording. No one seems to know what happened to Bell. I've pondered describing that voice, Bell's voice, for over seventy years, but find no way. I can point the trails usable to 'get to' the voice, but I can't make you hear it. A terminal loss.

These are descriptions to consider: No matter where one stood, in Village in front of Church door or at Hobbies Mitt's, Bell voice seemed to be same in intensity. It didn't seem, even to my Child's ears, to be loud closer to it and 'weaker' away.

Justifiably I think, I'd call its tone Spiritual, because even those of poor hearing-ability heard Bell. Or was it 'felt'? All *knew* Bell. Like SPIRIT, deny or accept but all '*hear*' it.

There was, in fact, a true spiritual communication between Bell and those of us who lived under its protection, its protective, gathering-power. There's a warning harshness to the ringing of a train bell… it penetrates by unsubtle force, and fire-truck bells. But Bell's voice was almost apologetic There was a 'mute' value to it, yet commercial-fishermen outside River said they had heard it "way offshore'. It wasn't high pitch in voice, nor basso profundo. From it came a quality of purity and beauty heard in many Oriental bell/gongs (heard shortly *after* the initial shock of 'the fist' striking, of whatever form). Bell voice reverberated after the last clapper-strike, finally disappearing in Air as does vanishing Mist.

First Shaker Church is gone. Bell is gone. Together with Village. Without Bell, Village died. No more calling together of *Po-oke*.

Shaker Church was old when I was young, 'born' in 1800's I heard. As far back as '90 or earlier? (Today, new Shaker Church stands where Old Church kept Ground dry). Beside it in those days was a meeting/eating hall. In both were old 'iron' tanks (or perhaps old oil-drums) converted to wood-burning Stoves . Even *Chutsk* knew the position of the Stoves and at Church sought the warming balm at Winter Tribal gatherings. Not for too long, however. From Stove, and with Hall filled with exercising Shakers, Building warmed fast.

Shaker Church opened to a bell-tower porch which was one step above the outside ground. From Porch another step up led in, through Door-way, to the interior.

Candle-stick-held candles lined the walls between the windows on each side and at the end opposite Door was Altar. Altar was a white cloth-covered table upon which stood a white crucifix perhaps four feet tall, or less, forty-two inches likely. (This was *not* a Christian cross, it was a *Shaker* Cross). Atop the ends of its 'arms' were candles and at center-top a candle. All pristine white. Behind the crucifix on Table, as back-light, another candle would glow lending an eery, an 'otherworldly' pearlescent light to the Altar area. Bells stood to right and left on Table, awaiting only the time for and arrival of an 'afficionado' Bells-ringer. Not that others weren't involved in the magic of Bells ringing.

Church was 'pure' white inside. Even the slight flicker of an old-style wooden match opened a new world, of ethereal light. On the Altar beside the crucifix, white candles illuminated both sides and under the 'arms'. At night with all candles lit the Senses were stimulated by a different 'realm' and Spiritual events occurred. Hall glowed white from the burning candles on the walls; from candles held in air on suspending hoops; the solid white of the crucifix casting glowing 'white-shadows' to ceiling; walls; faces of white-clad celebrants and/or seekers of 'help'. Yet from the burning candles there was no smell of hot wax, no 'lacing' candle smoke. In the building without a ceiling but the under-side of shingles on the roof I think the Cedar-shingles absorbed the wax. Not too fire-proof.

Shaker Church was the sanctuary of Bell. Bell's power with us? Bell 'pulled' us. It was a circular flow.

First was awareness of some conditional situation presenting Reality. Mists of thicker and thinner Fog swirling at the push of slight Wind creates wispy, shadowy figures appearing as human and/or animal-like forms, to witnesses. Mist's *Reality* thereupon becomes 'belief-in', caused by 'the Reality' becoming Surety. Bell was a man creation first. Second, but primary was Bell's voice, how Bell responded to the clapper. Spiritual for us. Shaker power worked in Shaker Church because it showed to us that it worked.

Isn't that the way 'Religions' work? Religion *works?* If it 'works' it works. For how many thousand years was Auser/Osiris, or the prayer ending name Amen a religion's hub?

Having been called by Bell for specific reasons, Church filled and we occupied a building of wood. Inside, a wood-floor with an ovaloid track literally shoe-pounded into it, rimmed the circumference at a distance beyond wall-benches and onlookers' outstretched legs. These might impede the movements of participating Shakers. Benches on Forest side held men generally.

Our Women used Surf-side benches. There they would sit, the awesome Humans who had crafted *Chutsk* in their bodies, who would sit nursing or rocking or cradling a *Chutsk* as the ceremonies progressed, feeling the assembly's admiration and love.

Always, to me, was a transcendental emotion caused by the presence of so many of these fabled creatures, whether little girls or Mothers or Grand-mothers, all together at one time, watching each of us without being obvious. We were trained that these were not ordinary creatures: These were *Women*. And so we gawked. Girls and Boys alike. Girls had to learn how they were to behave when mature. Boys learned to revere them. HobbiesMitt owned a Percheron stallion. It was unique, awesome. As were Women. We stared at 'Choppie'; we stared at them.

We were like 'fans' in the company of public 'stars'. One of our directives was to to pay attention to the presence of, to count how many Grammas, how many Mamas. *Did 'They' look at 'us'?* On Skoobus (schoolbus) next Monday we might brag excitedly, "I seen seven Grammas at Shake. An' they was thirteen Mamas"

We were trained to see them as they were: Majestic. There was Majesty in their behavior. To this day I feel awe in the presence of Female Native Elders. Of any tribe. (Non-Amerians are tribes too, ain't they?)

But Bell. Bell learned of our Births then announced them. Bell announced our departures for *'other side of River'*. Bell announced the grounding of the S.S. Temple Bar in 1939. Bell watched over us. Kept us gathered. And informed.

In a way, Bell announced its own death on 7 December, 1941, when it called us to learn about Pearl Harbor. Its importance diminished after that because soon many Villagers got quality radios and could hear Richfield Reporter news from KGO San Francisco. We didn't gather at Church anymore to learn about what the outside world was doing. (And Howeattle's store had a telephone [with two bells at top face and a crank on the side]. And Washburn's store. Ryan's. News was easy to get now).

Shaker Church had but one importance left: Services. Bell called us until demolition of Old Church. Then, Shaker Church-Bell disappeared. Perhaps because it was no longer needed it went to Bell 'heaven'. (Ain't they no Bell 'heaven')? Perhaps La Push was Bell's 'heaven'; and Shaker Church. To this day I hear Bell, enter Church, as I wish.

TRANSITION

L a Push is the name of a now mostly non-Indian village on East edge of Ocean, West edge of land. It was said the explorer La Perouse named it 'La Bouche', for what it represents: 'The Mouth', of Quillayute River. Our people pronounced 'La Bouche' as *La Push*. *Our* word for it all was *Tᴀ-ʙᴏᴋᴇ*: River, which was the whole system, *cK'lawah, Bo-cKacheel, Soulduck*, 'Dicky', the rivers which made Quillayute: *Ta-boke*. (All are 'branches' of *the Salmon Tree*, Quillayute River and branches).

Rivers surrounded us and all were *Ta-boke*: *Ta-boke Bo-cKacheel*; *Ta-boke Soulduck*; *Ta-boke cKal eute* (now Quillayute). Together they were *Ta-boke*. When Village had been established it was known as *Quillayute* until, as Dorothy Smith Klahn (born in that territory in 1908) said, it was renamed La Push near the turn of the 1900's.

When I was born and until 1941/42 it was Home for many full-blood Quileute, perhaps 40 or 50 mixed Quileute-*Hoquat* blood people, and *Hoquat* (White) men with Kloochman (Chinook jargon for 'Native women'), our Village on South bank of River, beside Surf. Outside Blood came from everywhere. Hank Taylor married a Quileute *Waysotsopot* (Woman), he a mix of Hawaiian/Indian Blood, but not Quileute. Coast Guards from all America married our Girls. There are few full blood Quileute now, only descendants.

La Push was a place of Mist; Rain; Fog. It became thereby a place of Myth, Legend and SPIRIT. There was one personality characteristic to La Push in those days: Wetness. That wetness shaped our world, gave it SPIRIT. We lived SPIRIT, felt SPIRIT, were SPIRIT.

Many years ago, at age fourteen, I left La Push, to Live there no more, yet La Push *Spirit* fills me. I'm from 'old' La Push, the old La Push of Quileute vitality, inheritance, Life style. That La Push had a short Life as 'towns' go, from re settling until World War 2 ended the near isolation of a strange little Village nearly unknown to the world. Less than 50 years?

The process of Indian re-settling began after The Smiths arrived and Village 'Quillayute' was the New Location. Then, the name La Push came to being. It existed for a lifetime, no more.

World War 2 killed La Push. When it started, English was about equal to Chinook jargon as language, rare, and for non-Quileute speakers. Quileute was the language spoken in all homes, even when several in a home spoke 'Boston'...*Hoquat*. But with the war came paved roads, electricity, 'modernity' (for the military invasion up on Quillayute Prairie). The U.S. involvement in World War 2 had been born. The primitive SPIRIT WORLD and reliance thereon became ill and began dying rapidly. La Push began to die visibly: Change changed change. Daily.

World War 2 put America center stage. Now, instead of a remote isolate, it was under the brightest of lights and the casual, the 'ordinary', the regular un-scrutinized life-styles were gone. Instead of a 'backwater' land without 'culture', it was under the World's microscope as *'The Salvor of Democracy'*.

So, too, the end-of-the-road 'world' of La Push. In came the military to Quillayute Prairie to close the doors of Yesterday and open the doors of Tomorrow. Our girls were popular with the military personnel who were popular with the girls. They brought an excitement and newness attractive to the girls, not to mention being the best of the best, uniformed, with regular pay-checks (which didn't hurt, they had money for dates). The future Mothers, the 'hub' of Quileute Life, welcomed the 'new, the exciting ways' and the language of 'outsiders' was birthed into the Children engendered by the new unions. Mothers teach initial Tribal ways and with their change to English, death reached for Old La Push. But it hasn't died in me.

The dying of La Push began when English worked to predominate in our homes. I don't think La Push has any memory of Quileute now, nor of Chinook jargon. Unused by me I've also forgotten Quileute, which words are spoken daily else the ability to formulate them diminishes. Lillian Pullen and Sarah and Fred Woodruff Sr., and Rosie

Black, et al, recorded the language with professional help from Dr. Jay Powell, a Canadian linquist who has helped to put the language onto tapes I've heard. So it remains to be learned by whomsoever; but it won't be essential. Without the Culture which develops the language it's meaningless but for those Loyal to their Base. Only dedicated practice can recall elements of a language superceded by another. The dedicated pursuit and practice of a language is its only source of being. After that its only worth is to those who 'dwell in academia'. Frank Herbert suggested I make a dictionary of our language in 1958 but that is a task more formidable than any I've pursued. I failed. Jay Powell PhD, et al, worked successfully but how to record *click*s and *hisses* and *gutteral breathing* overwhelmed me.

For the degree of success they achieved I'm forever grateful. The words they recorded are the words of Sarah and Freddy Woodruff and Gramma Lillian and the Eastman's, Hudson's; *all* my beloved Quileute people.

What depression can match that of seeing a vital, viable 'nation' (with its own specific personality, developed by successors to hundreds, no, thousands of years of BEING), disappear before one's eyes? I know a Woman from Alaska whose car-struck four-year old *Chutsk* died in Her arms at roadside. Her eyes hold unmatched Depression. Her 'stride' was forever broken. I have a 'feel' of some such great loss, but for friends and relatives, not for me, Childless. For me, today, to visit those I knew, I go to Cemetary. I go to 'the Hill'. It's carpeted with pure bloods, which I am not. Many of them 'up there' (on 'the Hill') were People who lived before *Hoquat*. (I have made a cemetary map and on that they are listed as 'Before Whites', BW)

Those were Quileute lands. For thousands of years *Po-oke* had ranged this part of Sacred Earth following a way of Life that left no mark as to where they'd been. As harmless to the environment as *T'dayokes*...Flicker. That way of Life was gun-crushed in one fell swoop. For which I hold no anger, just sorrow. We should have occupied two separate planets, unable to contact one another: one planet for Spoilers; one for Indians, who were moved to the square mile at 'The Mouth' (*La Push*). Thereby *Hoquat* made gain of the rich lands *Po-oke* occupied before 'the DISCOVERY!', the 'CONQUERING!' of 'the new lands'. Land now Forks Prairie, Quillayute Prairie; all the land up to the mountains and occupied by *Hoquat*. One legal but dishonest process after another was used by those who could influence

'*Govermint*' to grant 'patents' on lands surrounding La Push and the Quileute people. The patent on Lonesome Creek and the area 'up' from Beach was a condition of singular boldness. Research it under 'Smith, Mrs. A. Wesley'.

When Gramma (Lillian Pullen) and Freddy and Sarah passed, the Quileute of old were gone. Few Indians are left now, only their successors, Reservation Kids: Rez Kids. That too is a unique way of Life but dependent on the world of *Hoquat*. Which *Po-oke* did not want. (Joyously I hear about an upsurge in interest by the People, which I'm committed to help reveal). Today, a century and a third after Quileute ways began their decline there are descendents of The Quileute who make valiant and dedicated effort to reinstill some *Po-oke* (Quileute), ways, not the least is language. Very late but being done.

Reading some works of anthropologists who spoke no Quileute and took history and 'the ways' from interpretors is a base for this difficult effort to '*recapture the Quileute*' to see 'how Quileute Lived'. (Example: Ella Clark recorded our '*arranger's* (a man-god) name as 'kwate', not *cKwyeh-Tee*. So the 'now '*elders*" speak of 'kwate' [kwatee]. '*Truly*' elders? (Could true Elders have pronounced 'kwate' I wonder). Most Northwest Resident Indians face this dilemma. Sorry, but all we are today is historians in the same way Dr. Barbara Waterson is historian for ancient Egypt. The Mind-set caused by the Living Atmosphere of 'being Quileute' can never be regained. Mind-set is Village Brain and Village Brain is gone for all but the Aware...whomsoever *they* may be.

THE GHOST CALLED 'PAST'

Iremember La Push!, the Quileute. I remember the rich simplicity of the language, the sudden humor inherent in its being: it was funny to take Life too seriously because it all looked foolish later…helped by a language which saw humor in 'the serious Life'.

At La Push I first learned that there were Life imperatives beyond what came to *Chutsk* (Baby) (such as food, attention, care; the normal experiences of *Chutsk*. These the experience conditions for *Chutsk* because the sole experience so far has been cared-for adulation). Learning of 'other than I' situations, we learn AWE, of and for Life. I did anyway. (My first awareness of marvel-beyond-self came one night with Moonlight on *Ta-boke* which I tell of later).

At La Push I learned the Reality of MYTH by Living in it, with it; Living it. SPIRIT involves 'MYTH', (forgotten LEGEND?). Isn't MYTH the off-spring of LEGEND? It's all 'voo-doo' to *'the wise'*; it was actual truth for us and the potential of 'to become' became the backbone of our world view. LEGEND comes from some creature's doings. Our LEGENDs were the history of what we remembered about what we were from vaporous Mists of Memory, visits from the Ghost named Past.

Someone relating an 'experienced adventure' is accepted as truthful. A 'Hearer', at a later date retelling the adventure as it was heard (called 'Dreamer' by those with no idea of the Reality), is telling the truth known of someone *else's* experiences. Extremely old Legends become Myths, right?

So it was with *cKwyeh-Tee*, (a 'myth' to 'outsiders', as real to us as is Jesus to some; Allah to others). We viewed all related 'revelations' and explanations as Realities, this includes Jesus, Krishna, Jehovah, et al. Now, myths is what they're called, 'circular reasonings'. I accepted them then. I accept them now. I've seen nothing more 'reason-able'. The magic of human 'Reality' views (from the perspective of religions) is subject to doubt and question the world around. Why one more acceptable than another? Or, more realistically, why one *less*? And which doesn't attempt to dominate the rest by 'force'? *Which one is not 'the only one'? Where* are there contagious (contagious? *visible!*) examples of Love and Forbearance and Forgiveness? *Ruby Ridge? Wounded Knee? Trail of Tears? Waco, Texas? Kent State?* Et cetera?

At any rate, the 'place' and how it all came to be made us. SPIRIT concept is born in places like that, by the *unknown conditions* imposed on who lives there, of whatever family, Cougar; Blue-jay (*cKwash-cK-wash*); Deer (*Hawayishka*); *Po-oke* (Quileute two-leggeds): any and all other kinds of People. Isn't Spirit, Life Spirit, the impetus of the Kind *and* the Individual?

So now, today, from mists of memory, I sense an imperative to that world. A rush of near-forgotten Real World (here-now) pressures push themselves into my consciousness which resents stinking air; endlessly roaring mechanical noises; converted sewer water to drink; factory food with factory-impelled taste; doctors pushing petroleum pills.

Now La Push voice fills my ears: Bell, Village of drumming and singing and laughter from all directions; La Push, River-beach lined with Cedar Tree converted to canoes by Men of *Power*. (We pronounced canoe as 'cKeynoo'. *Po-oke* word for canoe was *Tabil, Tabil Ta-boke*, River canoe; as distinct from *Tabil cKwahleh*, Ocean [oshunt] cKeynoo). La Push with sorrow and joy. With bewilderment at *Ho-quat* ways, La Push is becoming a fading drum-beat for me so I'm Spirit-driven to recall those people and their unique way. This 'history' is more my own, out there, but it is mine. And about those whom I knew and loved, my People, *Po-oke*, the People of La Push.

In this today, I find that in me that memory-Mist Village is coming back to life, from the not-too-secure 'Snug harbor' of old age, but I hear the drums and singing throughout Village; the inevitable far-off laughter telling of someone working 'over there'; Mark Williams chasing his 'rustled' Horse(s) ('rustled' by some one of our young, but not

I of course], to gallop in Surf, which Horses loved). Too, being at Post Office when the big box from Monkeywartses comes for somebody.

Of course this work is only a touch of what there was, before La Push was born as Village, while it lived its unique Life. No authorities remain, myself included. Then recall for what reason? The pressure from those Memories brings the first imperative.

FALL

Sensed first is Fall. Fall of Year. Before the Change (the murder of Forest in 1939) year around Climate was predictable: Wet. Fall was less wet early on than Spring or Winter. But it was all Wet; some seasons just less cold than others.

I remember Fall because of LEGEND and wet Mist wherein lived Stick Indians, vague impressions seen at the corner of the eye as Shadowy flicker in Forest; heard through 'the corner of the ear' as sourceless sound; indeterminate, unidentifiable; felt in chill breeze, "You feel that chill?" "Ayyy, Stick Indians". Something that impressed the senses but couldn't be located: Spirits of their sort. Without the 'wet-world' we Lived in, no Spirit world.

'Four seasons' came with *Hoquat*. Before that our 'seasons' were based on what occurred at a given time. Some kind of Berry Season, Stealhead Season, Seal-hunting Season, etc. I'll tell of them, but for now, the 'four' seasons: *always wet* or Winter; *pretty wet*; Spring; Summer, damp; and sort of wet; Fall.

Fall began in August at La Push. Fleecy white vapors that were thinly spread rainless clouds (we heard there were eleven days a year of twenty-four hour rainless stretches) would move in on Coast in those August days and waning Sun's rays brought a warm kiss to eagerly waiting life-forms. The vaporous veil would filter warming Sun-beams into cool kissing fingers of Fall which reminded the 'basking' creatures that they lived here on this marvelous, mysterious, hidden-away Coast.

Fall, not yet exhuberant, basked almost asleep under early-Fall Fog, a late Summer chill in the air. Fog came, muting most sounds of 'civilized Earth', out-board motors; the single cylinder 'kuhbungh-kuhbungh-kuhbungh' of Salmons-trollers leaving or returning to *Ta-*

boke; barking Village Dogs; the rolling sound of Surf; any and all were Fog muted. These we recognized for their impact: Fall was wakening.

And Spider people were hanging out their nets wherever they found 'base' from which to start their marvelous embroideries. "Fall's come, Spiders is everstw'eres" some Elder would announce. Glittering diamonds of water-droplets glistened from Dew-wet webs in early day-light, these Spiders' 'nets', strung between tall blades of Grass, crossing trails, awaiting potential victims who could see the traps now and avoided them. Fields with small, edging trees and brush and tall grasses held thousands of these marvelous insect-traps. From house eaves; beneath overturned, drying cKeynoo; and especially from the 'baseball-diamond's Chicken-wire backstop': Webs.

Northerly, from across 'the Spit', (from Rialto Beach side), muffled Surf-voice was the only impelling sound to tell of Life. (Rialto Beach side has a steep slope and Ocean pounds there noisily). Even Woods and Forest were quiet. Many Summer dwellers had already tasted Fall and taken the cue: go South. Summer with Her colors and Bird songs and talking Insects was becoming quiet. Her arms were folding on Her breast, now overstrewn with falling leaves as if red-orange tears of sorrow for Her coming demise. Even Bushes were quiet, their inhabitants gone.

Yes Fall, you've destroyed the Births and Awakenings and thrills for the New Borns and even the Elders, and in your arrogance you bring more Rain and Wind. And bared Tree branches to make stark dark angularity against the pearl grey which is spread out as sky. But beware! Winter is rousing from the lethargy of hibernation imposed last Spring and awakening, as Black Bear does in Spring, to devour whatever it finds to devour and Fall, you beautiful, you arrogant, you ego-positive movement of the clock, you are to be the victim. (However, greatest Spirit of Forest, *Cho-Cho* [Wren] will not succumb to you, nor to you, Winter; *Cho-Cho* has Spirit beyond the power of Seasons. *Cho-Cho* is *cKwyeh-Tee*'s pet Bird! And strongest Spirit of all.

Soon one felt the potential for chill of more strength behind the feathery touches of approaching Fall's cold. In early Fall, when through thin vaporous clouds days were moderately warmed and brightened by weakening Sunshine, it was cool in shadows. Yet Air was warm by wind breaks. Drift logs on Beach were the 'hot places' to be among, in sunny, sandy patches between oftentimes towering logs.

It may have required wiggling or climbing or both, but the determined among us always found a hot spot (until Sun shined somewhere else) in which to bask sleepily, (or try to read Street and Smith Western Magazines), as neighbors to Chipmunk and Ground Squirrel and the rest of Drift-log inhabitants. It is so: Colt or Calf, Lamb, or Cougar cub; cubs of any and all Animals are born Sun worshippers.

And blessing not to be forgotten, transitional Sunshine was a 'time of eery light'. During those days of Season transition we loved to gather in groups on 'Oshunt' Beach; on dirt roads between houses, (we called them streets); at River bank where cKeynoo waited to 'go swimming for their owners'; to be bathed by the light's Spirit.

Po-oke in groups, five or ten, or perhaps two or three, would experience together the exciting and invigorating 'glow-color' light (today I call it Technicolor Light) which shined mysteriously in late, late afternoon, really in early evening, of many Fall days. The rare light made everything seem to shine from within, not to reflect from 'without'. Even 'other' Animals responded to it, *Byack* and *cKull-el* and *Cho-Cho*; *Hell-Divers; Shags*…it seemed all were energized by those evenings.

When the glowing colors of those rare and gorgeous evenings brought by Fall came to La Push mysteriously, we gloried in them, animated chatterings came from throughout Village. In the excitement of knowing that Summer and Fall would be having battles soon, to see who prevailed. Even *cKosscKa deedoh* (dogs) reacted, running, barking.

Fall's warning breath invigorated us all…as it inspired us to 'be prepared'. Fall would soon 'beat up' on Summer but in its ignorance fail to see the coming loss of its gains. Fall would be so weakened by the battle to evict Summer that Winter would eat Fall alive.

Fall never saw that coming but we knew and we knew we had to store food: regular, stormy weather was our La Push experience, the rainy, cold days, the screaming, wet nights lay just ahead, ready to weaken or even destroy the unprepared. Food was scarce, not to be 'found' in Winter, rather, had to be bought. Food and shelter were the Winter survival impositions on whatsoever of creatures would see next Spring. Then Spring, quietly, secretly, overwhelmed Winter's grip on our coastal world and 'stuff to eat begun comin' back to Life'). While Winter slept some calmness crept in pulling the soon to be born Spring. Awakening at times Winter would rage at the newly-being-born Spring but groggy from sleep, calmed even more.

These things we knew when the breath of Fall raced across Surf, along Beach, enveloped the unbundled and caused shivers to ripple the skin, quick, brief, but real.

The last foods we could gather were found now; the larder needed filling. So, we picked berries, preserved Salmon, Elk, Deer, Grouse, ate Salmon eggs as do Bears, fattening for Winter. My favorite berries were Salal, one 'secret' source was by Dungeness Spit.

So, away for Food gathering we went.

Even before "Old Sun come 'round", (the earliest of mornings on Food gathering trips), we would hear such as "Berry-pickin' time! Get up!" One long breath of words. "Don't you guys (youngsters) eat no berries what you pickin' today, neither." Of course we wouldn't. We were model children and would never have eaten those luscious berries until we could hold no more. (*We* were *just below perfect!*).

It was earlier at Berry Mountain where we camped, five auto-hours or more East of La Push, so we Young were still sleepy-brained. "You guys too comfortable in them warm blankets." In the cold mountain air, Sun said 'Hello!' a few minutes sooner and *cKa'a'yo* too and others who Lived 'Over there.' *cKa'a'yo* (Crow) starts talkin' earlier than at La Push. Mountain cKa'a'yo was 'lily bit' different, but talked same language as them at La Push. We young 'throated' cKa'a'yo talk to them and they responded raucously.

Herb Fisher and his Father finished heating an Elk-meat stew and we were at table (our laps) ready to do our duties for the cooks... eat everything. "Need good breakfast," 'Old Man' Fisher would say. He had known sixty-five or seventy years; (he it was who used to dip smoked-smelt into Vaseline, until Herb stopped it. So? Vaseline is grease; Bear fat is grease; Seal oil is grease. Grease is grease, ain't it?).

I liked to go to Berry Mountain with the Fishers.. They joked and laughed all day. 'Old Man' Fisher was the funniest person I ever knew, (and Herb inherited much of it). We youngsters loved him and hung onto him like ribbons. Everything he said was funny and what I see of harmless humor today was born into me from association with Herb's father. Cruel humor was not in him, nor the so-called 'humor' of humiliating nor demeaning personality assassination.

Once, before *Hoquat*, berries and our other foods were available nearby. No one had lived permanently at *Ta-boke* mouth until 'Bostons' moved us there. Upland, when *Po-oke* had Lived throughout the greater *Quillayute River-system*, hunting and gathering didn't require by-passing miles of nearly inaccessible Forest or poling cKeynoo up-stream to the Prairies past what had been ours since Time began, rather, it was near and on prairies where we had lived, so Life then was much easier. Forced to River-mouth to live year 'round made Life many-fold times more difficult. Deaths rose with the move to Quil-layute (to La Push), Little Bill told me.

Before being shoved to the square mile at *Ta-boke* mouth (where no protection exists from Winter's wrath), we, as rational people, had enjoyed up-river protection. For thousands of years we had visited River mouth in Spring, Summer and Fall only, while *Tss'y'uck* had hunted along Coast. In those days Trees had blunted the near hurri-cane force of unblocked storms six-thousand miles old and strong, and we had lived in the protection of the uplands, where our supplanters ensconced themselves as our superiors. On our lands. Without a dime of payment. But they didn't shoot us, California style, nor make us march on foot for thousands of miles to live on barren rock, Cherokee style.

Winter at La Push found food to be scarce. The 'dead of Win-ter' at La Push was a sobering experience for who had hunted River systems and Prairies the time of their history, knowing no such con-cept as 'money'. We helped each other in those depressing Depression years. Winter took its toll in the way flu did…(many in the Cemetary 'stopped being' in 1918).

Because of the dark and damp and cold, victorious, self-satisfied Winter snoozed deeply. By the time it tried to awaken and regain command, there was 'too much Spring out now' and Spring gave birth to Summer, which a weakened Winter could not defeat. Now food could be found again. Winter, too weak from Cold, too loggy from the deep sleep to 'fight away' Spring's youth and vitality, went away and hid. It went 'over there', (South), there to practice the art of being Winter, to get ready to return when Summer let Fall move in. Sum-mer, in its soft and gentle loveliness thought there was room for other weather and never learned not to trust Fall. Why? Summer never sees Winter. But Winter has practice defeating Fall. Winter can't defeat Spring, can't defeat Summer. Only dumb old Fall. It is so to this day.

We waited while Spring quietly, secretly, over-whelmed Winter's grip on our coastal world and we could shake off the 'fully-awake hi-bernation' which Winter gifted to us.

She'd let Fall move in without 'knowing about' Winter's coming Victory. She never saw it, how could She be faulted? Winter has long practice defeating Fall, has eternal history of victory over it. Winter was sobering. We knew that and almost worshipped Summer and Her Child Autumn, times of eating the 'fat of the land.' And for preparation of any surplus.

These things we knew when the breath of Fall raced across Surf, along Beach, enveloped the unbundled and caused shivers to ripple the skin...quickly, briefly. But real.

When the glowing colors of those rare and gorgeous evenings brought by Fall came to La Push, mysteriously, we gloried in them, animated chatterings came from throughout Village in the excitement of knowing that Summer and Fall would soon battle to see who was toughest.

In their youth-time Uncle Yum and Chris Morganroth Sr., were camped one night near Hoh River above Huelsdonk's place when the battle commenced and all night they lay silently, fearful, while the battle raged. In the morning, Uncle Yum said, he and Chris walked all over the battle ground, looking at debris from the rage of war between seasons. Limbs and branches and Fern plant debris and leaves were everywhere. Fall won they told me. "Summer don't know how to put up a deadly fight," Uncle Yum said. "All them branches an' leaves an' that was torn away from Summer when Fall sneaked up on Her. Parts of Summer lay all over the place", Chris added.

"We looked at each other whenever we come to a place where damage was bad, like big Maple Tree branches just plain tore out of place, flung to Earth like from a frenzy. They shrieked an' howled an' run upRiver, then down. It was a hell of a fight but Summer lost."

So now it would become more of Fall as Day died to be born as next Day; Fall, when River became more filled with upland rains draining through up-River valleys. Now *Sa-ats* (Chinook ['King'] Salmons, (not the same as 'Tyee', Spring Salmon), would begin to appear and excite who was captor of an Early One. "They comin' home now! Let's get busy!" Now preparation for First Fish Ceremony.

Every year we prepared a feast in celebration of Sa-ats' return. Berries and Camass and Elk and smoked Smelts and Seal oil...feast. (Even had potatoes). Sa-ats' bones were kept carefully: To thank Sa-ats for their return the bones were put into River with singing and drumming, all to show appreciation and to have Sa-ats feel our reverence; reverence is what it was indeed, our Survival depended upon *Alita*: Fish. We asked *cKwyeh-Tee* to send more Sa-ats. And all other gifts for Life.

After that the work of net-holding poles began. All up and down *Ta-boke* net-poles would be hammered into River bottom. On land by Coast Guard boat-house repair poles would be fixed upon which to hang nets. New nets needed lines (rope) tied top and bottom for floats and weights, thereby to hold the waiting nets upright in River. Wood 'sewing' needles holding sewing line for afixing new floats, new lead weights, patching holes in webs were whittled, although some were bought at Sunde and d'Evers or Pacific Marine Supply in Seattle. I imagine Howeattle and Washburn's La Push Store sold them also. Ruel and Hamnmer hardware store in Forks sold them. New pulling lines were spliced to netlines. Excitement's Spirit lay as Fog over and throughout Village.

cKeynoo were readied; oil-skins and hip-boots checked and replaced as needed: Morton Penn; Stanley Grey; Joe Pullen and his son 'P.P.' (Perry Pullen); Chris 'Big Jiggs' Penn (Jiggy's father); Fred Woodruff; Freddy Penn (Chris' brother); Billy Hudson and others, who ever saw them not wearing hip boots? These were the essentials for the Men as were 'Monkeywartsez' tennis shoes for Children...as were 'two-circle Keds' for Women, (the height of style). Fall rain and freshets heralded Salmon coming home and activity was from Crowcall to Sunset.

In Spring, cKeynoo paddles were lent, one family to another, and now owners sought their return or looked on First Beach for perfect wood for making new ones. At the same time *Tloquali* lodge men looked for Cedar pieces from which to make Spirit Board, "...where to set net this year?" *Tss'y'uck* and Tss'ay'whutleoke people did the same. Spirit Forks were checked for being present on the porches, or steps, even in front of the house.

Old ways took over and Essex and Packard and Hudson cars were forgotten. (There was even a 'Moon' and a 'Peerless' auto in Village). Poles and paddles for cKeynoo became essentials, as did outboard motors: Johnson Sea-horse and Evinrude, air-cooled Lawson.

All makes of outboards roared into life, or coughed and sputtered while sweating men wound starting cords and pulled, wound and pulled, wound and pulled, swearing and frustrated and angry at the balking machines. For whatever reason a motor would roar into action when it chose and the victorious 'master' would thunder up and down *Ta-boke*, to Mora, back toward Ahkalut 'tuning up', weaving at high speed through whatever remained of *Hoquat* commercial Salmon-fleet boats. These would be anchored, waiting out stormy N.W. seas or too broke to buy gas to get back to Seattle, or Astoria, or Westport... wherever.

Eager anticipation flowed into Village to drip almost as Rain from every one there. Dogs barked at the excitement, or howled at being left out. 'Salmon Spirit' was in our veins. Even for Children sleep came hard and was thrown off in early morning, *"cK'a'a'yo's* got Dawn awake! You kids get up!"* (Crow hollerin'! Dawn's comin'!) And we rose as if levitated. Who'd miss these thrills?

Memories.

Memories, silent as stealthy coastal-morning-fog to which we awakened regularly. Memories of deep, clear *Ta-boke*, luring Sa-ats from the wanderings of the Wait, (the Wait for calling by *Ta-boke*: "Come home! Come home! Make more beautiful, shimmer-skinned Sa-ats"). They had grown and matured at River-mouth, wandered to where no one knew, out into the vastness of *cKwahleh*. There, in *cK-wahleh*, that mystery of Earth-life, they faced Seal and Sea Lion and Killer Whale and Shark and *Hoquat* ways of mechanized catching. They learned and grew, if Fortune robed them with its covering, to return to *Ta-boke*, and *Po-oke*, who prayed to them that some might bless us as food with the wonder of their Lives. We waited, Fall to Fall, for *First Fish Ceremony*...it was in our Blood. It's said Muckleshoot still celebrates. And likely elsewhere.

Ah! the majesty of huge Sa-ats coming home to spawn! Marvelous. Sa-ats with golden and green and red skin flecks with spots of darkness like flicks of paint over their bodies. Opalescent. Nothing I know matched Sa-ats for beauty but Dolphin/Dorado, (not Porpoise). In the blessing that memory bestows I recall Fall, when they came home in their thousands to clean, clear water. And all perfect...no tumors nor lumps nor open sores; no disfigurements: perfect and gorgeous. By *cKwyeh-Tee*.

And still fresh in memory is Forest. Awesome, (silent to who couldn't hear it talking), inspiring in its eternality. Before 'misery whips', (lengthy, long-toothed saws which ate in short order what

MOTHER EARTH had developed carefully, then nursed for tens of thousands of years), there were Fog and Rain-pulling Hemlock and Sitka Spruce, all a noise-muffling barrier between *cKwahleh* and East, the *Hoquat Hoquat* world. Cedar grew tall and straight and offered self to be cKeynoo to who prayed at Cedar swamps for one to offer itself for that life. No Cedar anymore.

Alder with 'meat' of both white and red wood, huge, and older than time itself it seemed, was readied to smoke Salmons for winter, (and Smelts in Spring when they surged into *Ta-boke* to spawn and to be taken for eating fried or smoked). (I remember a factory near the old Ballard Bridge [by Seattle, to find Seattle go 150 miles East from La Push] where furniture was made using 'Washington Mahogany': Red Alder. This didn't last long considering the appetite mills have for wood). Other *Po-oke* constructs of Alder were bailers for cKeynoo; bowls; carvings; implements for the domestic Life of *Po-oke*.

In Forest we shared Life with the majesty of Yew Trees from which hunting bows were fashioned. These were used on Fall-migrating Water-Birds. When the hunger for better weather to South entered their Blood they visited us locally in stops from their flights. It was their exodus South we awaited. Incessantly talking, and in long lines they arched downward out of Fall skies as if a rain of feather-covered arrows, to land on ponds and small lakes which dotted the land around our primitive and natural Paradise. Their voices rang with the excitement of their migration. Oh the talking! Quack! Quack! Honk! Honk!

Their young, learning the route to their winter homes in the Summer South, stood out in the beauty of their young Lives, slick and clean and alert. Innocence learning confidence. Unparalleled is Great Spirit's creations if left alone. (Unassisted by Man Himself).

In truth we prayed to their Spirits for volunteers to help sustain those of us who couldn't get to the warmth of Southern Summer and constant food-supply. The Yew-bow provided silent hunting and a taken meal didn't terrorize everything as did 12 gauge shot-guns, a roar heard for miles.

However, in the worship of Gross National Product, outsiders bought right from someone, not us, to kill Forest and Forest died, River died, and what of Sa-ats? And myriad Forest-hidden small lakes and ponds even *Po-oke* never saw? Forest was huge and kept secret many of its intimacies for other than *Po-oke* life…where have they gone, the secret, enticing feeding and resting places for those incredibly far-ranging Geese and Ducks and their cousins of the Sky? Being Natural spots they stood in the way of *G.N.P. Progress* and now they are mud. Or baked earth.

Some Fall nights when darkness without Moon enveloped River and Forest, when Coast slept to lulling by Surf-voice, Plankton People came into River with the swell of flood-tide. Now the show of Burning Water came to us to view with awe. Nights without Moon's light and incoming tide sometimes brought this marvel of Plankton for Salmon People to stir, to swim through on their way home to spawn. This spectacle of 'Burning Water' was awaited as was the birth of new *Chutsk*.

We were told about it as Toddling Kids and taken to stand at River bank from which to see the glow, although it was from boats, or cKeynoo, that the awesome performance was seen best. I know of no similar sight to behold than that brought by all Salmon People at night, in phosphorescence, when they came home to make Salmons '*Chutsk*'. But it was Sa-ats alone who created the amazingly huge hoops of light. Elders knew which breed of Salmons made which streaking 'fire ball', "Sa-ats over there, look the size of that 'nother over there....Look, there goes Coho crazy fast ain't it."

Barrel-sized 'tubes'of phosphorescence glowing to rival Northern Lights filled *Ta-boke* in uncountable places as Alita (Fish) swam up-River, lacing it with tunnels of gleaming water at their passing: Burning Water. The long-lasting tunnels dimmed slowly, to be recharged by new arrivals. We would sit in cKeynoo in silence, afraid speaking might break the spell as their powerful tails propelled them like rockets through Plankton, watching as the glow diminished to be recharged as another and another and another would streak through the dark waters leaving countless tunnels of magical, mysterious, cool light. "Imagine what Sa-ats feels like goin' through that magic stuff," Old Man said to me several times. He was almost breathless "watching them tunnels them Folks is drilling through the water." The taste and smell of Home drove them as in the ecstatic return of a war-kept soldier now free to the arms of his loved ones. Death alone could stop the rendezvous.

And has.

On merchant ships in tropical waters I've leaned against taff-rails at night, in darkness as black as tropical nights without Moonlight can present, the ship's long wake-trail a diminishing glow proving that Plankton were present in mid-Ocean too, but the marvel of Sa-ats racing through Plankton-filled waters of *Ta-boke* was never equalled for me. However, never now, only in those days of clear, luminescent waters.

Dark nights, flood tides, Fall, *Ta-boke* and Sa-ats. No comparison. Sadly, in the shallow, murky water that flows over Wesley Smith's (WesleesMitts) long-ago farm-land, now flood- distributed between River mouth and the bluff at Rialto Beach, here that marvel of Earth-Life has been removed forever.

But G.N.P. benefitted! so they say. How sad the Minds which see nothing Sacred about those things which Earth-Life has spent Eternity perfecting. So the last time I went home to 'visit' La Push I found that the last time I'd been home had been the last time. With the passing of our beloved Elder Lillian Pullen, Jiggy's Mother, now there is only sad hole in chest. (Note: I returned for 'one more time' to Village in January 2007 and found interest to be high in the memories of their ancestors so I'll return again). Now another sad note:

Beloved friend Jiggy, Christian Penn Junior crossed the River in 2011. *Ha atch tlaks ala* Jiggy.

AWAKENINGS

Still another of the Time Ghosts roused by memory is the awakening to 'other than I' experience.

My parents were close friends with a commercial fisherman named John Wanska. I recall that John was Finnish, at least by parentage. His trolling-boat was named 'Faithful'. Occasionally he'd take us onto *cKwahleh* to experience commercial Salmon-trolling or simply for a boat ride to Sea Lion Rocks Northerly of Ahkalut. One trip we made on a flat calm Sea was to Destruction Island. We went ashore there and petted the tame '*Hawayishka*' (doe Deer) which the Light-tenders kept. (In earlier times they had a tame Bear we were told). Marvelous thrill to meet one of *Hawayishka* People and to pet it. It enjoyed having its ears and head scratched. Tame or wild depends upon treatment I realized, and resolved on that day to become a 'light-house tender' and have a Deer for a friend. I'm working on it to this day.

One time specific in my memory was a night-trip on 'Faithful' to Rialto Beach and Dance hall. At Rialto Beach was a store, cabins and in a secluded, Tree protected 'bowl' against the bluff, the dance-hall. Sometimes Mother sang with the 'Red Hot Red-snappers', a band made up of some Village men. I recall Fred Penn with a saxophone and Chris Morganroth Sr., singing. Jack Ward was playing some instrument now forgotten by me. Rex Ward loved to play the drums which were loaned by Wiley Duncan's family.

We went many times but one night remains. I was no more than four. Children taken to the dance slept on side-wall benches, self-flung onto coats and blankets strewn as beds. What can sleep as sprawled as young Children? Then to be carried home slung over a shoulder (as if a sack of potatoes) without awakening? That kind of sleep is the only thing that gets us through Childhood I think.

Most of the Children were awakened at dance's end to see Hob-biesMitt perform his 'rooster dance' in which he put the backs of his huge hands against his hips and with elbows out at his sides strutted and called rooster crowing and bowed and walked as does a rooster in the chicken yard. The young of all groups were giddy with delight see-ing this 'old *Hoquat*' do his rooster dance. Gleeful laughter thus ended the dances.

After the dance *this* night we left Rialto Beach for La Push, and Mother woke me to see Moon settling in the West for its nightly sleep. The full, yellowed glowing disc was low to Horizon and the silhouette of Ahkalut and land where Village lay was charcoal dark. Across *Ta-boke* the reflected stream of moonlight presented a flat, slightly undulating ribbon of gold, a gleaming path for 'Faithful' on a world otherwise charcoal dark. Across this charcoal mass, seemingly not vital and alive, came a liquid-gold ribbon drawing us into it. We weaved through boats, now unlighted but for anchor lights, moving toward the Shell Oil dock, there to disembark. I wonder if I dared breath, seeing that string of golden light pulling us toward La Push, silently, gently. That mystery of Life tattooed *exterior beauty* into my mind. It seems that what I recall of infinite Beauty was driven into my soul's recall at La Push. That was the first 'exterior' awareness for me. Something *else* was as wonderful as I. (*But no more, mind you!*). Moon didn't care whether I saw it or not, *it was being Moon.*

The second breath-stopping scene was miles of California Poppies, shimmering orange in California's San Juaquin Valley, as far as eye could see...my favorite color and Flower since my early Childhood. (Was I *three?*). Golden Orange like *Ta-boke*'s ribbon; like the wings of T'day-okes, (Flicker...Golden Wings); like California Poppies. *Delicious to the eyes*, as are the faces of smiling friends.

SLUG
Wednesday, 25 Sep 2002

Out here with Fuzzy and Re-Sun in gorgeous weather—'out here' being the Masonic Park near Granite Falls, Washington. (Fuzzy and Re-Sun are my guests. Neither are Masons unless there are Cathood Masons). Neither.

The chill of September later-afternoon has me cuddled with a cup of hot coffee. Half an hour or so ago I put a saucer of 'Kitty Biscuits' (which modern house-cats eat) on the ground beside this shelter. And 'just now' I was drawn in vision to the small pile of said biscuits and stared: it moved! Closer inspection revealed Slug, under several of the biscuits, munching on one in absorbed contentment, then I thought of a child-hood adventure involving Old Man, Slug, and me....

We were sitting on the front-porch of 'OUR' house when I spotted Slug. "I'm gettin' salt put on Slug," I said to Old Man, sitting beside me and stood to go into House.

"What for?"

"Kill it", I said. *Right thing to do to Slug!*

"Why you goan kill it?"

"'s a slug."

"You gonna cook it or eat it raw?"

I was revulsed. I'd heard that during famine times Slug was eaten. With full belly the thought of eating Slug destroyed my sensibilities. I was aghast. I'd die first. (Tough). (*Tloquali*).

"I ain't gonna eat it".

"Then why kill it?"

"It'll eat the garden."

"Why will it do that?"

Old Man had a 'milk eye'. His right eye saw like Hawk, the left one was dead. For emphasis he'd turn his head to the right far enough to hide the good eye, then turn the blind eye as far left as it would go, in effect staring with that eye as if it had deeper vision. Maybe it did! (Not having one, I don't know). Now he turned the 'un-nerver' at me. This was his 'emphasis' side. The effect? Always un-nerving.

"Garden is our food," I answered him.

"Oh." He was looking in the direction of Sea Lion Rocks. Pause. He tilted his head backward with a slight 'bob', then, " You make that food?"

"Planted it."

"You guys invented to plant stuff, ain't it."

I was becoming giddy in the way confusion is born in Children. His logic and mine were apart. "We planted the seeds what growed and Slug eatin' it".

"Why?"

"Why what?"

"Why its eating stuff?" He pressed on: suddenly I fell under the spell of his mind's power and stopped to think—the inevitable path he presented to me.

After a short pause of thinking I answered. All I could see was obvious.

"Because it's hungry," I said.

He smiled. "Ayy-y. It get hungry. Like us. We get hungry."

"But why it's eating *our* food?"

"You planted seeds, heh?"

"Ayy-y."

"You invent them seeds, what they'd be, how they'd grow up as food and all?" Seeds come from plants and 'ev'rybuddy' know how we got plants from seeds, seeds from plants. Who give 'em.

I answered in surety, "*cKwyeh-Tee* done it,"

"Ha-atch…(good). An' he caused Slug too, ain't it." Statement, not question.

"Ayy-y-y. Out a somethin' else…something Life-SPIRIT made first."

"Then it gots rights to eat too ain't it?" He put his hand on my seven or eight year old shoulder.

<How could Slug have rights?> <What's it here for?> <Who made it?> <Why?> <'Why' will tell what for.>

'*Must be important to Great Spirit who is perfect and don't do nothing without purpose*'. I'd heard that daily. <Then it did. It had rights too. Like everything Great Spirit designed.>

"Ayy-y-y", I replied. (Sure again that I was correct). (Hopefully).

"Should you hurt it if you ain't gonna eat it?"

"Waas. But can't hurt it, it just dissolves with salt."

"Imagine the pain salt burnin' into it brings. *Terrible* pain. Agony of pain. *Would that be fun for you*, to cause pain for it like you feel with soap burning you eyes? Only *not able to stop the burning pain*? Soap washes out. You have fun making *pain* for things?" He scowled at me.

I laughed. "Slug don't feel no pain."

"Ayy. They feel it. When salt get on 'em they twist and turn, writhe, in burnin' horror. It burn them to a melted lump."

"How can they feel?"

He was nonchalant as he looked at me with ' both' eyes. But there was that look of bland innocence, with that '*certain gleam*'.

He looked away, across River, as if toward Cape Johnson, north-west-ward. Then he gave a casual shrug, tossed his head quickly, as if I already knew, "How can they feel? Same way as when you pet them," he said, baiting the trap.

"*PET* THEM?" Pet a Slug?! I shouted with glee as if no more goofy thing had ever been said. I'd swallowed the hook.

An innocent grin crossed his face. "Oh! You didn't know about that eh? Watch!"

He rose from the porch-step we'd used as bench this half-hour, bent to Slug and picked it up. Immediately it withdrew into a ball shape, no end.

"See, this is head end," he said quietly, as if Slug might hear and run, pointing to a smooth, untextured area. "*Watch careful*". He placed Slug, now a tensed round ball of strange flesh, on the back of his left index finger. The smooth (head) end was close to his fingernail.

Although Childlike I was repelled by the sight of this 'sticky, slimy creature' on human flesh, I watched, spellbound. He blew spittle in a gust at the 'front end', spit against the ball of his right index finger and using the moisture he'd provided began to 'pet' very gently from the indicated front end toward the 'neck'—about ¾ inch or so. He blew spittle again as the moisture was absorbed. I watched intently…maybe he *was* a crazy old man as the 'christian' farmers said. I know for sure I was slack-jawed.

"See," he breathed as command and as I watched I felt 'hackles' rise on my neck, goose-bumps rose over my body—and once again I was transported into *Byack*'s world, for as I watched, Slug uncoiled slowly, its head elongated from its 'neck', eye-stems pushed out and the gentle soothing stroking of his wet finger removed its fear, tension, withdrawal, leaving instead a docile, pleased and enjoying Slug, waving its eye-stems, its body full-length and moving almost rhythmically.

"Well what you think about that" he said, as if totally surprised. I stared bewildered, unbelieving. Captivated. Awestruck. My brain was numb I'm sure.

And I was silent. *This* day brought a deep, a deep understanding. *Slug had liked* what *Byack* had done. I knew of a sudden what *Po-oke* meant: All Living things are People of one form or another.

BEACH; MIST; GLOW

Beach presented Mystery because, as we were told, Ocean (*cK-wahleh*), which made Beach, was and is MOTHER EARTH'S oldest Living Child. All which is, we were told, depends upon EARTH, *cKwahleh* included. Here are We, voiceless in Time, walking beside Surf whose voice is the oldest voice but perhaps for Wind...(maybe even before Surf was Wind's voice across parched rock). Beyond number, they who have heard 'voices of Wind and Surf' (when those voices were Time old already). One must wonder: Are Day and Night as old as Wind or Surf? The Mystery in total control of 'material destiny' in which we Live is answered by Surf; Wind: They've seen all things of Earth-time. And they who *read Spirit* are alone in comprehending.

Day or night I would walk Beach, beside Surf, often wondering whether Thought, when Thought came, could be Surf and /or Wind influenced. Beach (*Lawawat*) called to us when we wanted Thought to come. We felt ourselves to be in what *Hoquat* called 'cathedral' when we walked *Lawawat*. Our meditations were a form of prayer, 'help' from whatever we depend upon for Life, the 'Oh Thou, who man of baser earth didst make,' of Omar Khayya'm (or Whomsoever).

When we felt Sorrow, Beach called to us. Sorrow guided our feet to Beach. Who had lost *Chutsk* walked along Beach on paths of Sadness, the long history of *Po-oke*. Sobbing Mothers whose *Chutsk* had died in womb or died recently, walked Beach in the company of several relative/acquaintance Women. These ministered love and care and concern to the grieving Woman, that her Sorrow could be brought out profoundly, the sooner to 'dull the edge' of womb-deep pain only Mothers feel. Motherhood was the goal of our Women. We lost so many Babies. T.B. Small pox. Malnutrition. Unsought helpers to/of Death.

Too, Solace was bestowed upon us at and by that mysterious Beach. The occasions of late afternoon and 'Technicolor light' held magic but also there were dark Fall nights when **Glow** seemed to rise from wet Beach. Watching that it seemed to us that Eternal Mystery was combined with the common-place of everyday Living: Death and Life were one.

Always ahead, luminous Glow from Sand. Above and below Beach (from Woods, the side away from Surf, to Surf) was eery darkness which hid Ocean-wind distorted trees beyond the berm. From nights so black that no guide to Surf existed through vision, muted Surf voice was guide to itself. Nights came in which no light but the occasional 'lighter-ness' of a comber revealed a level from which we could judge 'where's Surf'? The mystery of *Glow* and the chance 'of seeing it tonight' drew us, so walkers went to Beach in hopes of seeing the miracle.

In that midzone berm above Surf, surrounded by darkness, Glow didn't appear each night. It appeared infrequently, unexpectedly. Times when Beach walkers were treated to the phenomenon, first to appear was a faint Glow, which stayed ahead of who was walking. Then it strengthened. Light, which appeared without apparent source, moved ahead as we walked. Turn around, there it was; or to the right; to the left: Glow. Simply, it was *just lighter than night.*

In recall it seems to have occurred on the darkest of nights, nights as far from full Moon as time could arrange, as in later Fall when Salmons came home. Few of us made nightly walks, beside Surf, other than pre-*Hoquat* Elders. But hope never failed us…when seen, next day who had had the experience would tell of it. I saw it perhaps a dozen times… probably less; I don't remember the number; they're unimportant. Important, the experience.

To be in Darkness which made Surf invisible along Beach, confronted by Glow beyond explanation from illuminant only Spirit could cause, which lighted a mere portion of the Living Sand upon which we walked, *was* Spiritual in all its aspects. Among the many things which made of us Spiritual People was that inexplicable Light: Glowing Beach.

It was an almost black and white world, the world of Coast. Except for Sunsets there was little of vivid color in which to immerse ourselves, especially before the '39-'40 murder of Forest. Forest was. Edged by Beach.

Then it wasn't.

Glow was its own phenomenon of 'color'.

Vaporous, dancing Mist rose from Beach Sand during fog-dimmed days as invisible rays from Sun heated Sand, and Mist rose. Mist, interspersed with the brown-grey-green of Spruce, Hemlock, Fir, together with the grey of Ocean, and the whiteness of Combers coming to rest after perhaps six–thousand miles of having been waves, were the major colors of our Lives.

But a glory of color came with a clear horizon at Sundown. The clear sky of evening which presented a horizon beyond and below the lead-grey stratus cloud mantle, our cover from Crow-call 'til Sun dropped, was awaited with color-hunger. The flaming, almost molten golden-yellow Day-star lighted our world with shocking contrast to the interminable grey displayed most of the day; the year. The heart of the sky was saying goodnight with beauty only it could present. Fortune gave that to us on many evenings so color wasn't denied us entirely.

In the six-month span between Sun-to-South and Sun-to-North the sights of charcoal grey silhouettes, J.I. (James Island—Ahkalut) and Cake Rock in Summer and the Needles, to the South in Winter, against blazing, brilliant yellow and red and orange with powder blue sky beyond, are still so captivating to me that speech while viewing is nearly a cardinal sin. I find no words for description. Go there. See it. No destruction of Sunset by our Animal-kind is possible. Yet. For which all thanks.

There was some rare other color to tease the hunger for vividness, brightness, in the passage of the year. In its season, in their seasons, Fox-glove lent color beauty, as did the subtle scarlet of 'Bull Thistle'; 'Canada Thistle'. Black berry; Salmon berry; rare-to-be-seen wild Strawberry flowerings gave subdued color to which we were audience.

It was on 'the Spit', the sand strip from Rialto Beach to Ahkalut, that tiny wild Strawberry bushes and their bead-sized prize of berries might be found... among the sparse driftwood logs, (much more sparse than on First Beach). Ocean on Rialto Beach side has an aggressive, hard charging Surf. Who knows whether the salt laden spray nourished or impeded the strawberry plants and berries? Anyway, there they were, gorgeous little berries, honey sweet. The tiny Berries radiated a pink blush against their host's green leaves. Against a nearly indescribable yellow-tan-grey beach sand, color--wise, the red-ness of decaying drift-logs against the grey of the not-yet-rotted trunk, the deep-grey of status clouds and their contribution to our Water needs, brown walls on local islands, color was there for who would see. But oftentimes the downpour trying to imitate Niagara Falls made everything a glistening grey.

But color. Permanent colors came in books; in National Geographic magazine Coast Guards gave to us; in 'Monkeywartzez' catalog. Color, as produced by Grand Canyon, other flamboyant Earth-sites, was unknown to Quileute people: *Po-oke*. Spiritual presentations such as Glow on wet Beach-sand were the sensual "color'-impressions of profundity' which in fact were uncolored light (Rainbow gave the color spectrum, when we could see it...rare and impressive).

Our real 'color' world was from white to black, with Rainbow or Sunset for awesome-ness. (With the sole exception of the wonder of *OUR* Women's minds and hands through the colors of their baskets. 'Our' baskets. Basketry I knew [even then I knew] to be True Art).

So to this day I see 'Spirit' appear in one of limitless changes from 'white' to 'black'. Undulating Mist produces Mist Beings, (only seen obliquely, but as observable realities. These exist as moving Mist to most, but not to who has been trained to know of this/these existence(s) and to recognize it/them). Swirling Mist presents the more momentary of Life's Existences: of 'Mist Beings', (to those who are *in Po-oke* terms), 'Medicine People'. That is to say, People of Knowledge. (To Amer-ians, *'Medicine'* is the term for Knowledge). 'Power', extant in Amer-ian cultures is simply 'Knowledge'. Including Knowledge of 'how to'; of 'what is'; of 'why'.

Who had Knowledge had Power. Thus, Power is Knowledge; Knowledge is Power. Aware that what IS is what is, observant Huminals observed and learned; becoming 'Knowledgable about': Knowing People; People of the Power of Knowledge of Natural TRUTHS. These had 'strong Medicine'.

These had *good brains*.

These with patience and compassion guided us to Survival.

And in those Mists at night, when the unfindable source of Glow lighted Beach and the path of the viewer, those of Knowledge saw portends of another Reality. (I wonder if this is the 'Separate Reality' of Carlos Castaneda). Lavan Coe and Doctor Lester ('*Byack*', meaning Raven, 'Old Man' for me), who were brothers and seen as equally awesome in Spirit Power by *Po-oke*, (laughed at by *Hoquat* mind, not *Hoquat* mind), could 'read' Nature and Mist and Glow. And Lavan's granddaughter Eleanor Coe who lived with him as a young Girl, told me of seeing these brothers conjuring beings before Her eyes, often frightening Her. Their conjuring of Wolves in the kitchen terrified Her She said not long before She died.

Reading Nature was Our Salvation Power. "How long we been here using 'Power'?" I asked. "For a million years, since (the) beginning of Time," Tyler Hobucket answered, "*Maybe* ten thousand!" Until 'flooded out' by guns/law expounders Power had served.

No villages exist along our Sacred Coast, Alaska to Mexico, wherever Human People lived, where-in Spiritual portents which 'came to' Medicine People didn't sustain them; us. This guidance we believed in (and do) as did Joan of Arc, whose visions were no less real, nor more, as 'visions from the 'God-force belief' which exalted *her*. 'Visions' and readings of SPIRIT have been experienced by Medicine People of any time in Human existence. "Spirit? Spirit?" I've heard the laughter and derision. "I've got a hunch them Indians are nuts!" Oh? And what do YOU call '*a hunch*'?

Johnny Moses from Vancouver Island had training which gave him deep Spiritual power. He doesn't exhibit the costumery of Indian-actors acting Indian. He is a *true Talking Chief.* A throw-back. Frequently when auto-travelling I listen to cassettes of his teachings. Though relatively young he has gifts of *Wisdom* to relate. His is the story of one whose path was SPIRIT designed. Others play-act 'us Indians' vainly seeking for 'old Truths' and 'dancing' 'as Spirit command.' Johnny Moses is not acting. What he says is of old. As told. He is a phonograph record created by old Medicine Women and Men. You don't hear Johnny Moses except as the voice put into him to replay for who will listen. With his 'power' he is a treasure of worth from whom to gain Knowledge of 'old ways'. Seeing Johnny I see a man living without his own being: He's a recording.

Against a battle called Forgotten, from the hill-top of age as vantage point to view 'our kind' I see no others, but the refusal to believe that it's all gone is power-prayer in me that holds my hopes permanently. For it I drum daily. For the many of whom I have no knowledge other than 'things heard' I bless in mind.

Individuals such as Robert Peele and the beauty of his traditional cKeynoo creations are part of the hope.

Anyway, Beach was our immediate contact with the Power of the Eternal for Mortal, dependent flesh. For 'things of Life' Water and Earth **ARE** the 'Eternal'.

Beach and Surf helped bring the meditative state of Mind which seems to be 'free-flowing'. The 'free-flow' of Thought compounding itself becomes Imagination and because we are the 'Cause and Effect-Law'-aware Animal, we have imagined our Creators. Imagination rules our Existences. Those of us, they of us, who have seen Glow on night-time Beach Sand are aware of 'Power' and the Undefinable. But undefinable is not the same as non-existent. The 'world' of Mist, and what it told to who Knew of its 'Realities' was/is 'Real'. As is World War 2 to who Knew it. As is who walked on water to his 'Believers'. How deny what was seen and recorded by the seers: The experiencers and comprehenders, understanders, *the guides* to Survival? When the Queen Charlotte Islands were a live Forest, I saw that Forest in person. In 1948 'Dad', (John Hansen, with whom I lived after I left La Push) and I went there on the new commercial-fishing boat 'Margie' he'd just built, to fish for Albacore Tuna.

I went rowing with a Canadian commercial fisherman to see some of Tasu Sound and absorbed the *thousands of years ago* **world**, as it must have been *without* 'man himself'. Rivulets and waterfalls and huge ferns, Deer the size of Collie Dogs, and smaller, so ingrown without predators; jumping Salmons…my only contact with un'civilized', *balanced* Earth was pre-cut Queen Charlotte Islands. I got to see it, enter its eternality. Here was Great Spirit's 'contribution' to one of gold's hungers: Forests only God touched so far. And I saw it. Walked in it.

Felt my true size in it. Saw Great Spirit's face in that Forest. Heard God's breathing.

There was the source of many of our La Push Beach drift-logs, La Push's First Beach. Incredible prehistoric Trees often became victims of violent North Pacific Winter-storms (which hurled themselves across thousands of miles of Ocean), without resistance but Ocean surface, before smashing their screaming anger against the West coast of the 'Charlottes'. Nothing to stop Wind and exploding Sea but 'the Charlottes'. Trees grew to the Ocean's edge and fell into the raging water. This in a way we cannot imagine.

Even more logs came as storm victims from Vancouver Island and the result was a drift-log beach of indescribable jumble at La Push, thousands and thousands of logs. The Rialto Beach sand-bar (the Spit) and Ahkalut formed a backwater eddy which pulled in the monstrous victims of Winter's rage. I can think of no more sobering example of *cKwahleh*'s might than witnessing huge logs of almost two-hundred feet, up to six feet in diameter, effortlessly tossed onto Beach to tangle with others of their kind. Southeast Alaska and British Columbia made the drift-log wonder of First Beach.

Fortunately those terrible old trees in Alaska, British Columbia, Washington, Oregon and California were cut away to protect G.N.P. *Thank god for the chain-saw.* The result is as anyone of vision could predict. Today our drift-log Beach is a nothingness of little logs and pieces of drift-wood. To fly over Vancouver Island or 'the Charlottes' and see the barren hills and valleys rolling hither and yon, tree-less, but not stumpless, is angering to any who saw that Earth before the 'Bostons' came. To tear away Trees that likely as not knew Jesus in person. But! GNP and chain saw. I've been asked, "But what would those people have done for a living?"

First, cut our reproducing. Too many people; too little concern.

However, as Little Bill (Uncle Yum) told me, "The time is lily ways (little way) over the horizon when who gets no *Chutsk* will be called 'Hero'. Time is comin' when *all us on Mother Earth* will be *part of the army to save Her.* Once time come when helpless to *repair Herself* come to our Mother, it's done. Nothin' but gra-a-a-ate time repairin' the damage. Mother Earth gonna enter a time when She can't support what ain't easy to support. That ain't us. Lon-n-ng time to repair the damage too many is bringin'. Humans alive at the time to help Mother Earth gonna be the end of our road. Human being developed during the course of events on the World. Course of events won't repeat theirself. So who don't make Children got two curses: No Child to watch grow; a unsavable dying Mother, Mother Earth".

Who knew those days, as did I, will recall the Life the drift logs sheltered. Thousands of Chipmunks and Ground-squirrels and Snakes. Strange little ponds held tiny Frog people. Large populations of Animals lived among the logs. And so many types of Bird People, vulnerably unafraid, flitting and eating and flying from log to log, nests nearby and protected. Garter-snake People ranged forth and back at ground level, seeking Slug and Frog and Mice and myriad Insects on which they gorged. I caught and lifted a beautiful Garter Snake one day and it vomited a large Slug into my hand. "Eat this, not me!" it said. If Mice eat grain and Snake eats Mice, and Slug, Insects, to stay alive, then Snake is good partner for mankind I decided.

The logs in those days were thrown above high-tide berm-line at First Beach. And I know that reports of logs piled fifteen-feet or more in height and well over fifty-feet from Ocean side to Tree-line sound unbelieveable. But until the Canadian Islands were raped of their awe-some stands of Forest, First Beach was unmatched on Earth for drift-logs as far as I have seen. I saw no such beaches on Canadian Islands nor Alaskan. Nor on mainland beaches. Just on First Beach. Having fished commercially from Alaska's Norton Sound to Southern Baja, Mexico, I bear personal witness, there was and is nothing remotely similar on any part of the western American continent to what La Push First Beach presented. Nor, anywhere on Earth I've seen from Merchant Ships.

It was that Beach which drew us Spiritually, not only in the 'glow of night', nor heart–tearing sorrow. Calm Sea, zephyr-breath wind with bright, sunny days brought out Mothers and their young, not excluding the marvelous Girls of ten or so, *the* surrogate Mothers. I see now that those gorgeous Little Women who so skillfully fulfilled the Mother role when it was necessary became wonderful Mothers later because of their experience with their younger Siblings. And the young of others. Being molded to steer Village health.

Mother guides that. As has been forever. The will and determina-tion of any Elder who pursues health is beauty in itself and those Girls grew to do their utmost to maintain their own, and families' health when they became adults and Elders themselves. That's one gift of isolation: Self sufficiency.

Often groups of us went to Beach on the lush, happy…halcyon… days to "let's look for agates for 'em bottles!", or, "We goan over at Lone-some Crick get Living-Water rocks," or, "We're goan over t' Headland to '*that*' Rock, pick Crystals," or "We got Medicine bag sand".

Frequently we got *cKwahleh* water in gallon jugs to pour into pans on our stoves, there to evaporate and leave Salt, which was then oven dried. This was to 'smoke' fish or meat, for preserving foods, or for Salt to make the *cold* Medicine bags…mates for the 'hot' bags of Sand. And for brushing our teeth, gargling…Salt was medicine. (Explanation of Medicine Bag use later).

At Beach we looked for Nature's gifts and never failed to look for 'Spirit Rocks'.

These were 'reminders' of beneficial things. Those we sought were naturally etched to resemble human faces or Animal shapes which, *naturally* cast onto stones, were said to be 'Spirit traps'. They held 'the power of the Spirit' of whatever resemblance there was, 'Old Woman Stones', 'Old Man Stones', 'Thunderbird Stones', 'Whale Stones'; these all were gathered and carried with near piety for the Spirit-trap Power they represented. "You got Thunderbird Rock in you hand you receivin' Thunder-bird powers". (These were not '*Soul Catchers*'; different. Frank Herbert liked that term so much he wrote a story about it).

I see statuettes of various 'saints' or 'power lenders' on dash-boards of autos as protectors of travelers, so wherein lies a difference between rocks cast by the Great Spirit and found by Spiritual People of 'Indian' heritage, and 'saints' cast in a factory (and sought/bought by believers of other backgrounds)? Come *on*! Come *on*!

Anything of 'Spiritual inspiration' was sought and carried for the 'inspirational power' it represented, (much as 'sacred statuary' in churches; 'beads' to pray through; or metallic castings reminiscent of *any* 'deity power'). Jesus' power is in symbol? We wore Cross Necklace to honor his gifts (although god of outsiders, it was honored in respect for them).

The 'spirit power' symbols are there to remind us of Spirit Power available to us somewhat like the crucifix is symbolic of the Power of Jesus in Christianity. Or through the representational embodiment of a god or saint or thing of Life valued anywhere: The 'saint' solicited today for its 'power'; previously, a minor 'god' prayed to by Egyptians. Et cetera.

We all have symbols of Benevolent-Power Bestowers: Rabbit's foot; old coat; old hat; lucky coin. Spirit Stones were actively sought by us, along Beach, more especially at South end by Bluff where Surf wore away Bluff and Beach at the same time. But Spirit Rocks were where one found them. Whatever coincides with good fortune, as, the lucky hat worn the day the record Steelhead is caught.

Kerr Mason jars (for canning Elk, and Bear, and Berries and Salmons, whatever we could get), were filled with Beach rocks of various colors and translucencies. We covered these with water and put them on the kitchen (or other) window-sill for daylight to project the colors into our living spaces. Every Village house had them.

We had cases of empty Mason jars stored and ready to can foods and never less than a dozen or more were rock-filled to scatter outside light into the house through the windows. Color radiated into the rooms.

Once, (before about 1930) the Headland was scalped to built the first jetty (at south side of *Ta-boke* mouth), there had been a hole through which one could pass from Beach to a small, rocky cove. There a different voice was heard where lighter Surf broke onto the cove pebbles. This the 'shshsh' of water over and through steep gravel as it flowed back to Sea after the small breakers had poured out their modest offerings of Surf-song. *Po-oke* were exhilarated by the cove and the abundance of Spirit Rocks there. Then about 1940 there was Tribal sadness when they heard the explosives roar which tore away the hardened rock of the tunnel. For *more* jetty-rock. *cKwyeh-Tee*'s little Beach where he hid from Grouse Woman.

Later, the crystal-embedded rock-in-Surf upon which we might clamber at low-tide to pick at the crystals was blown up to add to River-mouth jetty, to 'help stop silting from Ocean'. No one thought of the impending deposits from the Wesleesmitts farm, when the gone-away spongy tree-soil no longer sucked in the billions of gallons and millions of tons of Rain we had forever. So blowing away the face of Mussel Island and the Headland and our delightful little gravel beach were for nought in the final analysis. Once too, there had been a marvelous arching bridge from Ahkalut to a prominent rock beside it, (little James Island). Dynamite is tough. And *Hoquat*, determined.

But before that the magic of Beach, with the mysterious glass net-floats (now known to be Japanese net-floats), and the penetrating search for agates for Mothers, and the careful collecting of Salt-water/Fresh water pebbles at Lonesome Creek for making Living Water, was thousands of years in developing. When, in Summertime, did families not skim Beach? For us, we young, (perhaps for parents), to continue that ages-old tradition was almost unbearable joy. Sadly, exhilaration is unseen in the young, by me, anywhere, since then. Today I see only the blasé attitudes of Children not left to a Childhood upon which to grow. Legally 'socialized' to be profit-producing consumers.

The taste of *LOVE* (hand-in-hand with Mother) as we walked along Beach, the hugs of affirmation at discovery and analysis, the lessons given and the knowledge gained…how could *Primitives* have been so Human? So ordinary.

Human? How important to *Po-oke* was Beach. (Until Winter when Beach's face was aggressive, moody. And avoided except by Elders who needed Beach's 'balm'.

We were Babies on Beach with 'Mothers', (real or surrogate), learning *Love* for Love.

How important were Babies. No purpose existed beyond *CONTINUATION*. Babies, being *continuation* required the uttermost of preparation for to continue…to continue Life. Love received has greater Power to instill confidence in Self than any other. Guidance to ability to survive through loving education about Reality without the irrationalities of 'I believe therefore it is' as base; this their way.

Once upon a time.

Frequently *Hoquat* tourists fished Surf for perch and we young were inevitably drawn to any caught collection of the bright silver, vertically flat fish. Long casting-poles depositing hooked bait far beyond the first and sometimes second line of breakers amazed us. Too, we were fascinated by the experience of running our bare big-toes across the fishes' bloated bellies, causing 'dozens?' of wriggling, live, baby Perch to shoot out into the world which now was denying them the Life which Surf birth was to have given. We used our toes because our feet were inevitably bare.

Summer was the joyous time when the restriction of shoes was cast aside by young and old alike, Women, Children and Men. Anyone who wore shoes in Summer-time was pretentious beyond belief… except for Men who were in the height of fashion wearing hip-boots. These Men would stride along, boot-straps jangling, ringing, at every step. *These were Tss'y'uck*, who hunted food on *cKwahleh*. cKeynoo Men, who might be leaving to go to Ocean at any time. But none of the others of us would have anything under our feet but *flesh*.

Ah Beach! At Beach we challenged advancing Surf-foam to stop at our feet, then would retreat a modest few inches further until Foam settled into the thirsty sand and lay with crackling, hissing bubbles slowly dissolving by our toes. We had commanded Ocean and stopped it. (By way of calculated retreat).

On those nearly silent-Surf days I would oftentimes watch the slow, lazily curling fat little breakers and wonder at the difference between this and storms of Winter which brought its unbelievable seas.

How tall is Ahkalut? Over one hundred feet? The split at the 'West' end of Ahkalut is "where the anchor dragged and held during 'the Flood' which brought *Po-oke* here and sent ChemacKum over there". cKeynoo anchor for holding the People split the island at least half-way before it held and during *BIG* Winter-storms *cKwahleh* pours its power into the split and spray clears Ahkalut's top to settle across *Ta-boke* mouth and onto Beach way past the jetty. The 'boom' of breaking seas in the anchor-split end of Ahkalut can be heard during Winter storms as far away as Quillayute Prairie. When I had the hearing ears of Childhood I've heard La Push Surf from Forks.

How can Ocean and Surf be so changeable I wondered one day while Old Man (*Byack*) and his brother Lavan Coe, Vernie Black and I were on Beach. Old Man said, "You lissen to 'undervoices' of Surf…it tells you what weather goin' to be. *cKwahleh* got three voices. Deep voice, more like rumble heard on calm day; Oshunt-voice (Ocean-voice); Shallow-voice also like today. Deep voice allus there; been forever; that's heart-beat of Mother Earth. Other voices talk about weather now and weather comin'. Oshunt-voice is middle voice from breakers comin' from Over There… far away storms. Shallow-voice is Peaceful Seas. You can hear Deep Voice under Shallow-voice but can't hear nothin' else when OshuntVoice is soundin', that voice always loudest. But when you can hear *Deep*-voice you can hear Shallow-voice. At same time. Tellin' you 'bout peaceful Seas. In tunnel before train enter you hear an' feel rumble. Deep Voice is like that. Almost too deep to hear, so peaceful Shallow Voice says 'washhh-washhh-washhh' an' you can hear 'em both."

"Liss'nin' you hear what likely is oldest voice on Earth, *rumble voice*. On top of that sounds like boat-waves against *Ta-boke* Beach, little 'swishing sound', come to you. But unless you get local Wind pushin' bigger waves close by you, ain't gonna get no storm for two-three days. Two kinds of breakers an' rumble, one from far-off storm an' one from close-by storm. Wind makes waves. Breakers comin' which is even spaced is from 'way over there'. Big, unregular, crossing waves are end of nearby storm or storm goin' on right here. Lotsa stuff to learn 'bout *cKwahleh*' (if) you gonna live by it."

"And on it like *Tss'y'uck*," *Byack* added.

"Once Oshunt-voice drownin' out other voices you gettin' heavy weather out side Ahkalut. Whalin' cKeynoo weather. It don't pick-up more Wind in half a day, little more, then what's there is worst to be, good enough for Sealin' cKeynoo, for now. People of Those Days knew to lissen; knew about Voices of *cKwahleh*." Lavan Coe.

Vernie and I looked at one another, surprised. There seemed no end to the information Elders carried to teach us. It was as if Lavan read our thoughts, "Ayy...there's even a little more than that to know about. Lissenin' to Voice of *cKwahleh* tells about if it's safe to go for Whales, Seals, if it's safe for to go by shallow rocks fishin' for Snappers, goin' over to Halibuts Hole. Nobody traveled by cKeynoo until *cKwahleh said*, 'O.K., go'." Thereupon for two hours or so we listened to Surf to detect differences in its voices and learned to listen specifically for information about Weather.

"Who knows more about Weather than *cKwahleh* what knows because it help make weather. And it tell about it to who will listen and learn." Old Man was silent after that, but Lavan added, "Ev'rythin' talks to who will listen. An' learn." In Truth it is so.

PACK MIND

On Beach, above the line of ebbing high tide, hot Sun-beams baked drying Sand into a caked surface perhaps a quarter-inch thick. As we walked on the hardened Sand it broke even under Children's weight. Where small feet had trod we'd leave indentures. Or at times we would take a twig and create a circular break in the Sand trying to lift a 'Sand-pancake', crisp, hardened and challenging to get because of brittleness. For that time of Childish interest we contested to see who could lift the biggest piece of Sand-cake. I found that round pieces broke easier than pie-shapes.

This caked Sand floated on unrippling water into *Ta-boke* frequently. As incoming Tide carried Sand-clumps they'd dot River's surface as far up River as near Mora…as far as the old Sprowel place. Floating, crisped sand flowed under the foot-bridge by Hobbies Mitts house, way up Smith's slough. It literally lined River-beach shore-line with vast clusters of floating Sand cakes perhaps four or more inches in diameter. This in Summer when *Calm* was Coast's nature. Fullest high Tide brought this floating peculiarity into River and when ebb-Tide silently drained River, these small clumps of Sand from Surf Beach lay crisp for as far along both sides of River as high Tide carried them. They would refloat on high Tide again, but for minutes only as six hours on wet Beachs robbed them of much of their dry buoyancy.

When Sand cakes lay about, Sand-pipers swarmed-in to race along Beach stabbing at Sandfleas, in a frenzy of dashing, here; there; fly; land. Forth and back Maybe the Sandfleas were transported on the floating Sand cakes in to River Beachs, there to await their fate: 'grub' for Sand-pipers. I was told by Freddy Woodruff that 'swarms' of Birds and other kinds of 'swarm-types' have the same 'mind', called 'Pack Mind'.

"Look how they split, ball-up, rise, dive, explode then rush to settle on Beach. How can they each know to turn with 'em all, exact same second at a given second? Only way we figure is that 'Body' of the flock is as big as all the Birds in it. They're the cells of the Body. They obey a mind controlling them, like us, each by itself to turn exactly at the time one on other side of flock turn. They're a 'body' not joined under *skin*." Freddy was a forever source of honest response to the queries of the inexperienced young.

At times (for unknown-to-me causes), Sand-flea Empire ruled Beach. To walk in swim- shorts was to be bombarded by leaping Sand-fleas which bounced off harmlessly, (unless *they* got head-ache from bumping so hard). 'Pipers must have had telegrahy to transmit the 'news': BIG FEAST RIVER BEACH TELL 'EM ALL! SAME THING FIRST BEACH!!! (Maybe poor humor about the feast for Sand-pipers but the truth was that: Big feast for Sand-pipers at La Push)!!

Each area along Beach presented different Sand. Coarser Sand was deposited near *Ta-boke* mouth, behind Jetty, and became more fine further South. At Lonesome Creek, incredibly smooth, oval and dark colored (near-flat to bulging on a side) Pebbles were Sand-held in place on both sides of Creek. Fingernail sized on average the Pebbles were used to make Living Water and lay in/on fine Sand (which we used in Medicine Bags) while just above Surf were Pebbles of coarse, sharp shapes, much larger than on the rest of Beach.

(If 'Medicine Bags' haven't been described they were two 'bean-bag'-size soft leather covers for: 1) Salt, (dried from *cKwahleh* water, on Stove); 2) Sand, (from Lonesome Creek, oven dried in a second bag. [Put identifying mark on a bag as, 'red patch'? for 'hot', oven *heat* to about 200 d. F.]).

'Salt': Chill as cold as possible, (to-day these bags would be in the freezer until needed). We kept 'Sand' in warming oven above kitchen range, 'warm-ready' for 'big' oven. (Now comes Microwave).

The bags would be placed on either side of the needing place: Bad bruises, ankles, knees, etc., bruised muscle from a fall perhaps. Kept in place until *neither heat nor cold were felt any longer the* bags would be reversed. *This* until again no *further* difference could be felt. This might continue all day. One thing is guaranteed, kept at *it works*. '*Living water*' was 'regular La Push water' boiled in a glass or non-metal container, (a Kerr Mason jar mostly). On the bottom an inch of Lonesome Creek pebbles and the whole put into a metal pot with boiling water heating the Living Water. Boiled and cooled it would be kept for cooking, drinking, making poultices, moisture for Berry, Meat-Marrow 'pack-food', (used by who might be 'Over There', maybe Hunters). (At times pinches of Salt might be added to use for disinfectant, gargle, eye-wash, sinus-cavity 'snuffling'…). Are any of these skills used today? I wonder and hope.

SURF SPIRITS

One of the games our Parents played with us was 'watching for 'Surf Spirits". Inside the closest line of breakers smaller breakers raced nearly parallel to the Surf line but angled to one another coming from different directions. They moved at surprising speed and when two came together the meeting point leaped high in the air then both small waves and breaker disappeared. The racing little breakers "… are Surf-Spirits and they jump inta (into) Air when they meet". We were encouraged to watch for them to see them play. Of course we saw them regularly, but for too short a time to describe. Surf (Sea) Spirits are small and elusive but they can be seen…if you're a Child.

In recent times I told this story to a drawing class I was teaching and one of my students, tremendously gifted and surely capable of professionalism, made a picture for me as gift, a Surf-spirit which I'm including in the work, with Her permission, as example of Spirit impression. Beautiful input of Spirit guidance.

Even now in walks along Beach I look to see Surf-spirits which have chased one another in Surf-tag since Time began. I saw them as Child, and I do today, as an old man. (Even from home in Seattle).

MORE ABOUT BEACH; SPIRIT

What is now River mouth was a lagoon, we were told, before 1921, when *Ta-boke* still flowed to *cKwahleh* at Rialto Beach. Where a 'bight' formed near South *Ahkalut* a 'side-wheeler' steamer had wrecked and supposedly gold coins were found even into the twentieth century. Local history said this wreck had occurred after the 1860's. (We were told that from it stepped one 'Salvation Army' Smith, who liked the primitive and undeveloped area, [nothing here but Savages I presume], saw it as 'legally available' and sent for brothers A.W. 'Wesley' Smith, [WesleesMitt]; Oliver Smith, OliversMitt and young Harvey, 'HobbiesMitt' and sister Mina. I don't know the truth of that story, it was a story we heard at La Push about how the Smith family came to know about, settle here and take the land legally. In fact, much later I read in a book written by a pioneer child, Dorothy Smith Klahn, (daughter of Mina), that the man had been A.J. Smith and he had landed at Neah Bay, had not been ship-wrecked at La Push????

Tyler Hobucket told some of us who were playing on that area of Beach to look for gold coins. He said that in his childhood he'd heard that *Po-oke* had found such coins and because of their unknown value had used them as little wheels to roll along on Sand. He told us that as a Child his generation had been able to see parts of the wreckage, boilers and twisted metal, sticking from Sand at low tide. His brother Harry said the same thing. (Tyler was born on Beacon Hill Beach in Seattle in 1898 in a cKeynoo. His parents were picking hops in the valley). Of course we young looked for gold, but without specifics we lost interest and turned to making toy 'autos' of Bull Kelp, or tempted what we were told was poison at the end of the tails of Surf-tossed 'skates', actually 'Rays' (Manta Rays) of small size. These were a constant on Beach so that on any day one could see *cKa'a'yo*, *Byack*, *cKulell* in groups, tearing at the food supply given by Surf. An estimate: five or six could be found any day. Dog-fish (small Shark people) caught and killed by commercial Salmon fishermen drifted ashore to add to the Bird's larder. And in my early teen-years I came upon a fascinating rarity, a Sun-fish, round, strange top and bottom fins, no tail...another Beach mystery from *cKwahleh*. Having seen a pair of them swimming in *cKwahleh* I knew what it was.

Sea grasses *Po-oke* valued were shown to us with explanations of use. Elders still used what Ancestors had used and use by them constituted our regular Primitive schooling.

Some strange little buds of Sea-grasses, clustered somewhat like grapes, and filled with a thick, sustaining liquid, were carried in baskets by *Tss'y'uck* out to Seal 'channel', (twelve miles and more from *Ahkalut*) to augment the filled water-bags also taken. Who fished by Rocks and Islands wrapped their catch in this Sea-'weed' which kept the catch cool I suppose. I wonder: did the weed's 'slimy' coating have preservative merit?

Tss'y'uck prepared for the hazardous voyages onto *cKwahleh* carefully. Mostly mental preparation: Medicine: Power. (These voyages were made when Seal people were swimming North to Alaska.). The long journey for Seal-hunting was still on-going in my Childhood. Oftentimes Morton Penn brought roasts of the dark red, fatless meat to Village people. He and Grant Eastman were of the Men who saw to it that there was no hunger in Village. (Grant still harpooned prey). 'Father' trolled for Salmon from his cKeynoo (until he was able to lease a *Hoquat* 'troller') and provided some of this to others, more especially Elders, as one of the respected Providers. Today I salivate, thinking of the food we ate.

The bay between *Ahkalut* and Henderson Head (*cKuateata*) was called Whale Bay because Grey Whale entered the area during part of their North/South annual migrations. At their season we stood on Beach and watched them spout in large numbers, close to the Ocean area outside La Push. But not always did *Tss'y'uck* find Whale near Village. Deep Ocean routes by Whale beckoned *Tss'y'uck* to go 'way out'. Until 1912, when Joe Pullen took the last Whale by a Quileute. (By strength of arm, not by a nick with a sharp stick and some *Hoquat* with a high-power rifle to do the 'taking').

We were told that for their hunt all *Tss'y'uck* prepared themselves with physical and mental 'Medicine'. For *cKwalla* (Whale) it was year long preparation involving abstinence from gratification; Spirit quest in Cedar Forest or along Coast, isolated and meditative; fasting; Spirit Board study, all utterly fascinating. They were hunters for the largest food supply known: *cKwalla*. And for the few Men in a vulnerable cKeynoo the most dangerous. Onto *cKwalla*'s world. Perhaps miles from home on *cKwahleh*. *These were Men*. None questioned the valor and Spirit Power of who took *cKwalla*.

These *were* Men. They had no *Hoquat* with high-powered rifle to finish off the horror caused from jabbing one of these marvelous Whale People by a tavern-built throwing arm. (Then letting some 'stand-by' put the victim out of its long misery, later to brag about being mighty Whale Hunters. Rubbish). None but the mighty sought Whale and they took them without European 'arms' assistance, guns. And never in 'pride' nor ego gratification. They didn't swagger and sneer to show their 'superiority'.

Men were humbled by the majesty of the People they killed. It is and was to them, murder of another living Person. Sorrowful and thankful at the same time, they thanked *cKwalla* People for giving food to them for the lean times. Having spent a year in preparation for this 'take' from Mother Earth's Children, the Whalers acknowledged their dependency upon Power beyond themselves. They were not to take *cKwalla* unless *need* was there. *cKwalla* belonged to *cKwyeh-Tee* and to kill his children for 'sport' was to invite disaster. The more successful they were the more humility they felt. Their's a humbleness toward 'the Power of Life-Spirit' and the awesomeness of it; the total dependency on that power. And distribution was not at Village alone, Ozette, Hoh, Neah Bay, others received of this bounty.

Arrogance was seen in some Village *males* but not in the Men. No one ever called Joe Pullen arrogant. He was humble. The last Quileute to take *cKwalla*.

We were trained that 'good fortune' meant the pleasure of Great Spirit toward us and our actions. We were told to give 'all credit' to The Power and not to be proud…pride, we were told, is for who thinks that what they gain is accomplishment of their own superiority. We were warned by all to be humble about anything we did because Spirit *Power* gave the ability to us…not ourselves. What was given could be taken away easily…what then of ego?

"'About' 1912," Joe Pullen said, talking of that taking as we walked with 'Big Bill' Penn through Cedar Forest at Cape Flattery. There was no "I won the foot-ball game" ego/arrogance in his recall. "You don't like to kill stuff" he said. "When somebody think what they done they done by theirself an' their own Power without the mighty Power of Great Spirit in 'em an' brags, get away. Dangerous. 'don't need that talk."

I have several turn-to-the twentieth-century glass slide photographs of Quileute families and Village scenes which do not include the Whale beaching after that catch, but I'm sure someone has pictures of Joe's last Tribal feeding-success. I've seen a picture of Whale butchering on Beach near *Ahkalut*. Mr. Taylor from Mora had a daughter named 'Tealy' (sp), who had hundreds of area photos. Where are they now?

Incidentally, the Cedar stand at Flattery together with remnants of logs for cKeynoo downed long ago using fire-rings is now a stump-spiked barren-Earth mass of rolling hills…in that which remains after the Gross National Product was improved by Forest Killers. In 1958 I took the last photos of the old stand and what the People had used and preserved 'since the beginning of time'

LOSE-LOSE SITUATIONS

Daniel White was philosophical about the position/condition of all Native Amer-ians.

The 'brave ones', he told me, were all dead, fighting to the death against the disease of Money invasion. "Learn about the 'Trail of Tears' forced on Cherokee People. Grand-mothers, Grandfathers, pregnant Women, sick and young and Elders. Forced marching on foot for thousands of miles, much of it over rock in hot sunshine not their experience, overseen by gun-toting monsters on horseback. They drove them Cherokee from the *heritage lands* along the East oshunt to barren rock at Oklahoma, like cattle on a 'round-up trail'. Amer-ians all learned about 'concern', 'love', 'religious integrity'. The heros was the ones who died, *cKulell*, leaving none of the able Women and Men at the hands of the 'rat-like infestation' overwhelming them." Daniel shrugged.

"Them Natives remaining after the invasion by the Gunmen and their families cowered for their life and the life of their families. They was Cowards because they had no Choice: Enslavement to the Gunmen and their ways…or die. Dead, no help to family.

"Gun claimed the land for the Gunmen, an' their evil cunning. Gun-owners. It wasn't their better brains or decent way of Life (to get seen an' recognized for better way an' copied at once by us backward an' strugglin' Natives), it was their not bein' sensitive to the lands an' ways of the gunless. No way out for Natives. Even 'laws' didn't protect Natives; "law ain't *no law* which ain't obeyed by *Citizens AN' Govermint*".

"They was ruthless who overcome us. Cold; apart; no feeling. They saw no lack of virtue in their murders an' land grab. They loaded trains to go kill them shaggies (Bison) just to be killin'. Big fun. They took off the scalps of Indian kind to sell to gover'mint to prove they'd done in some Indians: *Paid*, for havin' the fun of killin' human beings. They run all over Cadipodia (California) killin' 'til the land run red. Ay-y, the invasion made drunks and/or cowards out of strong, brave an' independent people. Drunk washes away pain sometimes, for many. Indians was hunted down just to kill. Some law said 'Don't dig for gold in Cadipodia where Natives live'. So *kill* the Natives.

"*Then* dig for 'Go'd'. Read about Ishii." Daniel laughed when he finished this statement, so he wouldn't cry I guess. *Po-oke* have that habit.

SUMMERTIME

It was the La Push of 'scow days', Summer-time contact with the commercial Salmons-trolling crowd; of dozens of anchored Salmons-boats operated by Danes and Swedes and Norwegians; Finns; Greeks and on and on; of Pow-wows and bone-gamble and lodges of *Tss'y'uck* and *Tss'ay-whutleoke* and *Tloquali* and their joy by drumming and singing; of relating the deeds of *cKwy-ehTee*; of the mournful sound of Shaker Church Bell; of cKeynoo carving, of 'sweat lodge'. Because I never Lived in Village after it was diluted to full English speaking… full-blood-Quileute disappearance, I remember La Push as it was over 70 years ago, Amer-ian people living Quileute ways. I don't know the 'modern' La Push. But 'old La Push' is alive in me.

A thing I remember and liked about Summer was the arrival of the fish-buyers' 'scows'. These were plain barges towed to La Push from Seattle or Neah Bay or Westport for buying *Alita* during their seasons. On them were living quarters and storage in ice for fish, to go to Seattle every day or two in 'tending' vessels, 'tenders'. I recall the massive boxes of rock and cement used as anchors for the scows, four feet square and a foot deep. Cut loose when the season was finished the anchors remained on *Taboke* bottom. I wonder how many of them lie under feet of silt outside the 'marina' and toward *Ahkalut*. Scows were towed to anchor at specific sites by Salmon 'tenders', (later to carry boxes of fresh, iced Salmons from the buyers' scows to Seattle), which were of special interest to *Po-oke*. They might carry a Mother and Child to Seattle on some necessary trip, or Women and Men, but always with a friendliness the usual *Hoquat* encounter didn't bring. Outsiders were nicer than locals among *Hoquat*. Certainly they were more considerate in their attitudes and behaviors than was Hobbies Mitt with his attitude of 'poor Indians'…meaning he felt no sorrow for our plight of invasion and displacement birthed poverty. He was part of it.

One of the 'tenders' was the 'Harmony', which vessel I've seen even in more recent years in what was once Fishermen's Terminal by Ballard. Others were the George Washington, the Abraham Lincoln, the Gloria West (a World War one converted sub-chaser), the Rover, the Roamer…they all bought newspapers from me at one time or another as I sold newspapers from my little skiff 'Homebrew'.

I'd traveled to Ballard and through the Locks on The 'George Washington' and the 'Rover' and the 'Harmony' before I could walk. These and other tenders were part of our Summers and to this day the thrill of looking N.W. past Cake Rock and seeing the mass of squareness the scows presented as they came down the coast, racing to outrun bad weather, lives with me. We looked forward to them on *Taboke* for reason.

During Summer we Village kids tried, deviously, sometimes successfully, to sneak onto an end of some scow. Once aboard, "Don't talk or make no noise" we'd whisper to one another and lower our fishing gear into the clear water, to watch dozens of five and six inch Salmon-young sneer at our hooks. Bull-heads we caught, and flounders to take home to eat. Bull-heads we returned to River.

Among 'scows' I remember was Doremus Fisheries. One of HobbiesMitts daughters, Betty, married one of the men employed on Doremus's scow, one Art Munson, or Monson. He farmed on Beaver Prairie the rest of his life. And there was United Fishermen's Packing Co. scow, bossed by an understanding man named Bill Kirk. If 'BK' wasn't busy he would permit up to four of us to board while he oversaw our actions, watching out for us for our protection: Rivers don't care whom they drown.

A man named John Hansen (who later became my guardian) owned a scow which he leased to the 'FCA' or, Fishermen's Co-operative Association. It had been the Far West Fisheries scow when John ('Dad') bought and converted it. I remember his 'sign', John Hansen, Fish-Groceries. And there was Lars Anderson's 'Home Scow', which Porky Payne saved from sinking when a freshet driven log slugged into it at the water line and it began taking on water. And the Union

Oil scow with its bulk-fuel tanks ready to supply the fishing boats. I don't know *its* supply source.

'Home Scow' had pretty waitresses to serve food and beer drinks to fishermen. And boat-dwellers could bathe using Home Scow facilities. In Fall 1939 a new arrival was the scow run by two men, Butts and Pattison, who came to Village to buy fish for San Juan Fishing and Packing Co., and literally took over fish-buying at La Push. Others came and went but B&P were able to out-bid all others with San Juan's purse behind them. For years they were the only show in town. Pattison left later and Butts became the buyer by himself. Bobby Ward competed against them with moderate success. And a man named Zimson.

Most fishermen (in some cases with their wives, [or other 'long-haired boat-pullers']) trolled all day, sold their fish in early evening to a preferred fish-buyer then anchored in *Taboke* awaiting four things:

1: Me in my skiff 'Homebrew' selling the 'P.I.' newspaper, (the 'Times' was from *yesterday* evening and wasn't bought);

2: their evening meals;

3: their night's sleep;

4: the 3:30 alarm clock call.

Early morning darkness called them into activity for another day on *cKwahleh*, toiling for Salmons.

HobbiesMitts son-in-law, Wayne Richwine, had the mail-carrier contract for Forks-La Push for several years. When he returned to La Push in the afternoon with mail and newspapers I was at Howeattle's store to get papers from Mrs. Mary (Charlie) Howeattle, for delivery to the fishermen. With fifteen or so papers I rowed from vessel to vessel, at anchor, to sell the latest on the outside world.

Fishing Boats ranged in shape and size from the 'attractive' to the ridiculous. Depression dollars were rare and fishermen devised such 'rigs' as they could from which to fish.

cKlumbyuh (Columbia) River trollers with fore-peak accomodations; old life-boats of metal, from steam-ships, (surplus boats which leaked through rusting bottoms); cKlumb-yuh River gill-netters converted to permit 'living aboard'; World War 1 surplus boats of various shapes and sizes, all used for commercial fishing. These were the vessels awaiting me in 'Homebrew', selling the daily paper.

Strange accents fell on my ears from boat to boat. John Krocus, a Greek, had a lovely boat named the Potamus. 'Liberty Jack', boat

Liberty, (WW1 army vet who wore army issue clothing, heavy brown woolen trousers that flaired at the sides like 'riding breeches'); John Rudolph who fished from the 'Shamrock' after previous owner 'Sully' Sullivan drowned; Charlie Thorsen from the boat 'Rita'; Alf Benson with whom I fished at times, all spoke with heavily accented old country brogues.

Ta-boke was deep and clear in those days before Forest was gone. After that, Coastal rains flushed fertile Forest soil into Creeks and Rivers and deposited it between River mouth and Rialto Beach, just opposite HobbiesMitt's slough. (HobbiesMitt was Quileute pronunciation of Harvey Smith, who had farmed nearby the village) An exceptionally heavy storm in the mid-'60's was while Wayne Richwine owned and lived on his deceased 'Uncle-in-law's' old home property: The A. Wesley Smith farm and house.

This was up-stream from La Push, past Mr. James' Mora Park Resort. Wesley Smith's place was at 'the ox-bow'. That Winter one of the worst rain-floods of several years broke a 'short-cut' near (big, up close near) Wesley's home-place, mere feet from the house. All the earth removed is now bottom for a few-inches-deep-River outside 'the marina' at La Push.

Modern Rez-kids at La Push don't know the anger we felt toward 'them bosses in P.A' who caused the building of 'that marina', dredging away *our* mud-flats to drive pilings for docks. They cared nothing for Indian traditions; Indian sentiments; Indian desires. We knew they had less concern for Our ways than for the ways of migrating Birds. Indians, after all, are only half human. (No, let's see, they reasoned that Blacks were 60% human, Indians about 40%).

From where the mud-flats ended to a 'ford' across the mouth of Slough (HobbiesMitts), was a gorgeous and wild little forest in which we young practiced stealth. When 'that marina' was built it took away both forest and all the marvelous rivulets from tidal action within our beloved once-tidal mud-flats. Spring-time birthed young Crows (*cK'ay'yo*) through-out that little Forest and Old Man studied the talk of *cK'ay'yo* and *Byack* there as a Child. They found other places to raise Babies after that and with their early morning hollering for food left to go elsewhere

In an earlier year Cake Rock (about two miles from River-mouth) had 'run into' the coastal passenger-steam-ship H. F. Alexander. One of the souvenirs of that adventure was their (ship's crew's) unloading of a life-boat, which was then abandoned on dry land at the little Forest. Also left was a long piece of hawser which, from my later-on 'steam-shipping' Life I came to know was mooring line. I don't know why it was there but we young even went so far as to sail that life-boat out and across the deep Ocean, *clear to China!* (dragging 100 feet of steam-ship hawser, 'Cargo' of course). We sailed away from La Push to China many times. Many times. And to many other lands, Pago Pago; Mars; Strayuh (Australia); Gobi Desert. Places we learned about in school. I've dreamed of those 'hair-raising life-boat adventures' in later years. We were so young; so brave; so imaginative.

I don't have the bravery to depart on such adventures of Mind anymore.

I'm crazy now.

But back to *our* Mud-flats. It was a thick, slick, clay-like mud. For years the flats had provided hot mud and warm water at low tide on rare hot Summer days. On those days the mud holes were filled with ten-inch deep mud-gravy and screeching village young. After the exquisite joy of mud bathing, *Ta-boke* beckoned with stimulating, fresh *cKwahleh* flood-tide filling it. As the mud-holes began to fill with the chilling Sea-water we'd bound across the coarse grasses of the mud-flat tops (risking Bee sting from stepped on Bumble Bees) to enter the colder water of *Ta-boke* for the rinse off, then race for home and heat, if it was evening. Else we dressed and ran in now soggy clothes until 'dry'.

Before the last and huge freshet, an ox-bow had given wide protection to the 'A. Wesley Smith place', specifically fields (where cows grazed) with River surround on three sides and the house on the fourth. That was displaced forever by the breech and today the Quillayute runs steadily beside the house. In our youth *Ta-boke* was so clear that on uncloudy days we could see bottom and small crabs and flounders and bull-heads and young Salmons. *Ta-boke*, then, was deep enough that no thought of 'bottoming' ever came to mind for the anchoring fishermen. Fifteen feet at mid-tide is a reasonable estimate of how far it was down to the visible bottom. Even the lowest tides had reserve depth for anchoring.

No longer does a clear day bring visible bottom from fifteen feet above.. Today dirt colored water of wading depth flows from HobbiesMitt's slough to the dredge-maintained 'deep water channel' that passes the old 'Coast Guard boat-house'. The 'deep channel' is dirty even with the tide in and full. Coast Guard boat-channel serves for the marina as well, but it's not as when the Coast Guard Station was established

The 1921 freshet had sanded up the existent mouth of *Ta-boke* at Rialto Beach. A storm coupled with 'spring-tide' and flooding River blocked the normal outflow and River spilled into a lagoon that lay between Rialto Beach and *Ahkalut*, then broke down the barrier on the South end of *Ahkalut* where River mouth is today. This was a much safer entry to River, but needed to be maintained, thus a jetty was built of rock from Henderson Head (*cKuateata*) and 'James' and 'Mussel' Islands.

Less than a mile up-river from the present mouth (near the previous mouth) is the bluff from which a long 'sand-spit' projects out to *Ahkalut*. Where the sandspit swings North and becomes continental Beach, there a store and two or three tourist cabins were built. Then, closer to the bluff and north-ward perhaps five-hundred feet, amongst the wind-sculptured Beach trees, were a dance hall, several 'outhouses' and several tourist cabins which I think were part of the store/cabin enterprise. I've mentioned the dance-hall relative to 'The Red Hot Red Snappers' band and 'Mother' and the reflecting Moon-glow on *Ta-boke*.

THE COAST GUARDS

They began operation in 1931 when Walter M. Robbins arrived (with his wife Jessie(?), daughter Patricia Jean and son Phillip Walter) to take command of the new station. I think Robbins was 'Chief Bosun's Mate'. 'Cap' Robbins retired in 1936 and the station seemed to change with the changing of 'management'. The station was 'to protect the fishermen, and Indians in their canoes on the ocean'. For 'safety' no doubt. But in fact, rum-runners from 'north' ran booze to Quillayute River and Rialto Beach and the C.G. station put a stop to that.

Beyond the store in the direction of Mora and Forks, was and still is the road in and out for Rialto Beach. Above the road on the bluff was a 'mysterious residence', property of one 'Alexander the Great', a stage personality who traveled and performed on the 'Orpheum-circuit', we heard, (whatever that was). Beside his 'mysterious' residence was a look-out cabin on a tall stump, (from which to signal rum-runners, it was said). Rock and stone steps zig-zagged from the road-way up to the house which few of us ever entered. Later, and suspiciously, the place burned down, by accident or purpose it's impossible to know.

The stone-work is over-grown now, as if some Yucatan jungle… yet if you know where to look you can find it even in this new century. Anyway, Alexander never visited La Push/Rialto Beach after the Coast Guard station was functional. His whole enterprise became 'house-afire smoke signals' then disappeared.

When 'Cap' Robbins retired in 1936 the station seemed to change with the changing of 'management'.

Several 'Coasties' had young my age and we mingled on the school bus rides, first to the Quillayute Prairie School, then to Forks. (There had been a small school at La Push, between Morton Penn's 'alley' and the huge house which had been Dan Pullens, but inasmuch as one learns no English when speaking Quileute, that stopped; for second grade we were fortunate enough to learn about prejudice in a big way, away from Village at the Quillayute Prairie School). The 'Coastie kids' weren't like Prairie *Hoquat*s (Quillayute Prairie) nor like Forks and Beaver young. Coastie kids were like unto Rez-kids in their openness and lack of haughtiness. They took us all as People like them-selves.

Among the married Coast Guard personnel was 'Chick' and Mrs. Student. They lived in one of the five houses HobbiesMitt had had built near his farm house to rent to C.G. personnel. Their three young were Dorothy, George and Shirley. Dorothy was eldest, a mature and knowledgeable young woman of twelve or so. George, who envisioned himself as among the strongest of all people (after all he ate Ralston and drank Ovaltine) was perhaps ten, and Shirley, an adorable little elf, was about eight. Across the road from them lived Oscar Hedlund and his family. We village young thought highly of Oscar; he was friendly and patient. He fathered a girl-child with Zona Smith Richwine.

Another Coastie was an aggressive man named 'Dutch' Bundy whose son was Jimmy. We saw little of Jimmy, except on the school bus. He always seemed frightened.

Second in command of the station (and the second Bosun in charge of the station when Robbins retired) was Eric Rutekroner (sp?) whose son Eric Jr. was about my age. Eric Jr., was a vital, happy kid with a younger (baby) sibling I never knew. 'JR.' kept us entertained on the school bus rides by singing and endlessly telling of what the Coasties were doing. Big Eric and his family lived in another of the HobbiesMitt rentals. Mrs. Rutekroner was from Gracearbor (Gray's Harbor) and frequently her sisters Mary and Barbara Hasbrook (sp?) would visit her.

Our older boys were much taken with them inasmuch as they had no 'non-white' biases. Friendly and attractive, they 'smote widely among the Rez-boys'. Floyd 'Klumbo' Hudson was a handsome young man highly taken with Mary. He flirted with her constantly and his name for them was 'the Hasbeen sisters'. 'Klumbo' had a pleasant sing-ing voice and I hear today his 'Isle of Capri', and 'I like mountain music, good old mountain music, played by a hill-bill dilly band...' etc. Sung to Mary Hasbrook.

A Coastie I didn't approach if I could avoid it was a man I found to be, by my present outlook, Mucho Macho: "Look at MY kid, he's bigger'n them Siwash (Indian) kids two-three years oldern him." (Bigger he may have been, but astonishing to the Coast Guard personnel, according to Mrs. Robbins, was that the 'Siwash' kids who went into the military in W.W. 2 surprised the military dentists. Our teeth were almost perfect. I personally saw no dentist until I was 20, at which time the dentist said, "You have no fillings. When did you see a dentist last?" "Never"). Lloyd was the boy's name, his older sister was 'Dort', I recall...for Dorothy? We heard later that in some tragedy Lloyd drowned. At Gracearbor. We liked the Lewis kids. Lloyd's death sobered those of us who had lived near and gone to school with him. And Coasties were 'Village' now. Siwash by the way is supposedly from 'sauvage', said to be French for 'savage', which we were, to civilized folk.

In another of the houses was Wayne Richwine and his then-wife Zona, eldest daughter of Aunt Addie and HobbiesMitt. Wayne and Zona created a son, Victor, 'Vicky', a level headed and pleasant youngster. He was killed instantly through no fault of his own in a car wreck caused by a drunk from Puget Sound area, the day after he graduated from high school. By the time of his death Vic and his now divorced dad, Wayne, had moved to the A.Wesley Smith farm, there to 'ranch' cattle. Wayne was honored by the naming of the road to his (Wesley's) old place 'Richwine Road'.

Among others of the first stationed Coasties were Art De Soto; Ed 'Higgy' Higgen-botham, from 'Interbay' in Seattle, (an ex-navy man); and one we Rez kids liked a lot, Earl Elms. Dick Durburah enlisted at La Push I've been told. He wasn't among the original crew at La Push but was in a unique situation. He enlisted, spent his career there, at length becoming Chief at the station, before he retired to live at Forks. A 'neat guy.' His passion was model T Ford autos. All the unmarried personnel were housed in the station-house, where the Robbins family was likewise housed.

'Tex' Brumble lived on the Forks side of Bogachiel bridge close to where Bill Leyendecker and Nellie and their children lived. 'Tex' was a Coastie whose Mother, Sister and brother Dale lived with him. Dale and Thelma were 'older' kids who rode the school bus with us and who were universally liked. I think Dale was about fifteen in 1936 when he drowned under the Bogachiel bridge one hot summer day. His poems about Texas ring in my mind to this day, especially about 'Bluebonnet flowers' and 'the home of my Texas rose': "I'm going back to Texas, the home of my 'Texas rose', I'm going back to Texas where the Bluebonnet flower grows, etc." He was courteous and friendly to all, as was Thelma; school bus rides were subdued after we lost Dale. In that time period the school bus driver, Bill Leyendecker, a logger also, was killed by a felled Tree which bounced from a sapling and overtook him. Nellie, his wife, died in a fall from her Arabian horse crossing an upper Quillayute riffle. We experienced many depressing rides to school over such losses.

Of other personnel stationed at La Push, one was 'Red' Greenberg (sp?) a huge and gentle red-head. We liked the Coasties, (more expecially did our girls...they could take you to movies in Forks 'cause they earned money). Many of them married our girls. That pleased us. It was nearly impossible for Indian young to marry in the village because Wesley Smith's naming process gave brothers different last names and in a couple of generations it was difficult to know if we might be marrying one of our own first cousins. Bible or not, even Primitives know better than that.

The Coasties again. Earl Elms was a village kids' favorite. He taught us to tie knots, told us about boats, talked to us about how booze and tobacco were bad for health. He even advocated sexual abstinence "because that's a gift you should keep for the girl or boy you love and marry. Then nobody else can say they shared that treasure with your mate."

Earl was almost always surrounded by village kids. Daily some enlisted man would go to the post-office for Coast Guard station mail. Over their fatigues they wore canvas-like calf-leggings and a belt with a holstered .45 caliber automatic Colt pistol. To protect the government's mail. When Earl Elms was the courier he had a wake of as many as ten young Village admirers trotting along behind him, *at his specified distance*. God, we'd have loved to have seen more than the butt of that holstered .45! (Cowboy movies you know).

I can't forget the friendly and sincere manner of Earl Elms. He brought me into a sobering 'adventure' involving a drowning one day because I had my little skiff the 'Homebrew'. "You come help find him" Earl called to me that morning, as I walked along River Beach watching Coasties and fishermen dragging grapnels from skiffs to find the drowned man.

About one a.m. in the summer of 1938 a man named Frank Miller drowned while trying to board his anchored Salmon-hauling 'tender/packer'. Frank and a crewman came to La Push periodically on the 'packer' to pick up iced and market-ready troll-caught Salmon to take to Seattle. The crewman reported the accident to the Coast Guard and at dawn men rowing skiffs pulled grappling hooks, (with others of Coast Guard, *Po-oke* and fisher-men), back and forth over River bottom and Earl found Frank's body close by where I was rowing. I remember his call to the rest of the searchers, "Hey you guys, I've got him!" They put him on the Shell Oil float and placed a canvas over him, awaiting Robert Taylor and the hearse from his undertaking offices in Forks.

He had been an encouraging and friendly man who had always given a nickel for the newspaper I delivered and a nickel for me.. "Stay away from boats an' booze, Red," he told me several times, "you go to school and learn how to do something beside bummin' "roun' th' ocean'." But what does someone born to River and Ocean people do? Farm in Kansas? Being born within 500 feet of both Surf and River is fairly predictive for the adult Life.

I guess the drowning of Earl Elms in late '38 or early '39 was the first deep sorrow I felt for someone not related to Village *Po-oke*. He was *Hoquat* but not *Hoquat*.

He died in Surf near River mouth but wasn't found until a month later. Transported by Surf along First Beach to the bluff where he had been washed ashore, the Coast Guard belt on the remains identified him. I felt fortunate that I didn't see him. After that I paid less attention to the Coast Guard crew...I felt that Earl had been an elder brother and I wanted no more losses comparable to that. Even today, almost seventy years later, I think of Earl with both pleasure and sorrow. Very complex.

ELDER INFLUENCES

I was never caught by the 'fever' other boys in Village caught, those of similar age, the fever of sports/games. I was not and am not competitive except with myself. I wasn't inclined toward the 'seasonal imperatives', football, baseball, basketball, the like. These things came and were entertaining but of no practical use but 'time taking' to me. An athlete I was not. Am not. So athletics and seasonal games came and went without me.

But! To hear of 'Quest'! Of Power such as Uncle Yum's; his father Esau Penn's; of Tommy Payne's, to be taught about *Spirit!*, *that was the ecstasy of Mind which still hasn't diminished for me*. When I was with Elders I was over-joyed: True Elders weren't confrontational, challenging, as were most male peers. *Elders 'KNEW STUFF'; THEY TAUGHT STUFF, and above all, they were patient and kind in the way they taught.*

They told about what they as young had been told about Life. Many of their teachers had taught them *before Hoquat* came to our sanctuary. *Se-ic-tiss* Ward was born in1857. And Esau Penn, Mary Ward, etc., were said to have been born *before the American Civil War* with grandparents alive at the founding of America. They talked about Living, about how they'd examined the passed information to 'test it', made their determinations and then, to my great good fortune, told me about Truth as it displayed Itself to *them*. LIFE =TRUTH.

In truth', valid explanation for the process causing Thunder exists in *modern* knowledge, which explanations are accepted because they bear the important title of 'scientific knowledge'. But tell me, did *we* discover the scientific explanation or did some intellectually aware scientist reach us 'second hand' (via Book? Lecture? '?').

Ben Franklin proved lightning was electrical, not Thunderbird's flashing eyes. It is electrical activity which causes Thunder's *BOOM*, but, is that ALL there is? How does anyone know it *isn't* caused by Thunderbird's wings also? I don't. Willie Wilasie would say, "Thunderbird up there. Maybe we get to see it!" An *ANCIENT*. I believe him.

And even if the scientific explanation is totally correct without controversy, so what? What has that knowledge presented or created which changes the cause, the noise, the effect? When lightning flashed from Thunderbird's eyes and its flapping wings boomed across the heavens, high above the dripping grey clouds that covered MOTHER EARTH's face, we young (and perhaps some Elders) sneaked cautious looks to the heavens in hope of seeing that incredible bird flying forth and back above our searching eyes. And during contemporary thunderstorms I smile and say to Self, "Thunderbird going by." It may even have been carrying a Whale…our icon at LaPush was Thunderbird wityh Whale in its claws, *'ti stilol he-all'*.

When in early mornings Drum-voice throbbed throughout Village I left my bed, dressing as I ran, in the direction of the call. When a boy or younger man appeared at Lodge with curiousity about the songs, the dancing, the drumming, he was talked to, given discussion about Man-hood and the implications suggested by 'Man-hood'; stories about 'Round', (really a Wolf in human form, more later); about *Hooday-Hooday* Girls (*cKwyeh-Tee*'s daughters) and *HibHib*, (Grouse Woman); about how *Hawayishcka* (Deer) came to be; about prayer to Cedar Tree and why. In Lodge we learned why *cKwyeh-Tee* determined Cottonwood was useless to us. We learned about us and our relationship to Life. It worked until *Hoquat* (ships) came.

Quileute, *Po-oke*, had survived 'til then.

In lodge we learned about why the smallest Forest denizen had the biggest, most powerful Spirit of all: *Cho-Cho*, Winter Wren. Pass up *this* in order to play 'games' didn't equate for me.

Those were momentary things, seasonal, like New Years, excitement every few months. SPIRIT was all *Power, Eternal. Po-oke* lived knowing SPIRIT thousands of years ago. Ball-games were temporary, the interest of the moment. Before *Hoquat* came no one ever heard of those commercial sports. Nothing commercial about *cKwyeh-Tee*. Nor about our Life-style.

cKwyeh-Tee was Arranger for GREAT SPIRIT. *cKwyeh-Tee* altered everything, *after* Creation. He was *the Arranger*, (for us). Thank *cKwyeh-Tee* for the cooling West Wind at Cape Flattery. He rewarded acts of valor and value. But also *cKwyeh-Tee* was a trickster. If one was open and honest and helpful *cKwyeh-Tee* used his powers to help. One never knew if some funny old stranger might be *cKwyeh-Tee*: Be cautious, but kind to strangers; feed them if hungry; warm them if travelers, if cold; protect them if attacked. "It could be *cKwyeh-Tee*." Our five human skin colors were decided by him. Later I'll tell more of how *cKwyeh-Tee* functioned.

In lodge who sang a song sang a song which was 'given by 'the Spirits". Songs were 'presented' to the receiver as suddenly comprehended, insightful understandings of Nature. "It came to me when I was on 'Quest'" might explain the 'singer' of a new song. Really, insight into a principle of Life composed it. Dr. Lester's most repeated and Spiritual song included "I come from where Bushes are singing." He didn't 'give' that song to me so I can't use it.

No one could use another's song without permission, or 'gain' *Spirit disapproval*. However, to honor someone in Village Life one might give (a) special song(s) away, henceforth to be the song-property of the recipient, no more to be sung nor claimed by the bestower. (Unless the new 'owner' requested the Giver sing the song for all present).

Recorded on tape I have some personal songs of William E. 'Little Bill' (Uncle Yum) Penn, son of a man of great Power, Esau Penn. I have Esau's medicine poles, ('totem poles'), as personal gifts from Uncle Yum. He recorded some of his songs on tape for me for later proper gifting or museum bestowing, "…for preservation". Uncle Yum's two Children died in the 1918 flu epidemic and the day he gave both poles and songs to me it was with the stipulation that I protect them, "…until the day my Children ask for them."

LODGE TALKS

In Lodge the heat of an oil-barrel 'stove', (actually one barrel above another, radiating withering heat as it got hot enough to glow orange), was a cold day beckoning-call when meetings were held. Youngsters who showed inclination toward *Power* were lectured there and many Babies fell asleep on bare ground in front of the hypnotizing warmth while in the atmosphere of morality lectures, duty lectures, self-control lectures. Responsibility. A *Man* exemplified Responsibility. We heard from *Tloquali* about that symbol of Maturity. Over and over. And I never failed to heed the message about 'what is a *Man*', and what is a 'male'. Big difference to the People of those pre-war times.

Tss'y'uck and *Tss'ay-whutleoke* meetings were the same. Sometimes three or four meet-ings a month were held. Big Family gatherings really. There wasn't competition among these Elders for which had the correct approach to Valued Life and the Responsibility of the Mature to The People; the Tribe. Beneficial Morality is same the World around. Despotism; destructiveness; selfishness; violence; what name for immaturity, irresponsibility do you use? The action is the same in ALL CULTURES. Therefore, if the more' is for *self-projection and self-gain* (rather than the gift of Value [ultimately to self] from any contribution TO THE WHOLE to be made by the person), one becomes one of 'The Three P's': Priests of **P**olitics, **P**iety or **P**andering. We were told that misleading Words of Confusion produced just three things, Poverty; Privilege; Repression, i.e., Politicians; Merchants; Religionists.

Major discussions/impressions conveyed were about Dominance. Bullies dominate the weak, whereas the Mature dominate self. "Who is out of control in a group is in control", we were told.

Here, in Lodge, drumming and singing and "It came to me", followed by an insight into Village/Family responsibility and duty were the purposes of the gatherings. Shaman knowledge was revealed here. Only who held the respect of Villagers because of their known values were heeded enough by other 'Elders' to be permitted to speak of *values in Human Character* to the young. Who was not respected for evident and manifest Village-value was unheeded and couldn't speak about Mature Values. And might not even visit Lodge. Not at La Push. In civilization we listen to professional 'elders' using a rubber language There, backs were turned on the unworthy. The words spoken in Lodge were not carried to the outside from Lodge; only hoped for change in behavior left the meetings. Are we not inundated today with Immature prattling about *Mature Values*? Listen to 'office seekers'.

Which brings the subject of other in-lodge discussion to me. Now I speak of those silencing and ennobling times of Women speaking in Lodge. Even the Young of moderate experience by now held Women Elders in awe, who spoke not as often (nor as long) as did Men. At those times I fled my body and the atmosphere of the Lodge, red-hot stove and all, and entered ETHEREA, that place between the 'worlds' of the normal day's experiences. Between Sleep and Wake. This the world of Spirit, of meditation. Now I pulled into my being the Wisdom of our *Tribal Eternity, Women's Life Wisdom*. Absorbed it through my skin; into my lungs, my brain. *WOMANSES TALKIN' ' BOUT LIFE!!*

These speakers were they from whom came, in the long line of People from THE FIRST, the Civilizing ways which brought us to here. Compassion when it was needed; over-coming the Self; making and nourishing *Chutsk* from their own bodies AFTER HAVING CREATED EACH GENERATION IN AN UNBROKEN CHAIN FROM FIRST. If you fail to see the wonder of building a Child in one's own body, parting it and feeding it the perfect food for development from one's own body, Miracle means less to you than to me. What is *Life-Creation* but Divine? Sacred? Miracle? In Lodge we were educated to hold Reverence for these partners with Life-God in the 'manufacture' of *each* of us, in their own bodies…i.e. our Women.

One night after Charlie Howeattle spoke Mrs. Grant (Clara) East-man gave a message to us.

Perhaps I was nine or ten when Mrs. Eastman spoke about TREA-SURE. Meditating about that night I hear as clearly as if then the way She spoke, how the frail and ebbing Elder tried to stand to talk, and how Grant was able to get Her to sit, "You'll have more stren'th to give you message if you don't spend it trying to stand," he told Her. "Don't tell *me* what to do!," She answered, laughing, at which all the assemblage laughed about Her spunk. Then, "where's the chair?" Again, laughter.

Seated, She raised Her tiny, withered hands, which had created uncountable numbers of baskets; had calmed and assured uncount-able numbers of Young; an embodied beneficial Spirit. In the typical gesture of 'spirit feeling', Her hands were raised with palms up to 'cap-ture the spirit', asking permission, attention.. She smiled. Gas-lanterns hissed overhead; shadows 'lived'. A 'spell' began.

Every face directed toward Her as She announced, "*Ho ohwoosh*! I'm talking to the Young, to tomorrow now," She said, "...' rest ' you guys can go home." All of us in Lodge laughed. Pleasure from all at the vitality still in Her. She continued:

"You young takin' to *Hoquat* ways. Losin' *Po-oke* ways, you becomin' red-apples, red outside, white inside. The loss is to us all, Elders, who brought you here to this *day*, to you Young who is losin' *the ways of Val-ue*, our ways of Survival in Nature. Money replacin' Spirit. Our Pride in Ways of Value brought you here from the days 'Over There'," (ances-tral days). Here I remember Her looking upward with a slight toss of Her head, then back at us. "Soon, in the Life-time of many here, you will fight tryin' to remember the Old Ways, but you can't do it because Ways of Life is created by who Lives it. Not Lived, it ain't. It ain't play acted, like on *Hoquat* movies. You gonna live to see funny play-acting about Old Ways, in Lodge, done by who has no 'membrance of *Po-oke* except from *Hoquat* book writin'...not close to real. Nonsense talkers.

"Where the treasure is is where the heart is. With outside world it's money. How do we know that? For the *treasure,* for the god, same things, wars gets fought, people steal; lie; murder; destroy. For the 'god' money, for where is 'importance to the heart' pros-a-tutes works. Cheatin' an' schemin' is all parts of the outside world way of getting' to *their* 'god', Money. They fight to preserve their treasure.

"Elder *Po-oke* hearts is likewise with our treasures. We fight to help and preserve our treasure. By care an' protection our treasures is preserved for the comin' generations. *You* are our Treasure, you Young. With *Hoquat* fightin' wars for *money* even to die in that action, who destroys people's cities, wipin' out history an' people, (as our relatives Chimacum died and are lost because of old Sealth), we fight against hunger and sickness for *our* Treasure, which…is…*YOU!*"

Here She stopped talking and looked around the lodge at each post-defeat person, older or younger. I think She may have used this time for eye-contact with each of us, especially we young. And to pause for strength. I know that during this time of five minutes or more She looked into the eyes of each person present, a silent contact of Love, Compassion and Sorrow.

Then She spoke again. "We don't fight to gain territory or property, we fight to keep what we got left. Ain't much, with no place to Live the old ways. Before my parents was defeated we had tradition an' way of Life but defeat took it. We ain't got nothin' for you but Love an' our Blood. In the fight we fight also our own Selves and personal fear. Once we knew exactly what to do, each of us; how to survive like Charlie Howeattle just said. Now we Live Life directed by somebodies else (others) for *their* good (benefit).

"It was no small thing, to survive. It was no small thing for *Tss'y'uck* to go Sealin'; after *cKwalla* (Whale). Fearsome; take Lifetime Self control. None of the Elders here do 'stuff' they do without the power of Spirit. Among 'stuff', none learned without long hard study for how to gain Spirit needed for a particular way of Life. *Tss'aywhutleoke* faces Bear an' Cougar to find food and clothing-skins for us families.

"For us. Our ways never was to visit war on others, never was to win over others *except to keep 'em from winnin' over us.* Instead, our war was *battle for Life.. Tloquali* study all Life's things to see ways of Life unseen with eyes. Same as *Tss'y'uck; Tss'aywhutleoke.* Our way has been to survive as other Creatures do. But OUR way. *Hoquat* has his way, Cougar got his, *Po-oke* got his. That's Freedom. Maybe we din't have money but we had Freedom. You never goin' to see that. Sorrow in our heart 'bout that for our Treasure.

"We Treasure that in you is *our* Blood, from you will come more of our Blood. Nobody else got Blood like it. Doctor Ford told us, him an' Doctor Dever 'bout Blood. (Doctors at Forks Hospital) We hold that in pride. '*We lose our Pride we lose what we can become* in the new ways of bein'. An' Pride ain't *conceit*, *that*'s for Self Satisfied ones an' that's its own wall. Pride is otherwise. Pride is determination to raise Self to be of Benefit to all Life…ALL LIFE!

"*Po-oke* are proud, but not vain. Our history got heroes like all people have. Treasures of our past. Like our Young is treasures of our future.

"The Young is Quileute People's Treasure. Treasure of *Po-oke*, because in you is the Blood of all who made our history, who kept us ongoing, we who have protected you as you got to protect you own Young. It's gettin' diluted up now, but until lately our Blood was unaltered from THE BEGINNIN'.

"You our Treasures because to us nothin' is more precious than the Life we enjoy and decide how to Live…in you is that Life; *Po-oke* blood. NOBODY ELSE HAS IT. That alone makes it Treasure. Who on Earth don't feel that way?

"Without vanity we leaving what we have of Pride to you. These things are, Honor in Life making safe Village first, then Surf; Beach; *Ta-boke*; *Ahkalut*; *cKwahleh*. We leave these to you in different way than they was left to us…guns was in their face and is in your face today. Called 'govermint' but that's who got guns. To live as Human even if no longer Quileute, as *Po-oke*, you must obey Gun-People or die.

"Our lands for livin' in was once to mountain peaks, the ridges we can see. We never harmed it, EVER! Great Spirit loant it to us. Thunderbird (dTisdTilol) lies where we buried it up in Mountain. Layin' there now. We lived on forks of Rivers, smoke-houses holding families on Soulduk, Bocka-cheel, cK'lawah; lived down to Strawberry Point; Goodman's Crick; Jackson Crick; Hoh. Up Dicky River; at Ozette. Them was Our people until *Hoquat* gave them new history. An' living place. Quileute system was said to be Salmon Tree, 'reach into the waters and Salmons come from the branches'.

"*Hoquat* let us use a mile of '*their land*' here at *Ta-boke* mouth then them families which took our territory even got Govermint rights to Lonesome Crick. We got not much left to leave with you for your Life. Except that they took from us, we din't take from them. We got pride in that. Good for YOU TO KNOW *Po-oke* was rare on earth, din't humble none (Tyrannized none). Look back over you shoulders; who feared us?

"All the People of *cKwyeh-Tee*'s arrangements shared their lands with us, Cougar; Bear; Whale. Also these ones provided for us, so long as we behaved O.K. Where *Cho-Cho* lived we asked if we could enter. *Cho-Cho*, nervous, tiny, busy almost without visible reason, who keeps Life alive all Winter. Where it was the Living place for *Other* kinds of People, we entered. But not without permission. We asked Cedar Tree for rights where they lived. An' Deer, *Hawayishka*, a calm, peaceful and protective Mother what would fight Cougar to protect Her Babies. And Whale, *cKwalla*.

"*Tss'y'uck prayed all year* to *Spirit* of *cKwalla*, to go on *cKwahleh* for huntin'. We took nothin' without permission. We can't leave to you the places where we ranged to find lacamus and berries, what '*tobas*' (fish weirs) was, an' how to weave them with the help of Children to learn to pass to their Children. None but some Elders know about our places on Rivers an' Brooks where grasses for baskets grew and which we taught our Young to pick at the season. Out of our hands now.

"Quillayute Prairie was burned off by us since Time began for to make grow those foods which needed that action. Now cows all over up there. Even drilled a well for oil on Olliesmitt land…Hobbiesmitt's. Fences keep us away from places named by us when our time began. We can't show them to you, *Hoquat* dogs run us off, their kids swears at us and *tells* US *to 'go home'*. Ha! Ha! Sayin' bad kind of talk to Elders like Esau and Morton and Harry an' our Women who went to that place once to spend summer days gatherin' Foods for our Winters. Now look at a school an' hotel an' post office an' houses an' farm an' fences over what *cKwyeh-Tee* told us was to be left as we found it. And at Forks parts remain today of a smoke-house (dwelling). Little Bill lived in it a while. At Forks Prairie. That Prairie where we lived an' our Children played for a thousand of years. Today *Hoquat* cows eat at that spot an' where we laughed an' ran, where learning about Life took place you got to step over cow-pie. All that land, *Sacred* to us because what brought us to that point was Sacred, *cKwyeh-Tee*; our Elders; The Great Mystery.

"Part of our heritage is toilet for Cows, Horses, Sheep. We can't change that. That part of our Treasure Great Spirit gived away. You are Treasures to us because if we can leave anything of value to you to take it has to be what Treasure is: Irreplaceable. Honor is part of that Treasure; Love an' Patience part of that thing. Men of stren'th over theirself an' Women of the same character, these are parts of the Treasure. Many of our Young, seeing our 'war-defeat' by *Hoquat* hands will turn to the 'superior' way, letting the heritage, the Treasure of Honor, escape into the mist of 'once was'. But Defeat don't mean what was defeated was 'worthless'.

"*It will be.* our language goes. Their schools denyin' our language gift as they impose the new talk on you, not knowing this land, us, our ways, (*the reasons* for *the language)*, what built it. Them schools is 're-form schools' like where they put their young who is trouble. How can their language have meaning to us? They know about things like train, air plane; make automobiles. Their talk has meaning in that it is killing us. Too bad. Our language came from our way of Life, our decidin' how to behave under 'these circumstances'. Theirs done same thing. Both tongues made '*them/us*' people. One People cannot live Life for another People, control them, think for them. Cannot be that way.

"Only Chimacum shared our language on Earth. English replacin' it. An' *cKwyeh-Tee* goin' to be replaced by other Spirit Being what comes an' goes at will. But the Treasure will remain same if you carry with you into *Hoquat* world them things of permanent Value *Po-oke* lived by. For thousands of years of us livin'here. Here was the Worth of Honor and Dependability; these is big parts of the Treasure for you. Don't let 'em rot.

"We got to forget the loss of territory an' the destruction that follows as their god Go'd eats ev'rythin' in its path. All we pray for is that you, our Treasure, will not forget that Responsibility, and Love of an' to Tribe an' Family is Eternal Value. Human Bein' goes when that go. Quickly must you learn the meaning an' doing of Compassion; Forbearance; Gentleness. Whose *Chief* is *LOVE* is ruled wisely. Whose Chief is LOVE is ruled by GOD; GREAT SPIRIT. Whose Life is GOD!-ruled Lives in HARMONY— with all Life.

"One day that will come again but I don't think so for humans; maybe other kinds.

"You young boys must learn, you Greatest Stren'th is you control over you Self, *over* that stren'th, for to help those without that kinda stren'th. Only coward force his stren'th on them weak ones. You *must know* that *Men* is generous to ev'ryone 'cept themself. You must know *in you Spirit* that Family is not here for *father*, father is here to help an' protect an' provide for *Family*. Mother and Children ain't the reason for father except as he uses them to be MAN, to use his *Man*hood to HELP. *Man,* not just male. Little boy is male. Many times when adult they stay male. Men is growed-up males. Not all growed-up males is Men.

"You young girls must learn same lesson: All Woman is Female but not all Females is Woman. You also must learn: the excitement of 'new ways' is allus interestin', but one thing will be same: Motherin'. Motherin' you young; you husband; you Tribe. If we Elders know that that will continue, we will go into history to who gived the Treasure to us, first place, waiting for you to come to us in that day which is also coming for you, knowing the Treasure still lives where our Blood still flow. Hoh-ohwoosh."

She waved Her hand signifying finished. With that Grant helped Her to Her feet, Her son Harvey helped his Father with Her as they went to their car.

Chutsk lay on blankets as they had for the evening, none crying, some nursing, some sleeping. Young continued to run and chase and shout at one another, and those of us who knew Mrs. Eastman had given us a Treasure beyond normal lifespan, sat, in thought, sucking in phrases; words; meaning; re-hearing Her. Not a sound except from *Chutsk* and Young during Her gift presentation to us. We all heard Her, yet She spoke barely above a whisper.

I was less than twelve but I cannot forget how it was when Elders spoke in lodge.

Soon thereafter we put Her to rest in 'The Hill'. *cK'a'ayo* called one morning, and as from one heart came the penetrating, throbbing, cadenced beat of Drum…drumming throughout Village. All day the slowed, engulfing pulse of Village Life (slowed one more notch) re-sounded. Drums, and the doleful sound of Shaker-church bell penetrated every Village space as another of The Old Ones who had brought us to here passed to Our Past. Mrs. Grant Eastman had gone from our physical view: Now we would find Her in our heads and hearts when She 'came to us'.

The maturity of Men of whom She spoke was of such as Grant Eastman, Her near life-long husband, father of Harvey, (he father of Butchy, who earned a Silver Star in Korea), such as Tyler Hobucket and Stanley Grey and Daniel White and Mark 'Mock' Williams, Freddy Woodruff; the men Elders of the tribe (mentioned or not).

These had limitless access to the ears of young aspirants to any lodge, *Tloquali; Tss'y'uck; Tss'ay'whutleoke*. Others will be mentioned and given due credit for the conduct of their lives. Among these Chester Johnson was a highly respected Shaman in Tribal outlook, as was Lavan Coe and his brother, 'Doctor' Lester; Old Man to me, (whose

'*Tomanamus*' name was *Byack*, Raven (*Taxilit* power). Name and 'power' one. He was my primary teacher.

Later, one day on Beach I asked Fred Woodruff and Morton Penn what Mrs. Eastman had meant about 'males' and 'men'.

Fred answered first, " 'Male' means 'he', ain't it? Growed up 'he' is still 'male'. But growed up don't make 'Man'." I showed confusion because both laughed.

Morton Penn said, " 'Mature' males is Men." The silence that followed said I had to ask about that, so I did. "What's 'Mature'?" I asked, laughing. It sounded like 'manure' and had to have been a joke.

"'Mature' is being like so other people feel at ease about when they with you. You ain't angry an' threaten all the time. You do what your family need to get along. You sober, don't throw away money on junk stuff like horse-racin', you home with you kids an' wife, makin' 'em laugh an' want to be with you." Morton smiled hoping I'd gotten some of that.

I said to them that might be hard to figure out and Fred said, "It's easy to do. I do it this way: Ev'ry day I do what I *got* to do first, then what I want to do."

Morton said, "Make sure what you *want to* do don't wreck you from doin' what you got to do. Drinkin' an' crazy stuff like that will wreck you an' you plans for life. So do what don't put potholes in you way. That's *mature*. That's *Man*"

I was told in recent years that the son of a Lummi Woman was the 'Chief/King' of the Quileute because of *father's family's* importance to Tribe. The teller said that *Quileute are Matrilinear* and that no son of a Lummi (or any other tribe) Woman can bear a 'chief' for *Po-oke* respected though they might be. That all came with *Hoquat*, ('Chief' in *Hoquat* terms). Worthy offspring of traditionally respected families with long histories of contribution without Self-aggrandizing, *these* would be 'looked up to'. If that's '*chief*', that's chief.

Somehow there was failure to understand there was no 'political 'Chief" for *Po-oke*…the word 'chief' related to ability. One was 'chief' because of cKeynoo carving ability. Another might be 'chief' because of fishing skill. Elk-hunter Stanley Grey was '*chief* Elk-hunter. Professional, or 'journey-man' at what they did. 'Chief' 'do-er' of some skill. Quileute had no words such as 'professional' nor 'journeyman'. Beyond the ability to contribute to the overall well-being of *Po-oke*, no such thing as 'Chief' existed. But so it stands now in *Hoquat* history, the existence of a 'chief'. But incorrect.

Mary and Charlie Howeattle's daughter Pansie, (who married Dema and Bill Hudson's eldest son, Theodore), had *She* had a son, would have been the mother of a possible 'leader', if that person had grown to maturity displaying responsibility. And one to deal with *Hoquat* politics. Rosie Black's eldest son Roland 'Mink' Black would have been, after due ceremony, a 'blood-line' leader from a previously beneficial elder, Thomas Payne. Dalton 'Miller' Mason likewise was a descendant of a once beneficial elder. But not a Lummi Woman's child, (with respect to Lummi People for whom Quileute hold great reverence. "You got Lummi Woman for Wife? You a lucky man").

ELSA PAYNE and FIREWOOD

In those days of Beach-wood gathering for home fires, our Ladies had big baskets which were worn on their backs, strapped to a wide band of softened Cedar-bark placed against their foreheads. They put the chosen pieces of wood into a big basket and when the basket was filled, they'd place the basket onto a drift-log, turn so as to put the head-band in place on their foreheads then off they'd march toward home.

There were places throughout Village where groups of Women gathered on acceptable days, days of decent weather, thereat to weave baskets and as I see now, to keep tabs on Village affairs. The 'lead' Woman was likely '*the* Eldest'. It seemed that laughter was the biggest product of the gatherings. But in times of stress, from whatever cause, the groups were serious. There may have been six or more of these groupings at various places in Village during the few Halcyon days. One day, when I was about ten, I'd been to Ryan's for mail. Homeward bound I passed the basket-weaving Ladies and saw, down among the driftlogs, the small and age-enfeebled figure of Elsa Payne, wife of Thomas 'Tommy' Payne. She was heavily burdened even though Her basket wasn't half full. I ran down the slope to where She was struggling to cross the driftlogs and offered to take Her basket.

Man! This was *Woman's* work and no way would She surrender Her load. But I was going to help. The fight ensued with the Women watching from their places by the road. I lifted the back of the basket to take it and Elsa swung around. As She did so the line slipped and fell over Her neck. She rebuked me in Quileute and as we tugged for control, the basket spilled. More determined now, I wouldn't give up. She was not going to carry that heavy basket.

Laughter came from the ridge now while She and I gathered the spilled wood, and more. I filled the basket. Then, because She no longer had control of the basket, I took it and put the band on my forehead. That was a heavy load, but, tough Man that *I* was, I tried not to show that it was heavy as I carried it up the hill. Elsa berated me. The Women laughed. It seemed to me unfunny. "Tommy be wild when he find out you got new boy-friend Elsa, an' he sure good lookit. Tough, too!"

I felt that I was the brunt of unfair laughter and was hurt by the fact that I was doing what a Man should do by Quileute standards, help who needed help. But brunt or not I carried the wood to Elsa's house, there to deposit it on Her porch. I felt humiliated and turned without a word, to go and sulk I suppose, but in Quileute She said "wait" (vekawwa). She went into Her home and returned shortly with a package of something in a newspaper wrap. In it a huge piece of Elsa Payne's SMOKED SALMON! I was stunned.

She smiled at me as I looked at the fish and said, "Ayyy, *cKulell, ha-atch Chutsk*, ayy." *cKulell* means Sea-Gull (and guess what they think about Fish). What She said was, "Yes, *cKulell*, good child, yes." I was complimented beyond belief. The relief I felt brought a gusher of tears and Elsa put Her arm around me and squeezed, "Thank you little *cKulell*," She said. I raced home with my prize to share with the family.

Later, when I made quest for *Power* and returned to Village, La-van Coe was on bank of *Ta-boke* waiting for me. He said, "You home again *cKulell*." That became my name of reference. And henceforth as I'd wander through Village, from this doorway or that I might hear a moderately hushed voice and turn to see one of our beloved Women calling to me, " *cKulell! cKulell! Ha-atch ahlash*" (good eats) or "*Kola ahlash*", (come eat), or "*Ha-atch Sa-ats! Kola*", (good [smoked] King Salmon! Come!). And I'd be given Salmon-eggs or Smoked Black-cod or Salmon, or hard-boiled Sea gull eggs *which I loved*.

After my 'fight' to carry the load for a frail Elder, the Women of the Village let me know of their pleasure at the effort I'd made, but never with fanfare. Through assisting I had fought to honor one of our most important Village *Po-oke Waysotsopot*: A Female Elder of Quileute Tribe. They said no word about the encounter, but I knew no other youngster who was so frequently gifted by those Women as was I after that 'battle in the drift-logs'.

Then years later, one magic day Elsa gave a present beyond treasure to me: A set of bone-gamble bones which had belonged to Her husband Tommy. Her son would "sell them for drink, like somebody done with Tyler Hobucket's Eagle-feather/dentalium rain-cape, poor Tyler", she told me. Similar had happened with Tommy's *Tloquali drum*. Gone. But not the Bone-gamble bones. I have them and one of Her baskets to this day. "Say nothin' 'bout this 'til you become a 'teachin' *Tloquali*," She said, "Nobody try to steal them then."

In those days *Po-oke* were respectful of *Tloquali* Medicine. Today few know the word *Tloquali*, let alone respect it. The only People I know about who try to recreate their Medicine Power traditions are Skokomish People, impressive in their determination to recapture their heritage as they can. Respect is due those People for their efforts. Likewise of course there are other Tribes seeking *their* histories, their just and ancient heritages, I just don't know of them. Vancouver Island's Johnny Moses isn't a tribe but with his knowledge and training he is a heritage carrier of great value for all the People of the area. Johnny is worthy of praise. Respect that young man.

cKWIA

November brought storm-driven *cKwia*: Rain. Now began Rains which swept in from S.W. in waves of dull, dark grey drapes. Row after row of aggressive, wet 'draperies', undulating, fluttering, waves as Northern Lights flow, a self-repeating deluge, fell to leave Earth saturated, sometimes several inches deep, on any flat surface of ground, there to glisten under the nearly dark Sky. Then, fury spent, that curtain became drizzle, as if Rain was exhausted from the effort of the previous downpour. But in moments the daylight absorbing curtain would roar in again, thunderous voice hammering out from Soil;, boat decks; roofs.

At these times Childhood's energies were tried the most. Outdoor activities were all but impossible. Only Power Men from lodges were out in times such as these. (Village guardians were always vigilant). Now Mothers turned to their button-baskets. Chinese with coins sewed through square cut holes.

"Oh I wish I had time to sort the buttons to find the ones I want today. Maybe Vera Ward would help me sort them."

The immediate response was, "Let me! Let me! I know how!"

'*Ha-atch*,' 'Mother' would say at which out came the marvelous Chinese wicker-like basket filled with buttons. (We of Village were surrounded by the glorious baskets our Women made, but atop Chinese baskets square-holed coins were sewn. Mothers all had baskets of dime-store beads as well). The button-basket would be emptied onto the kitchen table-cloth with the directive, "See how many of the same kind you find."

cKwia was forgotten and seeking eyes and small agile fingers swept through the pile of buttons, leveling and turning up all, to be seen and compared. 'Look! I got three white ones with flowers painted on it!" Without question the same buttons had been sorted times without number, but the wonderful task of helping find as many of one kind as possible was ever challenging and eagerly entered as task. "Ayy-y! I remember this one!" Hours melted.

Where the Women found the buttons is mysterious to me. There were hundreds of them. A 'table-held' mountain of bone, and wood, and metal; of golden hue— silvery ones, painted ones, mother of pearl and tortoise-shell, round, dowel-like buttons, square buttons, huge ones, tiny ones; the button search took hours and passed the deluging day in the comfort of the living-room heater. Sometimes we might even *nap*, but just for seconds. Maybe minutes.

Each Woman in Village had Her basket of buttons, not just the Mothers. Additionally most had piles of *cellophane* from cigarette-package wrappers. Girls (and helpful boys) gathered wrappers from the discarded packets thrown about on Village roadways. To be ironed flat for storage they would cover a pile of the cellophane with damp-ened cloth and put tepid iron to the gathered treasure. The purpose was to fold each 'like-new sheet' later and weave the whole into a zig-zag web which became a belt or head-band or wristlet of shimmering, opalescent colors.

Another Rain impelled diversion was cutting colored paper from magazine pages, National Geographics given by 'Coasties' was number one but The Delineator and style magazines for Women were sought eagerly). Life, and Look were scoured for color but I don't remember seeing color in either.

Strips were cut from half an inch wide to two or more and these taper cut to a point, in effect a triangle from three inches long to six or even more…it depended on the designs the Girls made.

'Glue' (actually paste made of flour and water) on the back of each strip held the tapered paper. The wide end was put onto a wooden match-stick then the strip was rolled into a colorful tube, becoming high in the middle. The match-stick would be removed and the 'bead' set aside to dry. Later the beads would be strung onto such as shoe lac-es or tripled store string. The resultant beads were worn as necklaces. Who had clear finger-nail polish would coat the beads. They became shiny, resilient and attractive. Where did Girls get fingernail polish during Depression days? I know not. Sometimes varnish was found and used. At any rate on days after heavy Rain Skoobuss (school-bus) carried colorfully decorated Village Girls, displaying lovely beads, belts, headbands, etc.

However, there were times during heavy Rain when I wanted to be free of House and out, out to where *cKa ayo* scolded Weather and *cKulell* wheeled on Wind, high above River, challenging as if *cKwyeh-Tee* himself, "keep on blowin'! You can't stop me!"

Wearing oversize, hand-me-down knee-boots, stuffed with newspaper to make them more to size, oftentimes I slogged through mud-puddles on the road to HobbiesMitts, through fields now more like mud-bogs, soggy underfoot, soggy against the legs from soggy grasses, soaked from the shower of water from trees unable to hold more of *Sky as water-fall*, pouring itself onto Coast. The pounding roar was louder than Surf. The 'Heart-beat' of Mother Earth, Surf, was muffled by the Rain-roar from heavy clouds wringing themselves out onto our world.

I loved being abroad in Rain, witnessing the deep sleep Winter brought to us. Always surprising was the sudden flight of a remaining China Pheasant from some resting place in woods...silent but for *Cho-Cho*... or the occasional chattering of *Byack*, above the bog (HobbiesMitts house water). And the different tunes made by the dripping Trees.

Walking the old road again.

Un-altering pearl gray sky today. Weeping. Ceaselessly. The ground is shiny at any depression on the ground, water glistening under Rain. Rain-cloud goes from horizon to horizon without break....

It was such a day as this 66 years ago today that I left House early, to wander Land for the last time. I would be leaving for Butte, Montana, tomorrow morning, there to spend Winter.

Today I would go to Woods along *Taboke*, skirting Hobbies Mitts' land, and Maxfield's, past where Moore family lived (Charley and Marian and their little sister and parents) and upRiver where we young were not to go alone. We were told *DAWSKIYAH* lived in Woods by River. She preyed on the vulnerable inexperienced young. But I was *Tloquali*! *Dawskaiyah* would have been in trouble trying to subdue the likes of me!

I recall that every mud-puddle on the wagon trails provided rippling, concentric rings as the branches were busy dripping the endless supply of *cKwia*...Rain.

cKa cK aliyuh, (Alder trees) had shed its leaves; Elderberry, (our name for it was Sibuh), tried to maintain Summer by holding on—but the relentless advance of Time took leaves already advanced toward falling first but without replacement back-up, Elderberry gave up to Wind, Rain, Fall.

Even Fall was weakening its hold. Wind was more forceful. Because N.W. gales had hit us in September we saw 1939 giving up to its Fate long before winter struck, that day of 66 years ago (in 2005), as is today, is like that one, gloomy; wet; gusty; dim of light, this day has returned in bewilderment over those years with the question: Without having eaten breakfast, without food to take with me for snack, without thought about food: Why was there no need?

WINTER, SWAMP, WOODS and
Dawskaiyah

Hunger always arrived daily, but that day I recall Hunger stayed Home and let me roam without reminding me about Stomach. And thirst avoided me.

I heard *Cho Cho* that day, but *cKa ayo, Byack*, even *cKulell* were unheard.

Mrs. Owl hid from Rain as well. *Cho Cho* and *Dawskaiyah* and I owned the Woods.

It didn't take more than seconds to be soaked through by *cKwia*. I can still see the water running from my sleeves and hands in the steady downpour.

But I feel no memorable 'coldness'.

I wonder if the tragedy of killing the Trees and thus Forest was so numbing to my awareness that I had moved away from physical sense attention so that cold and wet seemed to have no effect.

The last day of the "old days' world', the old Life, as I had known it was that Sunday before my November 1939 birthday. Tomorrow I'd leave La Push to go to 'Beaut Mountains' (Butte, Montana) for Winter. I had to overlook *cKwia* and go find remembrances of La Push as it was *today*, this 1939 year which would change it forever. Everything was different already. Never again could it be known as it had been, un-touched; primitive.

I left House early in moderate Rain to 'go lissen to stuff' before tomorrow's planned departure. Ask me how I knew it would never be the same and all I can think is that the raping of Forest between Village and Forks was changing everything. Every day, from the school-bus to Forks we saw the huge logs bouncing through stumps and downed trees as the 'steam-donkey' pulled them toward the train load-point to take to some mill to eat. Relentlessly.

I had to go out, Rain or no. 'Ayyyy, *cKwia* ain't gonna quit',' I told myself, 'go out lookin.' As I left House, Wind driven *cKwia* attacked me and I thought of going back. Then I thought about the destruction ongoing with Trees and Forest, and hiked the road to Mark 'Mock' Williams' barn. I wanted to talk to *Kuitan* and Mama, his horses, before taking the woods trail to Hobbiesmitt road and Swamp.

I hurried now, thinking of all the places I had to visit and memorize; already *Change* had changed our world. A tunnel without sign of Sky, a tunnel half a mile long, of huge Sitka Spruce branchs, giants woven across the road-way, was now a war victim with massive stumps on either side, the cemetary for what once Lived here; the huge stumps were Sitka Spruce Forest's tombstones.

On the road toward Forks was a 'tee' where a left turn led to Quillayute Prairie. The right turn led to highway 101 and Forks. Where it angled right we could see the huge clearing in which stood the steam-donkey and gin-pole. In Skoobuz the shrieking whistle of the steam-donkey penetrated our senses. We all clamped hands over ears even before we heard it when in the distance we saw the steam issue from the whistle.

As the massacre progressed it was detectable in the attitude of we the young. Rather than the exhuberant exchanges between us on our way back home to Reality (from the suppression of the 'big town' of Forks) we became more quiet. The scene and violence of the steam donkey at work shocked us. I've wondered if Bill Leyendecker or Wayne Richwine, school-bus drivers, noticed what I...we...felt.

There's a video movie entitled 'The Never-Ending Story' which relates the battle a young 'Plains warrior'of about nine waged against *The Nothing*. He won. We had a similar battle in real Life. We lost

I guess on that last day of my 'scoutation' before all was gone, I knew I had to absorb what I could of what the area was: Pristine and virginal. As was I at the time. And bewildered by the approaching change to it all.

I arrived at Mock's barn...his horses were excited because they thought I was there to take them for a Surf gallop. Instead I held oats for them in my hand. In memory I can feel the velvety lips reaching for more oats, but I had been trained to be careful of over-feed so I gave them 'just a taste'. Or two.

Mock called his gelding *Kuitan*, which is 'horse' in Chinook jargon; Mare was Mama. It was early morning, no later than six. With *cKwia* overhead and falling it was still bleak with wet darkness and too early to see much outside. I decided to visit these People in their house a little while longer. In near pitch black darkness I sat atop a cow-stanchion Mock used when he had had cows, long ago. From there I told *Kuitan* and Mama about my coming trip. I hoped they felt sad over our coming separation.

I recall 'wading into misery' as if purposely, with some kind of pleasure; into the face of sorrow. Telling them how badly I felt I wanted to think they sympathized with me; enjoyed our talk. Even today I like to think they did. We were friends, Mama and Kuitan and I. Young as I was Kuitan let me ride him. With no reason to be, I wasn't afraid of him. Trusted, he loved. (Whose 'Chief' is 'Love'...).

I thrill today at the thought of galloping Kuitan across Village playground to Surf trail. The feel of exhuberant, exultant *Power* unleashed beneath me was ecstasy beyond physical; beyond transcendental. I became a hair on his hide. No sensation of pure exultation has been mine to experience since, *but I had it!* With only eighty or so pounds on his back he flew as if he were an 'empty horse'. At these times there was perhaps fifteen or twenty minutes before Roy Black (Village cop) and Mock would come driving down Beach after us. Seeing them I'd turn *Kuitan* toward a stumbly trail alongside Lonesome Creek. We'd jog along this trail, then a mighty gallop across Washburn's La Push Ocean Beach Resort property, (now La Push Oceanside Resort).

He'd gallop as if in a race with the mightiest Gelding on Earth, himself. It appeared to me to be great joy he displayed as he galloped around Coast Guard property and on home. He loved it. I loved it. I believe Mama loved it. She always nuzzled me when we returned, neighing softly before and after *Kuitan* and I went riding. At those times I rubbed him down and left through a loose barn board when Roy and Mock drove up. I think that Mock was pleased, secretly. Few in Village could ride Kuitan because he would tolerate no saddle. Anyone could ride Mama and when I 'borrowed' Her for the Surf ride She went eagerly. She was a sweet, loving person, Mama.

cKwia stopped momentarily, the day lightened some. I said good-bye to them. Today, as I recall our parting I still hear *Kuitan* whinny to me, softly. That entered my core. Both horses had been moved to Queets when I returned from Butte the next year and I never saw them again. But now, feeling a wistfulness with every move, I gave them 'just a few more oats' and left for *Ticksa*, Swamp.

At Swamp, (*Tiksa*) in wet semi-darkness, I watched for signs of Life. Except for *Cho-Cho* I saw none. Overhead a flight of Canadian Honkers called as they sped South; under the muffling clouds they weren't heard long enough to memorize their songs. . But without motivation I didn't have the 'feel' to try their calls anyway. The unaltering dark-pearl sky gave vague light to the blackened Swamp surface and 'scooters', those walkers-on-water of Summertime must have gone South with Canvasback people. Nothing.

The downed Spruce log I 'navigated' so carefully in Summer presented a forbidding look as its green-slime covering seemed to shine of its own accord. Edge of Swamp was nearly undefinable from the bent stalks and branches of brush and bushes which had lost their upright strength. Now some were bowed, head-end down, into Swamp. It was a planet of dripping, distorted forms. Soggy Alder leaves lay around Swamp a foot deep. Swamp seemed abandoned.

Without their identifying leaves to give warning, the sturdy stalks of Devil Sklub (Devil's Club) were easily mistaken for a harmless, steadying hand-hold. But woe to who grabbed that spiked stalk as 'assister'.

Frog People were there I believed; a 'PLOP' close by sent out concentric rings across Swamp face. Spooked Frog. No *T'day'okes* ('Golden Wings'/Flicker:) called, not *Shi-lele-ich-al*, (Kingfisher); not *Byack*; however, from here and there came voice of flittering *Cho-Cho*, Keeper of Life even where all seemed dead. *Cho-Cho* was like caretaker of a cemetary.

Swamp said that I should leave. I crossed the road to a little used trail leading to HobbiesMitt slough and a 'wade-able' cattle ford… out of sight of his house. Skirting low and slow at field-edges far from house and barn I passed upriver getting toward Maxfield's farm. On a previously unknown hay-wagon trail toward upper River from HobbiesMitts barn I slogged through water-filled wagon-wheel ruts in three and more inches of bleak water, beneath tall, leafless Alders. Leaves were an inches-thick carpeting over the ground: Alder; *Devil-*

sklub; Sam an' Sperry (Salmon-berry); slick pebbles as mud-puddle bottoms hid beneath deep leaf-beds. *These* were slick by both slime-covered pebbles and the leaf-bed coverings. Prudence said to step carefully, being unsure of the unseen beneath the mantle, Rock to twist ankle, or Branch to roll the foot…because I was trying to walk silently, like *Tss'ay-whut-leoke* (hunters on land). (*I didn't want Dawskaiyah to hear me*).

There was nothing on the wind of 'voice' but the first 'riffle' on Quillayute River, *Taboke*, its 'rushing song' coming to my ears as through cotton wadding. The winding trail fascinated me. I thought I knew the land hereabouts like Raven, whose territory it was. But I hadn't known it at all. A lesson in cockiness, I knew without *knowing* I did.

Then I wandered as in a fairy-land where green-golden moss overwhelmed the grey daylight, converting all to a green-gold glow, shadowless; directionless. Together with the needles of evergreens and Moss on trees the imparted light caused a nearly apprehensive alertness to wash over me: What if I wasn't supposed to be in this magic little world with the green-gold light?

Tloquali are without fear, however, so I pressed on, lured by the mystery of a place unknown. Ponds presented themselves as vistas through trees, crossed the wagon trail at some points; I wondered at their numbers. The sudden flight of a Chinese Pheasant tensed me with such a grip that it hurt, I was deeply frightened and shocked. In retrospect I wonder that I hadn't been alerted by my 'instincts' to avoid such vulnerability. I was being trained to be attentive to surroundings and to expect anything.

Recall tells me that I memorized the brilliance of what was not that bright a sky, reflected from mud-puddles. Everything of Sky not bounced from a flat, wet surface was as the surrounding 'woods', dark, nondescript. Some bright reflections were because of the bleak, dark contrast presented by everything around it. Good observation for later art work.

The occasionally silent, wind-less day was without 'voice' but for my slogging footsteps, *cKwia*, and the now louder sound of first riffle. And still around me, ponds without the songs of Frog People; these surprised me as I gathered my memories for forevermore.

Finally I wandered along River bank, shying away from Maxfield farm to avoid being seen where I might not be welcome…they had little to do with *Po-oke*, or even with local Bostons like HobbiesMitt on their neighboring farm, so I was cautious. Cows grazed or stared, with bovine intelligence, as I tried to be like *Cho-Cho*, flitting from one obscuring site to another. One would advance two or three steps toward me then stop and stare: curiosity or defense?

At length I made it to River and the 'deep hole' where I'd hooked my first Steelhead. And lost it in five seconds. Now peering into the bleak, sky-darkened water was like peering into a black, bottomless pit. In Summer under a clear sky the large rocks on the bottom showed plainly from a depth of eight feet or more, but now…nothing.

A crumbling dirt bank six or eight feet high with brush and grass overhung *Ta-boke*. Here the chance for a surprise attack, in this isolation, by, *DAWSKAIYAH!*

"*Learn about Dawskaiyah.* We young stayed alert for '*Dawskaiyah*', the old Woman of the Woods, the Witch Woman of the Hoh. She ate children who disobeyed, when She caught them, (cooked first though, She wasn't an Animal). Any Child who had disappeared nevermore to be found had been caught by *Dawskaiyah* no doubt. Disobedience was '*bussayy*', 'bad', and today, out here alone, I was '*bussayy*'. *No one knew where I was.*

"*Keep a constant lookout for any sight, sound or smell* that might be *Dawskaiyah!*" To a remarkabale distance She projected a smell to run from, , "Smelt Her a Hunderd feet or so, " Joe Pullen had said. She it was who would swoop down on an unsuspecting Child, plaster over its mouth with Spruce-Tree pitch so fast a scream was impossible. Then, pitch over the eyes, the Child would be popped into the basket She carried for kidnapping purposes and haul Her 'take' away to cook and enjoy. "She got a good appetite for *Chutsk*," we heard repeatedly.

As I wandered the woods on that November day I made sure no sloshing sounds as of footsteps in muddy puddles was anywhere in my hearing. Alert by golly. *As a Squirrel.*

Dawskaiyah never washed her mouth so she could be smelled before she caught you…"If you smell 'bad somethin' run for your Life!" we were told. She had weedy-mossy hair, terribly wrinkled skin and sparse whiskers, large warty face-adornments, a single, crooked tooth. (Additionally she was ugly)!

Dawskaiyah didn't find me that day…*Tloquali got Strong Spirit.* But I kept looking back, over my shoulders. (I was only glancing about. *She* didn't scare *me*, neither).

I ranged around Maxfield's alongside *Ta-boke*, then came to the small creek which was fed by a pond/lake of half an acre or so. On Moore's place. Then over to *Ta-boke* again opposite James' Mora Park Resort, and further upstream I wandered along the high bank overlooking *Ta-boke*. The bank could be eight feet above the flowing water and undercut by as much as two feet. From cKeynoo this had been pointed out to us several times with evidence of the collapse of the bank into River in many places. We saw sections of overhanging bank just fall, suddenly. Who would be standing on that bank when it collapsed was dead. We youngsters knew that because it was a condition pointed out purposely and constantly. Therefore I was back at least ten feet, in the line of Alders that grew along River.

Upstream above Big Pool was First Riffle and this day, after days of Rain, it was heard a long distance, easily over half a mile. River was swollen to almost field level. I wanted to see the heavy-run pouring over Riffle rocks and as I arrived at *Taboke* I saw a cKeynoo coming downstream like a Cedar bullet. It was Daniel White on his way to Village to set-up for seining. He always fished from Rialto Beach bluff to *Taboke* mouth. (When Fish Cops caught anyone 'above the line' in cKeynoo with net aboard it was 'take cKeynoo and all and go to jail… treaty or no treaty').

Unauthorized, someone took Rosie Black's cKeynoo , was caught upstream and her cKeynoo was confiscated forevermore. But the 'Lady' judge let Rosie have her paddle.

(We had learned long ago that *Treaty* was what WE obeyed, not *Hoquat* gover'mint. We learned early about balance in their Laws: you don't judge their Laws nor expect 'equality', *you obey them there Laws*. In addition to meaningless Treaties which harmed Amer-ians expecting to get 'justice' through *personally obeying* the Treaties: ('fish and hunt in the accustomed places' and like that) instead came harm from confiscation of essential equipment for Life sustaining with fine and/or imprisonment being the general result…(Rosie Black's cKeynoo, a secret present made for her by Her brother Walter Payne, was seized in an area of Treaty-grant fishing and kept. Then it was given to some undeserving town. And *then* the 'Lady' 'Judge' (whose name was 'Schlafer' [or nearly that]), in humility and with a burst of kindness gave *Her cKeynoo paddle* back to Rosie. Her cKeynoo was gone. [Starve if you have to, dig for roots, but we keep your property]. Treaty? Another of

Quileute treasures taken without concern. By the 'Law'. May not be honest but it's 'legal').

As Daniel shot down *Taboke* in his cKeynoo I thought I'd hidden myself but being the hunter he was Daniel had seen me and after shooting across Riffle he poled to River bank and shouted, "What you doin' here anyways? Who you with?"

" '*Kadido*'," I shouted back. *Kadido* (Dog) had appeared as if by magic while I trudged across Maxfield's farm. Dog belonged to Horace Bright's family.

"Then you guys get down here. Be dark quick. Come on." Dog bounded toward Daniel's cKeynoo and into it in obvious joy. I told Daniel I wanted to walk home. "Then get goin' an' stay away from *Taboke*!" I agreed to obey and turned to go toward Village.

They poled out into *Ta-boke* and carried by the rushing River they disappeared as by a wand-wave. A black-blanket of loneliness fell over me and I entered what I know today to have been akin to depression. I wished *Kadido* had stayed.

Sitting on a fallen Alder, away from the bank, listening to *Ta-boke*, not wanting to go to Beautmountaina (Butte, Montana), tense from cold and watching for *Dawskaiyah*; not wanting Forest to die; I felt the terror felt by *Hawayishka* and other Forest People, that which they knew as their home was taken to feed the endless hunger of Sawmill. No *Hoquat* change improved our world. When would it end?

Never. Go'd rules. 'Man-kind' worships Go'd...Gold.

Why would *cKwyeh-Tee* let *Hoquat* tear the world apart like was happening? (Today god-doubters ask, 'why does 'god' let war happen?'). *Doubt* about *cKwyeh-Tee* may have entered my psyche then, but I *know* that 'belief' in some 'good and benevolent Power' disappeared there near *Ta-boke*'s bank that desolate November day. There, in sorrow, I fell asleep to awaken later, Rain-soaked and bewildered. Where was I? How did I get here? I was experiencing a penetrating coldness and felt a strange upset.

"Hey you *cKulel*! Hey you!" I heard Daniel's voice from nearby.

"Ayy-y" I answered. Then there he was. "*cKola Chutsk*. You soakin' wet ain't it." He'd had second thoughts and turned to the bank a quarter mile below where I'd last seen him. He and Dog had walked back to get me. Back at cKeynoo Dog leaped in happily and I followed. Daniel pushed cKeynoo into *Ta-boke* stream and the three of us and

Great Spirit were together on River. Daniel wrapped me in a blanket but I couldn't stop shivering.

For my indiscretion the punishment of being ignored was due at home. But Daniel could sense a profound sadness in me I'm sure. I said nothing to him in contrast to my general non-stop jabbering. When we arrived at La Push he steered toward upriver side of C.G. boathouse and landed. I got out taking the line with the weight called 'anchor', (an abandoned engine's flywheel), to the end of the anchor-line, high on RiverBeach. Daniel said "Wait". Then he followed me across the rocks and added, "We go to your home."

The smell of roast Elk came at us when the door opened and the normal bedlam of laughing and joking people wecomed us. Mother said, "We wondered where you was! You get dry clothes on, you soakin' wet! You been keepin' Daniel comp'nee?"

"Ayyy. Him an' Dog helped me bring down my cKeynoo." No lying, just politically correct information. "I got to go now," he said. "Got to get back upRiver to eat."

"cKola ahlash," Dad said to Daniel and I too. "cKola ahlash Daniel."

"O.K. You gonna be like that I got no choice." And the evening passed. They spoke of Old Days and Life upRiver, of Esau Penn's Smokehouse (longhouse) on the cKlawah, at end of Airport (where Uncle Yum had been born in 1893) ; about Strawberry Point; Jackson and Goodman Cricks and bundled on a chair beside Stove I fell asleep hearing stories about 'Round', a great protector; about Hoh (Destruction) Island and the Woman who birthed Whalers; Days-of-Old stories. I awoke wishing I'd been able to stay awake to hear more, but Daniel was gone and I was in bed.

Hank Taylor drove Daniel back to his place between Hudsels and WesleesMitts. The next morning I left to go to the hell of living in Butte, Montana the rest of Winter.

I was sick on arrival in Butte two days later but 'played tired' and kept it secret for days. It was easy to believe, the tiredness, going from Sea-level to seven-thousand feet overnight made my nose-bleed so I was kept abed. Nursed by the whole household I had no 'hope I get better' thoughts: Paradise was gone forevermore I knew and cared little for tomorrow. I had no curiosity about this mountain-surrounded city without Surf; cKwia; Bell; drumming. Kuitan and Mama. Gone away forevermore.

If I'd thought that that November day in the Woods around La Push was bad Butte opened my eyes to *dismal*. There was *nothing* for a Child to do. *Nothing*. Dark skies and wind swirling over chilling, dirty snow from which there was no escape…I hated it. I re-call no color.

Even the arrival of a new baby was unrewarding. Chris Morganroth was a wonderful man. As a Child I loved Chris for his kindness to me. Chris Jr., had been born, but even the thought of Chris' *Chutsk* did nothing to enliven me. Jr. would be a year old in February and might walk before I got back home to teach him 'the right way to walk'… whatever that may have been. Hundreds of miles away now, *I couldn't rear Chris Jr.*, (as *I* had reared *other* Village babies…bottle feeding; holding; 'cooing' over). (Poor, deprived Chris Jr., I couldn't oversee how he was to be reared!).

Oftentimes I've wondered if my depression, spawned by the ruin of our world, was ever overcome. The change from isolated, wet Coast to important waystop for out-siders was almost instantaneous. To this day I've mixed feelings about those days and the sorrow then engendered. This day, in 2008, as I write, is the 69th year since then and this day, in Ballard, is as Rain-bleak, but without the dread for tomorrow I felt then.

Boyhood was passing as young man-hood approached, Elders were dying, drumming and singing and lodge took less of Village time now and sadness began to replace what had been near-rapture for Life. 'Happy' had been one name by which I was known but when I had finished my stay at Butte the constant display of teeth behind smiling lips was greatly diminished. The muck of 'civilized' Life was pouring itself over me, leaving the sorrow it brings and which I've seen the world around. Yet even in other lands where Poverty Maintainance is the political way, I've seen more happiness displayed than what I saw in Butte. '39 and '40 began my disappointments.

When we returned to La Push in Spring, Forest was gone. At times nowadays when I'm on Beach and feel the sudden, chill breath, the momentary breath just barely noticed, I know FOREST SPIRIT of this place is still 'there', waiting to swoop in and reclaim *Its Own*.

CHILDHOOD'S GAMES

Imaginative inventiveness is of all Children I feel; and we were that. An example is the emptied canned-milk tins, upon which we'd 'stomp' until the ends turned up to grasp our shoe sides. Our purpose by the stomping was to create 'horse-shoes'. (No, we didn't 'stomp' with barefeet).

Cans without both ends were valueless. To be used as 'shod-hooves' both ends had to wrap up and over the soles of our shoes. Canned milk cans were best. Once 'on', off we'd gallop, the clunking sound satisfying us that we were indeed horses or at least horse-back riding. (My favorite brand of milk was 'Pet', because of the label. Pet Milk labels were of a cow looking from a can with a smaller picture of the cow, while from that came another and on and on until the last was a tiny cow staring from a tiny can. All on the label).

Eight or so of us galloping along the roadways of Village must have been a spectacle, shouting, laughing, 'giddy-upping', and with many unconvincing 'whinny' attempts. At the tops of our voices. There must have been 'outsider' concern for our mental advancement but 'goofy' or not it carried us to levels of imagination from which we seemed to benefit. No one suffered other than by not being as fast as some others.

Except for George Student, who had a 'Tom Mix six-shooter' of wood, (fifty cents and box tops from Ralston Cereal), we played games of imagination which had no violence attached. George, a Coastie kid, wasn't violent with the toy, but wore it as a mark of pride. A 'true straight-shooter' [Tom Mix style]): "Straight shooters always win:

Law-breakers always lose! It pays to shoot straight." Tom Mix's motto. That was George's goal. I hope he made it.

A contribution to childhood games was that most of the commercial fishermen chewed 'snoose', the pungent, wet tobacco they called 'Cope'…Copenhagen Snuff, which was sold in round paper containers with metal tops. We looked for the emptied rounds eagerly, treasuring the round metal tops with which to play 'frisbee', (not the name in the '30's and '40's).

The lid was held between the middle and ring-finger of whichever 'handed' one was, then a supple wrist-flip launched the toy to sail away as much as fifty feet, more with proper wind, to a 'catcher'. We'd race after the spinning disc to catch it, in pride and satisfaction if we did. A collection of 'Cope' lids was in Native baskets of every boy in Village and many of our Girls. I had as many as twenty at a time, collected as *Hoquat* young collected marbles.

The edges of the lids were sharp. Carried in our pockets they caused nicked fingers so moderate Blood-stains on pocket-edges was standard for the afficianado: "He's a snoose-can player!" We took that label proudly. Teen-age boys from commercial boats taught the game to us originally; it became ours overnight, same as baseball for the Japanese.

Too, we gathered discarded cigarette packages for cellophane the Girls wanted for braiding belts, bracelets, necklaces, etc. Another use for 'cig' packs was, on the bottom fold of the 'Arabian animal standing by palm trees' package, were printed letters, 'C', 'D', etc., which a finder would try to confuse companions about…correctly guessing the letter would save the guesser from a hit on the shoulder. Incorrect guesses required that the guesser repeated the names of five kinds of what *Byack* called 'poison sausages', ('cigs'), Polar, Fatima, Spuds, Wings, Twenty-grand, etc. Having repeated these the guesser was saved from the hit. There were no 'PallMall'; 'Salem'; 'Windsor'; none of the recent breeds of poison sausages.

Card-board boxes were likewise treasured. The grassy knoll in front of Hal George's house, and the two Penn houses to the northwest, were slides for us when the tall Summer grass *dried* enough to present a slick face; wet didn't work. Sitting on a flat piece of card-board we'd 'shove off' at the brow of the slope and shoot down the thirty or forty foot embankment with the glee of a free-flier in space. Occasionally some ten or twelve year old ('a *big* kid') would come with a *tire*, the ultimate ride. One bigger boy would hold the tire vertically while another squeezed inside, to be rolled down the slope. 'Mink' Black and brother Verne were champions at this skill.

Rarely were we of the 'younger set' permitted the privilege of that ecstatic journey. The roll didn't stop at the base of the knoll as did the ride on card-board, instead zapping out another thirty or forty feet toward the drift logs. This area was where an original Rez Village stood. (It was maliciously burned out when *Po-oke* had gone to another village. All the very old, precious family heirlooms held by them were lost, that before 1900). The tire-ride path crossed the old site which time had absorbed.

For the making of the original jetty (1929-1931?) a narrow gauge railway had been used to haul huge stones from the South bluff (*cKwateata*) which ended First Beach. The rails had been left in place at the foot of the knoll and across the original village site. Later we covered a place with dirt where the tire-riders might roll. Laboriously we piled dirt for the 'tire-riders' to gain more distance in the roll. Also to avoid potential harm from a head-slam to a rail.

We were drawn to this area for several reasons, not for the card-board nor tire rides alone. Two or three carts, in retrospect 'ore-carts' from mines, were down by *cKwateata*, still on the rails. We tried to push or pull or ride them one way or another but by now, ten years after the jetty building, rust had claimed the bearings so all we could do was imagine what '*true railroading*' might have been like.

That line of 'action' from headland to *Ta-boke* was appealing to us, kids, and to me the best was the ride down the hill over slick, dry grass-stalks on the cardboard 'magic carpet'. Among being shod with canned-milk-can 'horse-shoes', squeezing out Perch young, straining to see Sea Spirits playing tag, seeking 'precious' stones, we never 'sought' for things *to do*…we living was a *doing* thing: La Push. It was filled with the 'never-ending.' Often-times to the apparent dismay of our seniors and/or Elders. (Poor Mark Williams and his 'rustled' horse(s)).

Fortunate indeed the Child of 'in those days' La Push.

SHIPWRECK EXCITEMENT

For Village *Po-oke*, April 13th (I believe) 1939, brought an incomparable adrenaline rush. That day, (in fog?), a British steamship had turned to go East toward Seattle…at Quillayute Needles. Apparently thinking they were at Cape Flattery they 'fetched up' forevermore.

Coast Guard bell ringing and running and hollering brought someone to Shaker Church Bell in the early hours and emptied the houses as by wand waving. "Steamer on Second Beach rocks, at the Needles!" was shouted from around Village and *Po-oke* piled into *cK-eynoo*, skiffs, trolling boats, anything available and "away all boats!" We were kept a distance from the ship, *S.S. Templebar*, by the Coasties as they helped the crew. I can't remember much beyond the incredible excitement and that as soon as possible **our** men were aboard the ship which had torn off much of its bottom but rested as if afloat. We were told it was carrying scrap metal for Japan, en route to Seattle to 'top off' its load.

At any rate the name 'Templebar', painted onto a small, flat strip of wood, once over the passageway door into the ship's wheel-house, was proudly displayed over the front door to John and Mable Jackson's house for many years. He had been one of the adventurers that boarded the ship. Now there were more Indians at one time on Second Beach Trail than ever before; Village was empty. How many Steamers wreck right outside Village? 1880's?…1939. I'd missed the first one but not the second. Lots of stuff to do in La Push.

During that 1939 summer, salvage crews came to La Push to remove the scrap-metal cargo from the ship. Divers, evoking starry-eyed admiration from Village young, worked long, dangerous hours to remove the cargo, which was put onto at least one barge to transport somewhere. I don't remember if the salvage-barge came into Village to transport away or was towed to Seattle. The latter I think.

In any event, Summer's salvage work became a financial loss. On the load meant as profit trip, a September storm broke the barge-cable from the tug. The barge capsized in Surf mid-way between *Ahkalut* and *cKwateata* (Henderson Head), spilling the profit load and leaving the barge upside down in pounding Surf. There it was reduced to waste. There would be no financial return for the salvors now.

Po-oke did what could be done for the bitterly disappointed salvage crew. Gifts of Elk meat, smoked Salmons, dried berries, even a few gathered dollars, were given to take home with them; perhaps to help get them home, whatever cash could be given. Some had purchased new cars which they had had to return, leaving themselves afoot because their old ones had been trade-ins. *Po-oke* who had grown to be friends with them housed some preparing to get them home. Several of them were from Portland, Oregon and *Po-oke* drove a few home back home.

The trip took them through Hoke-yum and 'Berdeen, where Village *Po-oke* had relatives. I heard there was a well remembered party at that time in 'Berdeen—*Po-oke* and salvage crew.

The salvors may not have been successful financially but they left La Push remembering friendly, hospitable, concerned people with whom they had associated for several months. One diver returned the next year as a commercial Salmons-fisherman and later that fall left with a Quileute bride.

Except for possible suitors for her hand, from La Push, none objected.

FEMALE SACREDNESS

Speaking of brides reminds me of a 'doing bad' lecture by Dema Hudson. One night at Lodge, actually the old meeting-house beside Shaker Church, Charlie Howeattle spoke of losing Tribal morality simply because we no longer ruled ourselves as in times past. When we had lived widespread over the entire Quillayute River system he said, close control of the young was possible because travel wasn't 'auto easy'. Going to another family's area took determined effort that involved cKeynoo travel to 'get there'. Or trail making, a task of great effort.

After Charlie had spoken, Dema went to the middle of the floor in the Church-meeting-house raised Her hand in greeting-salute which also requested permission to speak. Silence followed if the speaker was accepted, talk and attention to one's own activities continued, if not. I don't recall any Elder being shunned…or anyone else for that matter if there was something to be said. Babies excepted…They ran 'til exhausted while meetings were in session.

Before continuing I think it advisable to illustrate our attitude toward our Elders, more specifically Female Elders.

Lillian Pullen, widow of Chris Penn and the late Perry Pullen, was a revered Elder, advocate for Quileute and Children. Ill in later years She had serious operations. True to Female strength, She'd be home soon as if little had occurred. Her daughter-in-law Eileen Penn (Jiggy's wife) cared for Her and directed others in caring for 'Gramma'. Care and spunk prevailed. (Lillian was featured in a Seattle newspaper in the 1990's as one of three who still spoke Quileute).

Soon after a return home from the hospital, She attended a Tribal gathering in Village gymnasium where Children would be performing in Her honor. Lillian was seated at the far wall, across from the main opening. There She would be able to see Her beloved young people drum and sing and dance as their times arrived to perform. This within days of Her release from hospital.

Outside, gathered around the entry-way stairs were perhaps twenty-five youngsters of varying ages, both sexes, practicing 'roles', shrieking and behaving as do excited Children. At their entrance time, under the general control of a Girl about fifteen (the surrogate Mother) they filed into the narrow hallway at the same time Lillian decided She would go home to rest. With the help of Eileen and Jiggy, She rose to leave. The seated assemblage stood in respect as She was leaving and when She was at the exit hallway the 'surrogate Mother' saw Her coming toward the gathered young at the exit and turned to them, shouting, *'ELDER COMIN'!'*

As one, the Children stopped action. Infants and up, they froze tightly against both walls to permit 'Gramma' to pass through their gathering, smiling in appreciation and "Hello Gramma-ing" Her as She greeted each by name. With a loving smile to each. Among us all, adult or Child, She was The Elder.

Elder respect is Law among Po-oke. Woe to *any* group who loses it; or, who never had it. Respect and care for Elders is the wisest moral guide. Who has it not lives in chaos, buffeted by whim, impulse, confusion. In selfish competition for personal gain.

The night that Dema spoke in the meeting-hall is attached to my memory as firmly as is the night and speech-advice of Mrs. Eastman. She spoke to the Girls. And to males if they had sense to hear.

She took a breath, looked along the rows of familiar faces. Here were peer Elders; Her relatives and neighbors; the peers of Her Children. She missed no one as She acknowledged everyone with a nod of Her head, then spoke:

"Most you Girls to become Mothers; many older ones is now, married, caring for you own as you did for you younger brothers 'n' sisters (Sistuhs). Mother-hood come easy, make it easy to overlook importance of that role. But because it's easy, don't make the mistake of thinkin' it ain't important. Nothin' in the world is more important than that work of being Mother.

"Nothin'.

"If you disagree, what is *more* important than continuation of Life? Therefore who continue it is joined to Life and Life-Spirit. *Po-oke* see things of Life in simpler ways than many other peoples. If I ask 'what is purpose of Life', many say 'good job', 'good education', 'happiness', 'health'; *lotsa money*. But all are second purposes of Life. Truth is, *Pooke* know that Life has only **one** purpose and all other things that happen follow *that*: *Purpose of Life is TO CONTINUE LIFE.*

"If that ain't done no other purpose can become. Life continuing is the first purpose of Life. We have choices in what to do **in** Life, but Life itself is first. Because so many our People die as Babies it's natural for us to bear young at a 'tender age'. Common to us in Time Ghost days was Mothers of fifteen. To survive as Tribe we had to have young to replace the young who died, as well as adults who had also 'Crossed The River'.

"*Hoquat* come, tells about 'the sin' of breeding, 'your young allus 'doin' *bad*. We notice they didn't back away from doin' bad when the chance came for them to 'do bad' with our Girls. Otherwise how come so many half Po oke, half *Hoquat*s? Do we really see things different? Or like mostly, did we hear talk from both sides of somebodies mouth?

"The partnership between Life-designing Great Spirit and Females of *all things of Life* make possible that Life be continued. **WE KNOW** Great Spirit is Life in all things, Sacred. *Sacred*; Deevine. Then what Great Spirit *designs to become* is likewise Sacred. If Great Spirit's *Spirit* is Sacred, (*Hoquat* words say '*Deevine 'God*', the same as Sacred), if Great Spirit is *Sacred*, what can it *do* which *ain't Sacred?* Can that which is Sacred be non-Sacred? Only fools think so, or them *who prey on dumb minds of who don't think clean; clear.*

"An', what *the Sacred* uses to *continue* Life is *Sacred.* Great Spirit uses Woman, Female. Girls. As you become Women never forget your supreme partner in making new Life, Great Spirit. Its Life-creating partner, Female, is *Sacred* to SACRED DESIGNER/ CREATOR OF HOW LIFE IS MADE. Never forget: *Body which create Life is Sacred Vessel.* Life Creation is supreme of all deevine acts. Only deevine (divine) can make Life. Girls, you the partner with Creator of process to make Life. Sacred.

"Don't just "pass around' that Sacred Body to please who is not Sacred. Males can't never know the Sacred Responsibility *you* are crowned with...*carried as it should be you are a Life Creating Goddess. Don't put that marvel on some bed as toys. From born you are first partners with Great Spirit. Without you It cannot function. Without It you cannot function. You are Sacred to Great Spirit what designed you; it* used 'nother

Woman, you Mother, to build you. Male only *plant the seed*. You an' Great Spirit do *all* the rest. You are part of the Deevine, workin' for Life continuing.

"(If) Female gets trained to see Her Sacred responsibility early then She gonna Live as a Sacred being for Her parents, Her husband, Her Children, Her Tribe. She learn early on about restraint. Bein' responsible. Male also got to learn restraint.

"Don't think that as She is, Her Young won't become. Baby learn fastern anybody. They learn all languages of Earth quick. Aroun' the world they learn. They learn our tongue; Chinee; Makah; Boston, Chinook, all other languages before they walk. Let me know who among you here tonight can learn that fast. They learn from Mother, mainly. We know Babies understand talkin' real er-lee (early). Lot fastern lots of folks think…months old only.

"An' if language, difficult for grown-up to learn, is so easy for Babies, see how easy they learn things we do they can copy easier than language: violence; anger; hate; vicious; impatience; deception…what else? Possible *too* is Honor; trust; responsible Life.

"With THAT knowledge used, Tribe is led toward Sacredness if Mother knows what importance She has to Great Spirit. If She don't learn to understand responsibility of Her position as Mother, whether She become Mother or not, *Tribe loses*.

"Her *Mother parts* are Sacred to 'Great Mystery', Sacred Great Spirit. They are *Create*d by Great Spirit to be partners in Life making. Nothing but Mother Parts of Her body can make more Life. Nothing. How do you explain Deevine; Sacred?

"Those parts of you Girls which create and carry Life are given to you by Great Spirit. They are supreme gift to Human Beings. Males don't get more than brief encounter with that process and chases it 'most their Life'. But for that reason male can go away from what they cause and deny what they done. *Them who chase the most are them saying about 'doing bad' the most.*

"Male can deny their part in Child making. For Woman, *yakado* (the contact with Life creating) begins partnership with what *Hoquat* call God. If She has Baby, it may leave Her body, but never Her being. If it leave Her body before it can Live alone, She will carry that departed one in Her mind an' soul forever. That Sacred Life-being within Her is burned into every part of Her body Live or die. Her contact with male may be ended when that contact is ended, for male.

It begin and last the rest of Her Life for Female, with *yakado. It cannot end for Her.*

"The Blood is the Life. When Sacred, Living Blood issue from you then no longer are you same like boys, no concern 'bout what you do an' where you go. Now you can become victim of *Hoquat* things; violence; anger; rapin'. Because the most important thing about you is that you are Motherable, the most important thing that happens to you is the first issue of Life's Blood. As *Po-oke* that is all you came to Life for, as Woman.

"Once we celebrated that first happening with gra-a-a-te ceremony." To emphasize 'great' She made a circle with Her hands from joined at the top out both ways meeting at the bottom, "...did ev'rythin' to celebrate 'Sacred happening'." She paused while She looked at various friends and relatives. "Sacred happening. No one in Village at that time was more important so there was important things to do to impress on You! and the rest of *Po-oke* that you had entered into the time of Life when great Tribal responsibility had come to you. Sad, we no longer celebrate that marvelous thing. Now it's just a happening, like being hungry, sleeping. Our girls no longer get that sacred ritual of 'getting' to be Woman. In *Hoquat* world first Ceremony to show Importance is to win football game...to come out of school...graduate. Our way was, *you got to be*, at that time, like them butterflies, beautiful change from somethin' else. Big change." Pause. "Big change."

"To defile you Power for sheer pleasure, or for gift of any kind, risking the Sacredness of you body to become a non-important toy is to give away the Partnership with God-Power within you. Above all things remember that now you are a most important of things to Great Spirit, now you are WOMAN! Don't lose that gift. It ain't just nothin', preserve what you been given, *MADE TO BE WOMAN! Continuer of Life!*

"Not to understand (that) you Sacred responsibility *isn't thrown to males* is to lose the Power and beauty and purpose of the gift of Life-bearing *which is yours alone.* Is to make of you like any drifting piece of somethin' unknown on *cKwahleh* (Ocean): *Hoquat.* No greater pride can exist than to be Woman...not just female. You can build Life!

"The issue of Blood is bond between you and God of Life which is Sacred. *Life is in the BLOOD* so BLOOD is SACRED. Failin' to understand that, failin' to be proud of it, protective of it, is to be male with Woman parts: pleasure only. *You must come to know that you are*

Sacred. To distribute that Sacredness as unimportant is to be like male. Protect your Sacredness for who will be your Man, who will father Babies with you. Not to give to just any male. Give to *your chosen Man* the treasure of your exclusive Sacred-ness. A Man cannot be more honored than to be the trusted, chosen, Life-creating mate of a Woman *waiting for him.*

"To you males I say this: It ain't your right to bother Female for you pleasure. If they want you for their mate *'they send out 'sparkles''.* When you get chosen you gonna know. Be Men, not male hound dogs. Be *Men.* Have Self-control. I have said it." At which She bowed, waved Her right hand to assembled *Po-oke* and returned to her seat in the hall.

How sad that these wisdoms should pass; that *Hoquat Hoquat* ways prevail. Far more reasonable that Women, the civilizers of humanity, should be seen to be the reasonable ones of any tribe, *Hoquat* or other. I see male dominance as from violence; coercion; intimidation by strength of muscle, not brain. I recall an explanation about 'our' (we Huminals) way of Survival...*brain is stronger than muscle.*

And those Women not learning their importance, (instead trained as play-things for male pleasures, [and then uncomfortably for males, conceiving and *causing disruption in male Lives]),* how sad they won't know their importance in partnership with the Life-Law making force of the Universe. How sad. How sad for ALL that *muscle* and *prostate* rule our world.

TIKSA: BIG SWAMP

Leaving his farm toward La Push, the last two houses on Hobbies Mitts' land were *originally* rented by Coast Guardsman Oscar Hedlund and on the right, 'Chick' Student and his family. A few feet beyond, onto Village land, was a log bridge which covered a brook two feet wide. Small logs crossed the brook and more logs crossed them, onto these dirt was piled and gravel for the road out of the Maxfield farm and Hobbies Mitts, (called Thunder Road now).

Toward La Push, to the left of the road and very small bridge was a miniature swamp where Frog families lived and played, which little swamp, together with big Swamp, (*tiksa*), was an orchestra pit of Frog music heard throughout Village when it was tuned up and performing. Day or night, the orchestra was performing except when an intrusion to the performance came and Intermission was called. We knew something different had occurred near Swamp because everybody shut up. Frogs. Watch-dogs good as Geese.

I remember hearing that no Tribe of any sense has Permanent Camp not close by to swamp of some kind…always upwind to it. Swamps are full of, teem with, Life. Swamps draw Life to themselves. Swamps eat anything decomposable. Marvelous, fertile soil bottoms line any Swamp.

In birthing season, large, gelatinous globs, Frog-egg masses, crowded side by side in moderately shallow water along the periphery of the 'little' swamp, likely seeking Sun-light. To lift the masses was a challenge we young tried to accomplish, without success. Hands side by side we'd succeed only in splitting the masses, capturing none. The feel of the cool, gelatinous egg masses was as interesting as the cool, Living 'feel' of Garter-snakes.

The source of *Little* Swamp may have been Swamp, (which we longed to explore). As in little swamps, (several existed, most unknown to the young), uncountable clusters of eggs lined the 'shores' of Swamp. Polliwogs darted forth and back in the cloud darkened waters, to be seen only on sunny days, when a ray of sunlight brightened a spot in the water clear to bottom, eighteen-inches to two feet down. This always revealed abundant Life.

Occasionally we would wander down HobbiesMitts road to both the small, brook-fed pools that were swamp-like in their Life production, or, rarely, (we were warned *to stay away* from *Swamp*), rarely, we entered the path-opening beside the huge, up-rooted Sitka Spruce stump which lay on its side to left of Road. Once inside that forbidden, actually dangerous 'ground', we crept carefully along the huge log which lay more than half-way across Swamp. Our handholds were large, upstanding limbs...once branches on the huge tree.

From the log we stared at the magic action ongoing in the sometimes brightened water. Wriggling Polliwogs; darting small minnows of whatever kind; strangely wiggling bugs which later became mosquitos; and enthralling to behold, the dive and emerging of Kingfisher with minnow in mouth. Across the surface of Swamp, long-legged, black spider-like bugs ran as if on dry land. The sign of contact with surface of Swamp was the dimple where each foot rested. In sunlit spots the over-laid leaves lay as carpet on Swamp bottom and there to be seen in places, a voracious bug attacked anything that might pass its gullet.

Bobcat and Mink and Cougar and Bear wait to grab the vulnerable small and young of whatever kind, we were warned, so we kept senses alert, ready to dash for the safety of Road if any sign of danger showed. We weren't going to be caught off guard. Especially was I alert: *I* was *Tloquali*.

The true danger of Swamp was the slippery 'ground' of Rain soaked moss and slick mossy surface on slippery log, all danger to small, inexperienced young who could fall in and drown in seconds.

Birds of so many kinds nested and hunted and protected territory around Swamp that recalling them seems to be an exercise in imagination...invention. From nearby hay-fields came Redwing Blackbirds on their food quest. The thrill of hearing a Meadowlark remains within me though I don't remember them around Swamp, frequently from one of HobbiesMitts fields, (like *Honey one could hear*): the Meadowlark. Oregon Juncos splashed color in quick flashes throughout HobbiesMitts fields, occasionally visiting Swamp, on the rare occasion of clear sky and bright Sunlight flooding the Natural Animal food-basket which *was* Swamp. Chickadees were akin to swarms of feathers. Songs came from all directions to excite the ear…many of these birds spilled over from hay fields to populate Swamp for the incredible numbers of insects available. Springtime catching to transport to hungry mouths in limitless nests. Overwhelming *cKa-a-yo* babies screeching with inimitable raucous demands. Rarely during the daytime we heard the 'hoot' of an owl. Kingfisher chanted.

One creature which riveted my attention on Swamp visits was Dragonfly. There was such a majesty about these incredible hunters as they skimmed Swamp surface, or zoomed in lovely curved arcs up toward taller trees then zoomed down again to land, apparently weightless, on a slender stalk of a bush. All else was overlooked as I imagined mystical power being displayed before my eyes. From what inner light came the shimmer of green-blue beneath the humming silver wings I wondered. I would try to 'sneak up' on any one of them, so still as to be nearly unnoticed (I'm sure), going closer to whatever branch was the landing site but the decision by 'darning needle' bug to move was made: I was too close and away it would dart, wings a shimmering semi-transparent flash in whatever of Sunlight came through. The word to this day for Dragonfly is 'Majestic' as far as I'm concerned. There were hundreds of them in that Swamp territory. Bug eaters.

Throughout the area was *Byack*, seeking vulnerable and unprotected young Birds or unhatched eggs; screaming parent birds announced the robberies. Red-tailed Hawk silhouettes were bold against the blue sky on clear days, the beautiful red-tail feathers easily seen, not opaque to direct overhead Sunlight. Or they perched on branches awaiting the unwary. There was no Eagle family at La Push when I was young, they'd all been shot, (*as well they deserved to be, darn things*). Who knows what that beautiful, that majestically gorgeous creature may have done to some farm animal. Maybe. Don't even kill it for *the potential danger. KILL IT FOR FUN.* "Yeah, got me a big Eagle last week". Thousands of years of Life in their own territory and dislodged, as were *Po-oke…* "we uns all have to be pertected from you uns all". They were protected from Animals and 'savages' by gun-power we *ab-*

origine inhabitants were shown. What bone-deep Fear. What 'religious' hypocrisy.

To us the Eagle is likewise aborigine. They were protected from Animals and 'savages' by gun-power.

In particular when Frog People were bringing forth young, Garter Snake was busy not only on the ground surrounding Swamp but, in what was to me a marvelous discovery, Snake could swim! I thought I'd discovered something never seen before when one day I had sneaked to the huge log and lo! toward me from dark shadows 'over there' (other side of Swamp) came a strange rippling reflection and a wriggling object (like a stick) causing the ripple. On recognizing the 'stick' as Snake I panicked from surprise and left the scene as if rocket propelled. The most disappointing part was that I couldn't go and report *my amazing discovery*. A dismal day. The same condition as *River visits without chaperon*, Swamp was off-limits to *Po-oke* young.

A subduing day was the one in which I saw two ducks land in a tree and one enter a hole. I went home to bed stunned, to 'get away from it all'. My day when confused. Mama recognized the signs of trouble and finally, when I told about Ducks landing in trees She laughed until I worried about Her. "What you seen was Wood Ducks! That's where they nest for new ones!" O.K. then. I got out of bed and went outside again. Who knew that Ducks could live in trees?

Owl People lived close by, but separated into territories they protected. Two in particular had separate trees from which to cast longing stares at MissisMitts 'garden' hens. "Can you shoot a gun?" She asked me one day, and of course at twelve years I was a 'marksman'. At least in my own mind. I aimed with great care to miss and fired, whereupon Owl 'split', bringing forth from MissisMitt an, "Oh wonderful, you scared it away!" I had already been trained in Village: Don't kill unless it is to eat. Owl was not on the gourmet bird list. "Owls won't eat Owls" *Byack* said.

It was a thrill at night to walk along the road-way past Swamp, toward HobbiesMitts farm ('fahm', HobbiesMitt called it). I loved to hear rustlings in brush on both sides of Road, and more especially, to hear the 'Hooo...Hooo...Hooo" of one of our Quileute Owl-People as they talked to one another from unseen vantage points. I was told that what Lived within the confines of La Push was/were Quileute People...*Po-oke*.

To hear it all was worth experiencing. The spooky mystery which night beside Swamp projected: splashes; shrieks; moans; hoots...*it was scary*...only a coward would have shunned it. Or someone with common sense. But who could resist that mystery of sounds from creatures which lived unseen by us in Night, as we without proper night senses live in Day? After nights by Swamp, 'scary' movies were boring. I yawned at 'Dr. Jekyll & Mr. Hyde'; 'the Hunchback of N.D.'

ANIMAL

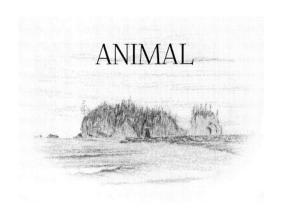

A lesson in Life Reality came to me via Tyler Hobucket when I was about twelve. And his brother Harry...who had two beautiful Greyhound dogs which I learned were as partial to 'nicecream' as I. Ed Ryan, postmaster and owner of Ryan's store, (once Cully's Hotel)(then Eversman's) dispensed a large ice-cream cone with a sprinkling of tiny chocolate cylinders over its top. For a nickel.

In addition to my summer 'newspaper-route' to anchored fish-boats for that income, I 'gutted' Fall seine-caught Salmons for Butts-Pattison's fish-buying scow. Some-times given a nickel from Mama for myself (after I had given Her my pay), I was a 'rich kid'. We were paid a penny a fish cleaned and I could clean even King in thirty seconds and wash it in another fifteen, eggs into a container and on to the next fish within a minute. I was fast enough to earn *fifty-cents an hour* if pushing. Full grown men couldn't match that pace and I have no idea from what source that skill came but I never met close competition.

So with that unending source of incredible wealth I might buy Hersheysalmon-bar (Hershey's almond) or GREEN RIVER 'pop' (soda), or nicecream cone. Maybe even save the money and drool over pictures of bicycles in Monkeywarts or Searzez catalogs, hoarding the coins I might otherwise have spent. (Sometimes a hoard of twenny or thirdy cents). Charlie Howeattle had a printed sign at the soda cooler: 'We don't know where mom is but we've got 'pop' on ice'. I thought highly of the twisted meaning and often bought Green River.

One day I left Ryan's with a chocolate-sprinkled vanilla cone and stopped to talk to Tyler and Harry, (whose stucco house was beside Ryan's to the north-west). Here two lovely Greyhounds, both my height, simply snarfed the cone from my hand…I was holding it for them, obviously.. "Crunch crunch" was what I heard relative to the cone. Part of it hit the ground and was gratefully retrieved by one of the dogs.

Having learned the essentials of English in school, I informed the two happy dogs that I considered them to be mere animals, in one manner or another. Harry and Tyler, standing there as audience, laughed. But I didn't. "Salmonlabeech! Them dogs took my nicecream!" I told the world. "Dang dumb dogs!"

"Never mind," Tyler said, laughing, as was Harry, he'd buy another, and with his daughter Helen took me to Ryan's where Helen and I *both scored*! Outside again, Tyler tapped my shoulder and said, " 'Sco to Beach". Helen entered the house and Tyler and I crossed drift logs to Beach. He had in mind to open my mind to the obvious, as yet not obvious to me. Thanking Tyler for the replacement of nicescream I offered some to him but he wasn't hungry I guessed. I couldn't imagine not hungry for nicecream.

We turned toward Lonesome Crick and he said, "Don't swear at Animals for bein' nacheral. Their Spirit gonna turn 'gainst you."

"What you mean, Tyler?"

"When you was holdin' the ice cream how they know you ain't holdin' it for them? We hold things for them to eat. They expect it when we hold it."

"Don't know. Didn't offer it."

"Think about this: they think 'Dog', we think '*Po-oke*'"

"That 'cause they're dumb?"

"What's dumb 'bout knowing what's good to eat?"

"Ayyy." I laughed. No arguing '*ha-atch Ah-lahsh*'. "Nothin', but that ain't dog food."

"It gets made in a factory it ain't nobody's food. It's fake".

"How come we like it then?" 'Fake food' bewildered me.

"Inventors figured how to make it taste so good is why. It don't make you healthy like Smelts does."

"How come govermint lets 'em?"

"Comp'nys *own* govermint."

"I thought *we* was govermint, *Po-oke* an' *Hoquat* both."

"I'll tell you about it sometime. Somethin' else now. Both with Two-leggeds and other Animals each gots its own thoughts for to survive. They is just three things for survivin': 1) Eat don't get et; 2) Safe shelter; 3) havin' young to come along behind us. Them Dogs eatin' you ice cream is obeyin' the way to survive by eatin' stuff. What don't do it that way?" That had to be absorbed. Then I saw the reasoning behind it and that ended the lesson.

We waded Lonesome Crick searching for round, flat rocks. These to skip on *Ta-boke* when we returned to Village. Tyler said, "Figure when money can get shuffled back and forth even govermint listen to it clink. Nothin' is honest about money gain in the world. Them who s'posta be most honest is richest ones of all, like churches. Two things is sure: there ain't nothing constant but Change and Corruption, always wrong, always greedy, always destroying the nation. Who got lots of money can give some away to buy favors."

I stopped and looked at him. "But them people talks about how god (Jesus) was poor when he come here. What they need money for if 'god' dint?"

"That's one god. There's a god in Mind for every human bean (being). Two-leggeds also talk about how two-leggeds is more important than animals. Ain't we Animals? Just like you talkin' about them dogs as dumb because they wanted somethin' good to eat, just like you. We're most important because we say so. *No other reason*. All which Lives is most important to itself. Remember, if everything had a name for itself its name would be 'Me'."

I thought about 'Animals' and that we were Animals.

"How can we be Animals, Tyler? We don't act like it. An' we think, ain't it."

"Ayy-y we act like it. We fight for grub an' territory an' matin' like Elks do. We' get babies like them. We got Blood an' guts like them. We got hair an' teeth an' eyes, ears, bones. We croak like them do. They make decision about what's happenin' 'round 'em all the time. They look to see about jumpin' over logs, if they can or can't. That's decision. That's thinkin'. Difference is we need brains what analyze more than other Animals."

"How come?"

Before he answered he was silent for perhaps five minutes. I looked at his face and saw he was inside someplace. When he came outside again he looked at me and said, "I think it's 'we need it most'. We're most vulnerable Animal because we're weakest. Deeper thinkin' is how we survive."

That hurt my human pride because to a child 'our' everything is best, 'our' parents; 'our' country; 'our' Tribe; even to those who own one, 'our' car.

"I thought humans is toughest an' best. What's better?"

"We can't out swim Sea-Lion. We can't outrun, out-jump Cougar. We can't see like Dog or Cat, can't smell stuff they smell easy. Owl-people see in dark, like cat does.."

"We don't hear like other kinds; any. You wanna find out how tough you are, pick a fight with twenty pound Wild Cat. You'll find out who's tough faster'n you want. Or only a house-cat. You'd lose, toot sweet. No, *human way* is deep thinking in order *to make it* in a world filled with tough, hungry creatures, mostly tougher'n us."

Thinking about that I laughed. Then, "Old Man told me 'bout how Animals think about things we don't know nothin' about, like sound and smell and things; they hear what we don't an' they think about it. That ain't too dumb."

"Ayyy. Swearin' at somethin' you don't understan' is what's dumb ain't it."

"Ayy. You sayin' ever'thin' sees stuff different, ain't it. Just because I see this way ain't got to be right."

"Ayy. When we get back you tell them dogs you sorry about you misunderstandin' them an' rub 'em good. Their feelin's won't be hurt no more an' they'll forget about it Otherwise next time you see 'em they gonna be unfriendly, maybe bark."

"Tyler," I said, stopping in my tracks, "how they goin' to know what I'm tellin' them? They don't talk our language."

"They don't have to, language just make sound out of thought, they 'hear' your thinkin', whether you make sound or not."

We walked to *Ta-boke* and skipped rocks. Tyler skipped one thirteen times. I made four. There we unloaded our rock-burdened pockets then returned to Harry's house. The two Greyhounds 'woo-wooed' to us in happy greeting. I apologized to them and we made friends more than we were before. I knew by their behavior *they understood* and I felt a bond with them not experienced before. After that there was no mistaking *they* knew *I* knew *who* and *what they were.* They'd begin to 'WooWoo' when I was still at the corner by Hank Taylor's house. I'd 'WooWoo' back and it almost became a 'yowling' match. I always had at least a small piece of bread for them with me. Henceforth they behaved as friends behave after being apart. Only with them it was just as exciting day by day, or even hour by hour. I too felt it grow.

That bond has passed to all other Creatures for me. Even more than before. I had learned a new vision from Slug and its friend Old Man. I saw Spider, hanging in shimmering webs in uncountable numbers around Swamp, as People of *their* kind going about *their* way of Life. Dog taught a lesson. And I bonded with them all.

What can SACRED GREAT SPIRIT/GOD make that *isn't* Sacred to It, as Dema had said thus is Sacred *in fact*? I haven't enough ego to condemn what GodPower has created. I haven't enough stupidity to harm it. If Great Spirit made *it* I protect *it*. Thus *all*.

HUNTING

Only *Hoquat*-mind would kill a huge, magnificent Bull Elk to hang its head on the end of a barn to show how powerful a bullet can be. Big, 'chief' bulls, were never taken by *Po-oke* because *they* sired Animals of strength. Killing them and leaving the weak and inept to breed is *Hoquat* (*Hoquat*= crazy, no honor; *Hoquat*=White, honorable). Their off-spring become weaker and weaker as the power Animals are taken to hang on the barn. Same as in War, the best die. Habit of who kills for power-gain. Soldiers, politicians, '*sport* killers'. Imagine the twisted minds of who KILL Life-creatures as sport. Including fellow Humans. God's makings.

We asked each hunted group if any of the creatures would volunteer to save us from hunger. We took no Babies. What might come forward of forked-horn bucks or three year olds we would accept in gratitude, *leaving no part to be unused.* Years after it would have died a *natural* death, those *volunteer* Animals were held in reverence by *Po-oke*. Bones were used, hides, some made drums, horns converted to carvings, frequently about the Animal itself. Hoofs became rattles and from thigh bones came 'Soul Catcher'. Everything was used. From *bone marrow* came medicine we made for blending with salt and plants to use for pain reduction; to put on burns (without salt); to put on unhealthy skin; to use for making pemmican. Everything was used. With unending gratitude.

Before we were permitted to hunt we had to learn to shoot. Only with deadly accuracy would the death we caused be *non-reflexive.* We accepted *Hoquat* rifle gratefully because it caused instantaneous death in skilled hands. The aim was to penetrate below and behind the ear where the backbone entered the head. The Animal taken didn't wink. We learned to 'pray' *for* it afterward, and *to* the Animal for understanding of why it had been taken, before and after taking it, and thanking it.

Great sympathy for the Animal and its family and friends came from the hunter. We knew they all would be sad. I never took an Animal I didn't cry about. I would carress and pet and kiss the poor dead thing and realistically, become more depressed about it as time passed. I did this the first Elk I took and as I sat crying, its dead-head on my lap, Fred Penn and Fred Woodruff touched my shoulder and I looked at them wondering if I was to be ridiculed for my 'childishness'.

Massive sympathy showed in their eyes, and wetness. 'Woody' said, "You goin' to be good *Tloquali*, good *Tss'ay-whutleoke*, *cKulell*. You got heart. You gonna be considerate an' careful. None of us don't feel like you do. Nobody wants to murder nothin' but we dint plan it. Great Spirit showed the way". Fred Penn said,

"*Tloquali* talk to and listen to all creatures of MOTHER EARTH. Same as *Tss'y'uck*, Same as *Tss'ay-whutleoke*. All *Po-oke* know all Life things are Children of one Creator. That's why we touch nothing for to harm. If you ain't gonna eat it leave it alone. If it wants to eat *you*, run. It's natural to be sad when you got to kill but we got families too. That's why we ask them for volunteer. Cougar don't like killin' Fawn but got to make milk for Her Babies…dint (didn't) *invent* Life, we just got to live it like how it started. It's Natural to be Natural. Best thing for us: If Great Spirit made it we respect it."

Tloquali and *Tss'y'uck* and *Tss'ay-whutleoke* considered conversation with non-two leggeds as like the Spirit conversation other people call 'prayer'. Successful 'in the hunt' these Warriors against Hunger talked out loud or in their head to thank what had volunteered to die to feed other Babies' milk. Call it Prayer. I asked Woody, ' What's Prayer"?"

"Prayer is lissnin'. *You* do all the talkin' Great Spirit can't get in a word. *Great Spirit knows you' needs*. Prayin' is keepin' you' mouth shut an' you' ears open. If you ain't *playin' some game for other two-leggeds to see*, *Great Spirit* will talk to *you!* Be alone when you lissnin' for Great Spirit. Shut up an' listen. Let God talk. Same with non-two leggeds. Lissen. Jus' like *Po-oke* they talkin' to one another alla time". "Them ain't noises they makin' when you hear 'em, it's talk," Charlie Howeattle told me. He was Shaker minister. He knew about that stuff.

Isolation and fasting and drinking Living Water is what puts the mind into the place that Great Spirit can come talk to 'seeker'. In times of great hunger in Village lodge people try to find volunteer creatures to eat and if none volunteer they don't eat. That's why all Lodge People train themselves not to be hungry if there's nothing to eat. "Why be hungry if you can't satisfy it?" Chester Johnson and *Se-ic-tiss* Ward said that to me over and over. "When you get hungry, an' got no food don't think about it. There ain't no feeling where you' mind don't give attention." Even today I don't get hungry unless food is there. Nor thirsty without water to drink. What would be the purpose? To concentrate on the uncomfortable is to increase its strength. Worry is that kind of thing. Stanley Grey told me that worry is the lowest form of human thought. "Life is like *cKwia* (Rain)…will do what it does. Worry can't stop it." Two Greyhounds which ate my nicecream helped me to learn these things.

DISCIPLINE

Those who resembled neither *Hoquat* nor *Po-oke* bore the brunt of Ignorance from undisciplined Village *Po-oke* as well as 'outside' *Hoquat*, in Arrogance. Especially in School: "Hey 'Breed'"; "Hey 'Siwash'"; "Hey 'Savage'", and on and on. Ask Kenneth 'Porky' Payne.

Those who were products of neither group, but rather both, were likely to have the red-hair, blue eyes, freckles, etc., of those enlightened and self-less bringers of the benefits of Civilization, (among which were booze, disease and greed and selfishness; violence; deception; those valuable elements of gun-toters from where ever they came, with their guns as 'civilizers'). They who *enjoyed* making crossed blood lines had no thought of other than gratification in their 'good' God spouting minds. Who *would* suffer, (other than the compliant Girls predestined by centuries of custom to be 'ready' at the proper age), were the 'Breeds'. Ask the products of Negro/White mixing; *any* other 'splits'.

Porky Payne and I could be twins. We've talked about the prejudice of who trained us to behave violently *(for our self-protection)*. It evolved to a hit to the mouth or nose, broken teeth, blackened eyes, a fist-smash to the larynx, by the prejudice victim, us, elements of Ignorance compounded, and relished by the performing vengeance seeker. Both 'worlds' seemed against us, whether we deserved punishment from the stupidity of 'Me superior to you' or not.

A *consequence* (of the 'edicts' by *Ignorance*, that non-*Po-oke* or non-*Hoquat* products of 'doing bad' [half-breeds or less] resorted to) was *violence*, engendered by and visited upon those who *pushed their superiority*. We evolved to violence. Booze and drugs also came from there.

If you can't fight them, stupefy yourself seems to have been the result. Seeing the obvious consequent tragedies. I was never drawn to this knocking myself out with booze, I preferred to see blood. And not mine.

One day I was 'corraled' to be advised by Grant Eastman, one of the most peaceful, un-violent of our Men. Walking on Beach was the way to the discussion and I hear his words ringing forth to now.

"You getting' mean *cKulell*. Word comin' to us you pick fights and bust folks up at school. You kicked out of school now, ain't it."

I felt the sadness to his words and was washed with regret. Excuse crowded excuse, and alibis which seemed reasonable earlier, to my mind, were seen by me now as mere excuses to see blood. *I wanted blood.* He asked me to speak up when I answered and I realized that of Men in Village this one deserved great respect. "I got kicked out," I replied so he could hear.

"How come?" His hand was on my shoulder as we walked, gentle, warm, soothing. "I busted XXXX's nose. He made hock-tooey (spit) on my tablet."

"How old are you now *cKulell*?"

"Lebbum".

"You been trainin' to control yourself seven years now. What you learned, if you did?"

"Elders tellin' me 'bout not lettin' stupids make my mind work."

"What that means to you?"

I remember seeing two other Village Men 'over there', meaning a ways behind us. Their walking strides told me Stanley Grey and Daniel White were out Beaching too.

He repeated the question. " *cKulell*, what that means to you?"

"What you all been tellin' me. I let somebody else make me mad they runnin' my brain. Got to remember *Discipline* like you said. Can't let nobody else think for me." This came intellectually. Yet a rush of impelled emotion burst like a dam. "But they call me names an' throw stuff at me an' bust up my stuff. They cut my new tennashoes and my stuff in the gym locker got cut up…they never stop. Dog poop get in my lunch bag. Ev'er'day at school from getting off skoobus 'til school's done I get to be target. I figure if I bust enough teeth I'll get left alone."

"We all gone through that *cKulell*. They took us babies from home and fam'ly to 'boarding school'. They beat who talked Quileute…any Indian language. We talk *Hoquat* poor (badly) we got beat. We got lonesome for home, cried, we got beat. They musta got fun like in ma-kin' babies the way they beat on us. We never got what all Baby needs, hugs an' love. Keep 'em in the kennels they belong in, 's what they said to one and other. They tried *training us there was no such thing as cKwyeh-Tee, told us about their god what walked on water* and that stuff and beat us if we dint believe it.

"'God of love', they said, tried to break our spirit with beating if they could. That way we'd have a god to be afraid of. Instead of respect and love, to thank for Life-gifts, to go to for help as we would to our parents. 'F we fought back, talked back, they beat us unconscious. They used little kids in beds like their wife. Kids died of broken heart. We learned to deceive: Play like you believe that but keep what you could of *Po-oke* ways. Older ones didn't have same chance we had, didn't know nothin' else." My mind swirled to think of what these Elders had suffered before '*Boarding Schools*' were stopped.

"Talked to us lots about god's loving even savages. Like us." Grant smiled. "'S why I go to church so much…miss the talkin' came from boarding school." He laughed again. I was in church more often than he, which is like *all three times.*

"We didn't get home for so long we forgot sometimes we had young brothers and sisters. We was barely past *Chutsk*, baby. They tried trainin' us to believe our Mother and Father was stupid. Backward. Ig-norant. Savages. That *Hoquat* was superior in all ways. But we watched 'Superior' destroy Forests an' saw Rivers suffer. We watched them plow Forest floor up and plant garbage Land dint know. We gone through what you're going through. But you goin' to end in jail you keep goin'. *Once you get there* you mights well die because they love having Indian victims nobody can see them destroy. They feel guilty about nothing except missing the chance to steal, or harm; beat, ridicule. You let them lead you mind and you going to end up just like what they want: you in jail, punished for their evil by their evil. You doin' what *Hoquats* want."

Desperation at my plight took hold and I began to cry. "What can I do? What can *we* do? They *make* us go to school. They don't let us stay home and learn *Po-oke* ways. We got to learn 'bout demokercy and equaliddy' and them things *none of them* believes anyway; why should we? None of it ain't true or there wouldn't be nobody hungry."

A rush of despair took me almost to convulsions of sobbing. I had nowhere to go, no way out of the penalty of going to the *Hoquats* for mercy they didn't have. *School*, I saw clearly, was for *subjugation* and *stupifying*. It made consumers and nothing else. I saw that at ten. Now I was almost insane with hopelessness.

"What I'm gonna do?"

"*Tloquali*, *cKulell*. You got to take pain an' don't flinch. *You got to* **rise above** *what oppress you.* You got to have mind so strong nothing outside you can control it. You got to be like 'Round'! You got to have *Wolf Hair* 'round you heart." His voice became stentorian: "You all we got left *cKulell*! ' rest (the rest) all drinks, smokes, playin' *Hoquat* an' *Hoquat* games. You got to open you *Thunderbird 'Taxilit.'*. When you talk it goin' to be as Thunder, ev'rybody goin' to hear. If we didn't believe in you to be above them and their power and to *carry what we was* with you to keep and protect we got no hope at all. You *got* to rise above them and like *Tloquali*, like Round, be able to suffer any pain because you are Black Face. *PAIN DON'T EXIST FOR YOU!* You got to rise above you' body and be MIND ONLY. *Pain don't touch mind.* Can't. *YOU'RE BLACK FACE! DON'T NEVER FORGET IT!*" He was almost sobbing himself and a resolve was born in me. I was *Tloquali* and only dying could stop it.

I had buried my face against his chest, sobbing deep sorrow, standing on the curative powers of Beach. His arms held me against him in gentle love and I marveled that both my shoulders were being patted in sympathy. It was then I realized that both Stanley Grey and Daniel White were beside us, trying to pass strength to me for for-bearance to face an ordeal not unlike what they had already suffered. It was boarding school but I got to come home every night.

I remember the anguish of that day, how my chest ached from sobbing. I remember also that much died in me that day, standing on Beach with three marvelous old Men of the 1800's whose sole hope lay in the last boy wanting to be *Tloquali*. I remember too that something previously unknown to my psyche was born. I knew that Childhood's things were behind me. From now I had to have strength and resolve which I'd not had before. That was the finding of something else, outside myself, which existed known or unknown just waiting to be found. As the shimmer of golden light pulling us toward La Push from Jon Wanska's boat once had awaited me, so too was my *Taxilit*, Spirit Animal guide.

Tomanamus is *awareness* that other power exists, *Taxilit* is that other power.

So on that 'today', from the cocoon of Childhood, a Man was un-winding slowly from the threads of boyhood's Yesterday. Three Men and a boy walked to Beach earlier, now four Men left the incubating and healing power Beach presented. Tears for no longer shedding tears of Childhood were part of the catharsis, I recall, and for the saying good-bye to Childhood. Forced, by Ignorance over which I, nor *Po-oke*, had any control. As 'they' would do, I knew now, 'they' would do. We could do nothing to protect ourselsves from them. We must obey the gun-backed laws *they created and interpreted*. In over seventy years of observing I see no error in that conclusion.

MUSIC of the SUNSET

It was evening now. Thin clouds moved by. We four *Tloquali* (!) (we four *MEN* mind you) marched past Lonesome Creek and found a log to sit on. Daniel White said, "Now, this going to make you feel good. Big Show comin' from Great Spirit, give you Power."

"What kinda show Daniel?"

"Once you get to be past Boy you learn with Lodges-people 'bout lissnin' for the Music of Sunset…Sunset Music."

I whirled to stare at Daniel. He was facing out to Ocean but his eyes were turned to watch me. What I felt was Shock at the recognition of a reality which may well have been but which had not occurred to me. "How somebody gonna hear with their eyes?"

"Seein' an' hearin' goin' into same brain", Stanley Gray said. "Them colors which is brightest is loudest, real dark ones is quite (quiet). 'Hear' the music in you Spirit. More of it you 'hear' further on, you gettin' to Balancin' you *Mind*."

"Sun down now, watch them colors an' 'magine what they sound like to Great Spirit. If *IT* can hear it, we can try." Explained thus I understood: Mind expansion to feel that a sight we *saw* could be *heard* by God. Knowing that *it could be heard* presented a challenge Great Spirit put there so we could strive to master it. 'Impossible' of course, but I learned to *hear* the Sunset Show on rare occasions. As rare as 'glow' on Beach.

"Watch how it come to be that blue sky melt into orange sky, how orange sky melt into blue one. *Where that happens?* Think you can point at where they changes? See as if you hearin' music while you watchin'.

Where that *color change happen* is pure melody to Great Spirit. Now, don't say no more. Lissen."

After today, I sensed, I was a different person. I had reached a plateau of some kind, I saw, but of what?

AWAITING SPRING

Stark, bare branches stood out, leaden, wet, lifeless, (but for the movement and voice of ChoCho) since Winter had first gained power over our world. Skunk cabbage leaves had shuddered slowly in slight 'Summer' winds against their water surrounded stalks then had died and rotted all Winter in every water storage-pond around. The broad and repelling Devil's Club leaves had dropped leaving a sticky-sharp floor across the woods wherever Devil's Club had grown. And huge Nettles. There were areas into which we didn't venture. Devil's Club stalks with long, heavy and extremely sharp spikes wait for the unwary in the same manner as Nettles across the top of Ahkalut. The leaves themselves are spiked and ready to battle intruders into their realm. (We harvested tall nettles on Ahkalut).

In Fall, Alder had dropped a thick mantle of leaves for Rain to soak and rot and turn into soil with the exact nutrients required for Alder. And for what would come to grow in those sites when Alder was overwhelmed. In Fall, everywhere in Woods where a foothold had been gained, Salmon Berry, (having had red, yellow or orange berries in their season), stood as if remnants of the dying of a planet. Their lightly greyed stalks looked painted against the backdrop of dark, wet Woods. But for Evergreen Trees, and *Cho-Cho*, Life may have gone away forever.

Even in Summer kids' trousers were wet below the knees. In any season, but more in Winter, trousers which at night were put to dry behind heater or stove were mud-stiff from knee to foot in the morning. And only apparently clean from knee to waist. Wherever we could roam, we were in at least knee-high, wet grasses. Soaking wet grasses. Soaked 'tenna shoes' squirted water from holes worn into them on both sides where toe and foot bent. The tennis-shoe sound 'squish-squish' was heard with the actual footsteps when someone was approaching.

I remember the apparently bloodless, pale and wrinkled flesh of water soaked toes and feet which came out of tennis shoes on removal. "Soak you' feet warm water or they gonna fall off" we were told almost as ritual of the day.

That may have involved going to the water spigot by Olive and Pete Clark's house. He was second generation Coastie, (son of Prentice Clark, an early 1900's Coasty from Neah Bay), She part Quileute. At the corner by their lot stood the spigot from which we in the area drew water. It seemed our journey always took place at night during which time we would be Rain pelted from the dead-black night sky.

Inevitably.

The spigot delivered water through a six-inch wooden delivery 'pipe' from a wooden-box 'collector' by the entrance to Second Beach Trail a mile away. Wonderfully interesting creatures came forth with the water during the driving Rains of Winter. The interesting creatures likely were centipedes or sow-bugs or very young, very dead 'water puppies', orange and brown and torn from the ride down the pipe-line to the spigot. Bark pieces and rusty brown Fern fronds certainly added vegetable nutrition. All this was carefully filtered through cheese-cloth so we'd be sure to have pure water. Benefit *had* to come from that. Most frequently we boiled the water. (A *little* benefit had to come from that too).

Debris of one sort or another seemed to plague the system's flow too frequently. With Bucket beneath Spigot, turned full force, sometimes Water streamed forth, at other times it might take five minutes to fill a bucket. Or the pipe might be blocked.

Or worse. Spigot stood a couple of feet in the air without support so when occasionally hit by a careless driver, the broken pipe emptied the box up on the hill, then in Rain more like a wall of water than drops from the sky, people gathered to repair the break. If at night, kerosene railroad-lanterns with flickering, yellow light or hissing, brilliant Coleman lanterns cast unimaginably active, distorted shadows of people against houses and cars, people who would be working to repair the break. (And *rarely* someone might swear. [At the 'good fortune' of having to repair the water line]).

At any rate, with two buckets of water, the water-bearer would slosh along toward home, likely arriving with buckets just two-thirds filled with the prize. Now I see it would have been more simple to put two-thirds bucket in each to have less slopping, less weight, but unless you've been a kid yourself you may not see how folly sometimes goes with Childhood.

Then home with the buckets. We'd heat water to soak our already soggy feet. This made us sleepy; it was off to bed with trousers by stove drying for tomorrow and another day of being soaked to the knees, and a chance to laugh tomorrow night again, at one another's 'dead-man's' feet.

So Winter had darkened and further dampened our Coastal world, the deciduous plants and trees bare and interesting to see. Ghostly stalks of last years Salmon-berry bushes, light grey against the dark woods beyond were curious winter forms that had been Summer's lush, green-tinged bulbous shapes. And Vine Maples, Alders, contorted trunks and arms dark-grey against a light grey sky, awaited Rebirth.

Yet through Winter which brought sleep to most, or drove other kinds to other places, the gigantic Spirit of *Cho-Cho*, talking in apparently dead brush, dark little body flitting throughout the slumbering tangle of leafless stalks and branches, kept our sleeping land alive. *Po-oke* held that the most incredible, the biggest of all Spirits, was that of *Cho-Cho*: Winter Wren. With her pert little tail flicking betraying her location. And Her 'peep'.

And as Winter increased its effort to deliver a final strangle-hold, bringing from the lake we called Sky, more chill, more Rain, stove-wood piles diminished increasingly and so too kindling. In moderate 'anxiety' more like increasing awareness, we watched South-west skies which brought the draperies of Rain, hoping for the break which called out 'Spring!' And waited eagerly for when newly-sprouting area plants began to show the wisps of green they brought.

Sometimes it was dry enough for wood gathering. During occasional un-Raining spells we cKeynooed up Dicky River to search the banks and side fields among downed and rotted old trees for branches which now resembled no more than spear-points. These, a foot or more in length, were sought eagerly and wrested from the rot of the log, or sometimes chopped free. Uncle Yum said that such pieces can be taken dripping wet from lake bottoms or creeks or streams and will burn hot and smoke-free without 'drying'. Pitch is in these branches and they burn as does nothing else of wood, so-called 'wet or dry'. Not brilliant with light nor choking with smoke, these burned wonderfully. One in Mr. Majestic would last hours.

We would gather as many as possible and after Forest died thousands of acres of these fire-brand producing trees were available. The few raining trunks rotted and the 'spear points' could be retrieved from the rot. On a 'wood-gathering' day, perhaps with no more than a week's supply of this material gathered we might be driven out by Rain again, to return home with the booty. Meantime we watched the Southwest horizon for the weather break announcing Winter's death. All eyes were also scanning the Woods close to home…looking for the buds of Spring.

Then came the thrill. Village exhuberance bloomed as green buds poked out of branches everywhere, almost too small to see individually. Looking at Alder and Willow woods from a distance, the multitudes of buds presented a slightly shimmering yellow-green color to our world and in eagerness we sought Salmon Berry, for 'shoots' from the ground. These new stalks we peeled and ate. Gorgeous, crunchy and satisfying vegetation we hungered for by Spring.

Now even Salal, never very revealing of its purpose, seemed to present more surface 'fuzz' on its leaves. To *Po-oke*, waiting for Salal Berries was nearly torture. I know of none who didn't desire Salal Berries above almost any other. I treasured them. Waiting for late Summer and the harvest of Salal was stressful to any addict. *Se-ic-tiss* Ward taught me the joy of Sa-lal eating: Crush a bunch of them, dilute with Living Water for a great fruit drink.

When buds began appearing…and 'shoots', cKeynoos which had been kept dry since seine season for Salmons were 'righted'. From end of Salmons seining 'til Spring they were kept upside down on *Ta-boke* Beach or beside houses, small logs under each end (to keep the inside dry of rot-causing Rain-water (*kwia*) over Winter,).

Holes were patched, holes which may have been knot-holes at one time. Copper tacks side by side held pieces of sheet-lead covered tin in place over the holes and were wonderfully effective. Usually some fisherman had sheet-lead to spare.

A rapidly developing (but almost religious *avoidance of*) interest in the next sign of Spring was the hungrily awaited appearance of Smelts. (We believed that concentrating on '*which* prey' sent thought Spirit to them and they'd make effort to avoid who was seeking them.

After deciding which, "Don't look at or think about the one to be took until that last instant, the act of 'capture'". Elks or Smelts). At almost any time before the middle of June Smelts might swim into River or be at Surf. cKeynoo, with new or patched seines piled in preparation, were readied at River Beach, awaiting the smelts, some to *cKwahleh* side of Shell Oil dock, some taken to Surf and First Beach to await Surf Smelts gathering in Ocean.

When Smelts came they swarmed into River with right tide, close to mouth, there to be caught before getting to the oil dock. From *Ta-boke* Beach experienced fishers watched for the flashing-silver of darting masses, the surface flipping, as the schools moved along close to Beach readying for to spawn.

"*cKetocks!*" (go) the 'boss' would call and upstream those waiting in cKeynoo pushed straight out from River Beach to make a 'U' turn fifty feet out and then come back to Beach a hundred feet or less, downstream. Throwing out the net to stop the school's up River passage, the downstream return to the beach surrounded it and the work began.

The up-River section of the net was held in place by several helpers (who acted as holding anchors) while the net was dumped overboard. Others took the downstream haul-in line for the net and pulled it ashore, effectively holding the school in place. Now as many as could pulled the two ends of the net until the Smelts were brought close to, trapped in Beach and dipped out into boxes. And for helpers, into buckets.

The 'pullers' were each given a bucket of Smelts to take home for their pay. Or, their 'take' might go to 'the smoke shed', there to hang by sticks through the gills in racks above a smoky fire. To smoke them we put them above the smoke-fire and kept the smoke flowing up and around them, four feet or so above the 'fire', (more smoke and heat than flame), until they were hard smoked for winter. We ate them dry, as they were, or sometimes boiled them to eat with peas and small, round, boiled potatoes. When Smelts were fresh we gutted them, tossed them in flour then butter fried them. Smelts were *cKwyeh-Tee's* gift in Spring-time.

Someone always took Smelts to MizzizMitt to trade for butter. Their 'pay' was later, fresh *butter*-fried Smelts.

The net/cKeynoo owners might box their fresh catch for rapid delivery to Seattle/Tacoma area, to get a few cents a pound for the delicacy. Whiz Fish or San Juan Fishing and Packing Company, or Strand, from 'Berdeen, were principal buyers.

During 'the smoke' we young hung around watching, for the days it took to cure them, hoping for samples when the Winter's storage was ready to test...Child test. To eat them, when at last Smelts were smoked dry we dipped them in available Seal oil, (or bacon fat if no Seal oil), and munched them down. Chocolate cake could be as enticing I suppose, but I'd be hard pressed to choose if only one could be had.

Herb's father, 'Old Man' Fisher at Hoh River ate them dipped in Vaseline until Herb put a stop to it. Grease is grease and oil is oil if you aren't of the mechanical world. How does Vaseline differ from Whale blubber, Mazola differ from Seal oil?

When Smelts not yet 'schooled' came to Ocean Surf in long, strung out lines, hip-boot protected fishers with dip-nets awaited the delicious prize. Boxes of heavy wood were placed above water-line on Sand so the successful 'dipper' could empty the Smelts into the boxes then go to Surf for more. More often than not a fisher was inundated by a larger than expected breaker where the fishing took place and had to go sit on a log to remove the water-filled boots for emptying. Laughter inevitably followed this experience, other fishers who had been more fortunate awaited their turns, knowing the breaker for them was soon to arrive.

When *schools* appeared in Surf, someone with cKeynoo readied, net in place and stern to Beach, patiently waited for the right 'flashing' to show in the wave that peaked just before it broke. Then the fishing crew , generally three, went into action and the 'surround' pattern of River fishing was re-enacted in Surf.

Here, swamped cKeynoo were common, but the 'polers' continued to push cKeynoo in the 'U' circle, a ton or more of *cKwahleh* the added burden, one or two people bailing rapidly to lighten the vessel in order to drive it as far ashore as possible while the net continued to be tossed out. Then 'pulling in' the school began and Smelts were brought ashore to readied boxes. Always amazing to me was the roadway taken by the fishing group to get to Beach through the jumble of drift-logs. But in whatever magic manner, they found an opening and appeared with cars to carry away the 'take of the day': box-loads of Smelts.

I don't remember the man's name who bought a new Packard auto every two or three years, removed the back-seat and seat-back in order to carry up to four boxes of Smelts to market in 'Berdeen or Seattle.

One time I went along when he and his wife picked up a new Packard. The name of the car company was different than most names, Packard Seattle Company. To my mind it would have been Seattle Packard etc. I hope to recall the names of the couple.

The trip was fascinating. We stopped in Port Angeles to eat in a café entered by going downstairs from the street. ('Me, I had me a waffle'). 'P.A.' was a city of minor mystery to me, 'Duck Inn Café', Monkeywartses store, a long spit of land out into the straits on the end of which was a lighthouse, ferries that went 'over there' (to Canada)... great place P.A. So big! This trip was special to me because I sat on a board, in back, atop four boxes of Smelts to Seattle, then got to ride back to La Push in a new Packard with the seat not yet removed. We ferried from Ballard to Port Ludlow then drove to P.A. passing through what I called 'funny name', Sequim. And got to eat waffle in that downstairs café. All because of Smelts.

Sea Gull eggs were gathered in Spring from atop such places as Cake Rock. I've not tasted eggs to match them. The beautiful speckled shells and brilliant yellow of the yoke made them lovely foods to see and delicious to eat. Gathered in Spring, for days there were eggs brought to Village from islands as far north as outside Cape Alava leading to Ozette Reef, as far south as Rounded and Alexander Islands.

Before *Hoquat* ownership of Destruction Island, except for *Po-oke*, no destructive predator could get at the eggs three miles offshore, so from Hoh River had come eggs for multitudes.

Once gathered the eggs were boiled, scrambled, (they didn't spread across a pan as do storage eggs, because they stand, almost as if still in the shell: *fresh* eggs); baked cakes with them, which were inevitably yellow as butter; used them in bread, also always a golden yellow, made hotcakes, hey, what are eggs used for? Sea Gull eggs are better.

A circle of women weaving baskets.

Canoes through the surf to go for seals or whales.

A river canoe (*Kwia ta bil*) for ladies.

Axing stem and stern before adzing.

Axing to shape for canoe.

Charlie Howeattle and Chester Johnson nearby where the
women gathered basket reeds, at the river mouth.

Poling across the river.

Setting net to catch smelt.

Smelt fishers in canoe with net.

Tommy Payne
showing opponents
a 'miss' in guessing
at the 'bone gamble'.

Ada Black's husband
drumming for 'bone
gamble'.

Tyler Hobucket
drumming at
'bone gamble'.

Teenage participant
in 'bone gamble'
with rhythm sticks.

'Big Bill' Penn
drumming at
'bone gamble'.

Fire rack for
burning down
canoe tree.

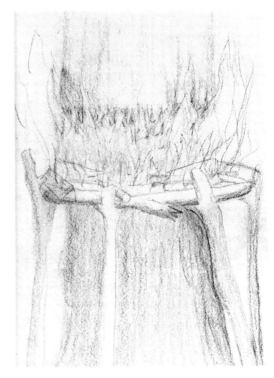

LAKES

Before the Parks Dep't came with their outsider unconcern and wisdom there was a marvelous, a wondrous little lake near to James' 'Mora Park Auto Court' (where Supreme Court Justice William O. Douglas stayed when he was free to do so, mostly in Summertime).

The James family lived upriver from Dicky River a third of a mile at a bend of the road toward Forks and Quillayute Prairie. Rather than to maintain the original road to Mora and Rialto Beach Mr. Goverment broke in a new road which straightened the bend of the original. Now, instead of splendid isolation the beautiful, unspoiled lake has a fine paved road racing beside it for outsiders to dash along toward their 'rights' at Rialto Beach and points North. Forget the isolated beauty…uniformed and uninformed, Smokey Bear hat wearers talk of the benefit to all of the 'new route'.

Originally there was a trail to the lake which wound for about half a mile through sparse tree growth, and several old stumps where Fern garden beauty bordered both sides of the trail). Once close, unless one knew the final entry to the lake site proper it's unlikely that the delightful experience of a visit would be had…a lake would not be suspected.

It was about two hundred fifty feet long, less than three hundred anyway, Easterly-Westerly, varying from forty to eighty feet across. Wind-downed trees lay at odd angles from the shore, half submerged, some with the far ends underwater. The entirety of the logs, partial bridgeways to the deeper water, showed spines of dead branches, standing somewhat as if a Dinosaur's backbone. We would make our way out to near the submerged ends from which to cast fishing lures which never lured anything to my knowledge. Yet fish jumped frequently, snagging insects skimming the lake-top.

Rimming the lake were stands of Skunk Cabbage so plentiful that we gathered them in season. And Cat-tails. Those older Women who knew how used the bulbs from which the Cat-tails grew to make a 'flour' which made delicious food.

We never hunted migrating Duck and/or Goose People there. It was their sanctuary. When *Hoquat* hunters from ouside learned of the multitudes of Birds gathering on the little lake, bird-stamp bearers were near elbow to elbow around the lake, blowing birds to pieces, fighting over whose kill was whose, leaving cigarette packages and butts and empty beer and booze bottles of one kind or another as beautification projects.

Garbage dumps never appealed to me so I never went back after I saw the mess. Red and green shot-gun shell casings littered the shallow waters around the various downed trees which were 'piers' out onto the lake. Beauty left. It's just as well 'Mr. Govermint' opened it to Sky.

But before the spoiling, Duck People, Brant and Canvasback and Mallard and Ruddy all had their Paradise. Before the Ruddys mated they performed marvelous dances,to win admiring Females I'd guess. With puffy white cheeks and bluish bill the males would thump their chests with their bills making an indescribable whopping noise. Excited the ladies no end it appeared, there were more each year.

And 'Honkers' (Canada Geese) had James' lake on their maps. It was thrilling to see the long 'Vee' lines of Geese both Spring and Fall as they broke to circle near the lake, then come in at miles an hour showing their skills at 'how to land' amphibian sky-travelers: themselves.

It's one thrill to have heard the calling of these travelers, in late evening or early morning, from the distances of their high-flight, but the astonishing power of their voices from two or three hundred feet away as they called warnings to those now water-borne below, that thirty-mile an hour projectiles of ten or more pounds were coming in, "watch out!", one word alone describes: Awesome. First viewing of this always got full attention. Feather covered projectiles coming straight toward you then dropping with very little splash then wiggling their tails.

In truth it *was* a 'birder's' Paradise, 'James' little Lake'. To the healthy and susceptible ears of Children the bird songs were overwhelming. I wonder about listing the many there were to avoid repeating what Peterson's marvelous 'Western Bird Books' reveal.

Species so varied it was almost impossible to separate the calls. Stellar's Jay (Blue-Jay [*Kwash Kwash* to *Po-oke*]); *T'Dayokes* (Flicker); Red-headed Woodpecker; all nested around James' lake. Too, nests of Wood Ducks had the lake for view sites. And Ospreys atop a tall old snag owning a huge nest. Red-headed Woodpeckers cadenced their beats against trees as they sought food. 'Chipmunks' 'chirped'. Occasionally from a direction unfound came the beat-sound of Grouse wings, '*cKic salaws*' (Thumpers). Crows, at times Doves, and the seasonal announcements made by Ducks of one kind or another, Green Winged Teal, Canvas-backs, all by James' little lake, blessed the peaceful Visitor.

"Learn to listen to Woods as it talk to you", I was told repeatedly. Over and over I was advised to 'Listen to (the) stuff what it's tellin' you'". "What you hear in Woods today?" "What Black-berries bush told you?" Or "What about Alders? What they sayin'?" Or, "What did voice of Riffles tell you goin' on out there at River? Riffles got (have) voice depending on what's goin' on with *cKwia* in mountains. There's message in what water does to rocks of riffle…sometimes 'clink', sometimes 'clunk', water movin' rocks of Riffle". One said, "Hear ev'rythin'. Unnerstan' it". Other said, "When them People like Birds, Elks, who Live in Woods talkin', (to one another about what's happ'nin'), learn to understand it like they do. That talkin' is full of Life information, learn what it says, the more you learn the bigger your Medicine. Otherwise move to city an' live like *Hoquat*."

A book about the Life at that little lake could be written and be unbelieveable for variety. Certainly the richness of different breeds surpassed even Swamp at La Push for its Life gifts. Although Animal Life abounded there as well. Muskrat populations as well as Wild-cats nearby, ("You hear Baby screamin' that's Wild Cat"). Fox People no doubt, Squirrels and Chipmunks…on and on.

Another lake was found before arriving at La Push. *Bo-cKacheel* bridge was by the Klahn family farms. A mile and a half past the bridge over Bo-cKacheel was Moore's farm. Their place was approximately opposite James' Auto Court and on it was another little lake, roughly round, of about an acre. From it flowed a small brook. It was the height of Indian-ness for some of us from Village to go by cKey-noo up to the brook-mouth and 'steal with stunning stealth' along the brook to the lake. There we'd fish and amazingly, catch from six to ten inch Trouts. The isolation of the lake and the rareness of fishing there was beneficial to fish production no doubt. Strangely, directly across *Ta-boke* James' lake gave us no return for our 'fishing expertise'. I loved to visit lakes.

Moore's lake was about a third of a mile from the house and barn. Their dogs barked the entire time we were there but no one ever came to investigate the cause...*which was marauding Indians.* (Ten or so years old). After the Moores left Wayne Richwine and his son Vic lived there before moving to WesleesMitts farm land).

REEDS

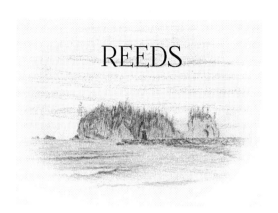

Reed, grass, bark gathering days began before dawn for the La-dies. In fact all things began before Dawn. Preparation for Baby-tending (for those with recent-borns) began the night before. Among needs were: knives for cutting rushes and grasses; binding materials of Cedar bark or Nettle fibers were set out to take; water and food; rain clothes; all the things needed by the Women for a day upRiver. Large gathering baskets were put into cKeynoo. Winter gathering of Spruce roots and mud grass was primary and Bear-grass, which grew in the mountains, was prized and traded for.

Putnam and Rit dyes in their little envelopes were in the houses of every weaver. Not all Women were weavers. Many didn't know how to color the materials naturally. South of the 'Needles' (rocks in Ocean nearby) was a clay bank above the shoreline which produced an elusive yellow. (This clay bank was part of a sighting point on the way to the 'Halibutses' hole). Oregon Grape and this clay were used together to make a lovely yellow. The clay was more in use as a facial cheek-col-orant than dye. When Elk grass was protected from Rain and left in sun light (and moonlight) it became white and took dyes beautifully.

The clay was heated in a kettle with the white Elk grass and then wrapped with Oregon Grape in Skunk cabbage leaves and buried in 'Slough-bank' mud while still hot. When retrieved the Elk grass was yellow. How long in the mud I can't recall. Experiment.

The 'Slough' was tidal, a small river-like body, a mile or so in long, that wound its way past Hobbies Mitts house and barn. The river had a thick, brown mud as bed for its entire length. From it grew a basket grass which was brown colored. The name I know it by is Mud Grass.

I think it was the grass which when buried in Slough mud turned black. Cold *stove-ashes* were mixed with this grass and it was left for the needed time, which I can't recall. The grass color was black when 'done'.

The Ladies who weaved these baskets were in groups generally, and in these groups were 'color secrets' which were either discovered or learned from 'long ago'. Salt and Salal berries were mixed and blended and heated and crushed and endlessly experimented with to get the beautiful purple of the berries but I know of no success to have come from the years of labor to 'find the secret'

I called Rosie Black (Mrs. Roy) in early 1970's (while I camped above Dungeness Spit) to tell Her of the masses of Salal which grew there. She and Roy drove to the campsite and we picked berries by the pound. "With this many berries we can get fat and get dye too," She laughed when She and Roy left that evening for La Push. I don't know the outcome of that adventure.

Putnam, Rit, and another dye (Diamond?) prevailed with the baskets made for *Hoquat* purchase, but for *Po-oke* use, baskets were colored as much as possible in the 'old ways', however old that may have been. Sadly, these 'natural' dyes faded if direct Sun-rays touched them, in fact even indirect. Many of my baskets, protected as much as possible, show only faded remnants of once brilliant colors: some one hundred years old or more.

When the materials had been gathered and were ready for the next phase of preparation more hard work began. Mud Grass was prepared as told earlier, as well as bleached Elk Grass. Winter-gathered Spruce and Cedar roots were stripped from wet ground and cut to proper width-size at home. Tools included paring knives and the inevitable 'D'-handled cutter by which all grasses for a projected basket were made to be the same width. They had several of the cutters, depending upon the size of the weaving to be made. These were to weave around the 'base' material, stripped Cedar-bark or root, or root from Spruce trees.

Fortunately for the interested, a New York actor from Skokomish reservation was instrumental in forming a N.W. weaving group and many N.W. Natives and non-Natives are involved and producing beautiful works of art Native-style as result of his foresight, this includes fiber arts. Susan Pavel, Ph D excels at this skill.

The artists who created the gorgeous baskets which were for utility first, then sale, gathered bundles of grasses of various species. These were at hand throughout the houses of weavers. The cut ends were bound with a piece of the grass and then hung to dry with the cut ends up. It appalls me to think of the labor intensive basket production and the *Hoquat* disdain for these beautiful folk art pieces. A few cents apiece. Many I saw sold for fifteen cents.

How industrious these artists were, and only now is there shown any appreciation for the contribution to human creativity made by them. I know of no more beautiful handcraft than baskets. Is their perfection in the art of basketry less impressive than that of 'old masters' in painting, etc? Or tapestries? Or tapa cloth? Not to me.

When basket making was in progress during Rain, Mothers and Grandmothers and Sisters and cousins gathered in a functionally appropriate house (roomy enough for the gathered Women) and the party was on, laughter the most impressive 'product'. It became a game of socially happy people in producing what they loved to make, notwithstanding the labor-intensive element involved. Social parties every day.

Among them at these times the work and learning by Girls brought the most laughter. The training was directed by love. I think my favorites to this day, as possessions, are the baskets by Girls I knew (who became proficient Artists later). There was pride about their work. Expressions of encouragement and admiration for a beautifully executed and functional basket was likely their chief pleasure. The great reward was admiration from their peers...and their teachers...from the Tribe.

From such as Susie Morganroth, Nina Bright, Dema Hudson, Mary Howeattle, Mary Ward, Clara Eastman and on and on, deftness was the never ending goal, ever increasing deftness. 'Gramma' Lillian Pullen and Her daughter-in-law Eileen Penn dedicated themselves to continuing the skill, Lillian holding classes in cities and towns away from La Push, teaching *Hoquat*s as well as Native Peoples her skill. I think Eileen is likewise involved. Mary Ward Eastman makes lovely baskets. Her husband Harvey Eastman Jr., known as 'Butch', (or from me 'Butchie') won the Silver Star in Korean/US warfare. (Out of less than 50 military personnel en toto from La Push in two wars. Butch Eastman).

Several weavers have banded together to continue their traditions by both weaving and teaching in classes and seminars away from La

Push where interest shows its head…in spite of the continuing and increasing difficulty of finding materials…so much of the previous free-ranging territory is now *Hoquat* land and off-limits, so materials are often-times unavailable. The Northwest basketry skills are ongoing due to the imaginative leadership of the man from Skokomish. Many N.W. Natives and non-Natives are involved and producing beautiful works of art Native-style because of the work of this man's followers.

GATHERING MATERIALS

The search for materials was tedious because of the loss of former range. At times we went to Cape Flattery to an old stand of Cedar for weaving-material bark. There, still laying as felled, a Cedar which had been felled (now) a century and a half ago, in the old way of burning away a position near ground level to 'hour glass' the stump-to-be. A Tree selected for cKeynoo would be girdled around the tree just above ground. The 'girdle' took away five or six inches of bark and inner bark. Bark would be pulled from the potential cKeynoo tree up-ward, in strips up to fourteen inches wide at the 'girdling'. Held on each side of the fourteen inches the picker coerced the material from the Tree, gently; gently; gently, backing slowly. This pulled an ever-narrower strip of bark from the tree which, when removed was processed further so as to be easier to roll and carry for the weavers.

Because girdling the Tree 'made it sick without cure, like T.B.' (Big Bill Penn) there was sickening Power around it. Thus, for cKeynoo it would be left until it had died before it was revisited. No one would work the dying Tree out of concern for the sickness around it which could be transferred to the unwary or ignorant. Dying Trees were avoided for a year as sap drained. The sap having drained the Tree was 'dry' relatively. Then the burning platform was built for Fire. This high enough to tend easily. Moderately dry, the tree burned with a char-surface which was scraped away. The fire drying the area inside as it burned made it easier and easier to burn as time progressed. A line (rope) which had been attached high up the Tree was strained against, increasingly, in the direction it was desired the Tree should fall and one magic day, "Tree fallin'!" was shouted victoriously. Fire might have been applied to one side only, the Tree falling in the direction of the 'undercut'.

What have been called 'toy canoes' were really models for cKeynoo to be built. No two carvers had the same arm spread; no two cKeynoo models were the same. (These models later became serving 'bowls' for Potlatch and pow-wow and other feasts when their first purpose had been served).

With arms spread wide, finger-tip to finger-tip the model would be built to 'half the spread', (called 'waloowa'). They varied in dimensions. Six times the model size became River cKeynoo size.. If 'waloowa' was seventy inches the model would be thirty-five inches and that times six made for cKeynoo of about eighteen feet. I don't know if ever I knew waloowa for Ocean cKeynoo. Of course these cKeynoo were made 'with Spirit power involved' so *had* to be as prescribed.

'Impulse cKeynoo', not intended as *cKwalla* hunter or *cKwahleh* hunter's (*Tssy-uck*) cKeynoo (Whale, Ocean fishing/hunting People), were made to satisfy the builders intent. I still lust for the twelve-foot Sealing cKeynoo model Mock Williams built.

When the builder had rough-hewn the ends, (with ax in our times), and had likewise 'roughed-in' the sides and bottom, some amount of rough hollowing took place to reduce weight for the trip to Ocean, (which might be miles away, as at Cape Flattery; mostly down-hill), or, to Hoh or Quillayute Rivers if near home.

This took help from other cKeynoo men and was done only as if it might be a game they were playing. Work converted to games was a way around drudgery. My White guardian said several times that *Pooke* didn't like work that couldn't be made into a game. Correct.

Once to Village the truing for balance and beauty took place. I remember Charlie Howeattle scrutinizing a cKeynoo as the work progressed. And talking to Joe Pullen about the 'flair' of the bow of his new cKeynoo (which I helped transport to Village) before shaping it further. Many area cKeynoo builders sought the advice of Billy Hudson, who built fabulously beautiful cKeynoo. His racing cKeynoo were sought widely by various Tribes which 'felt' the Spirit of his art. His eldest son, Theodore, was likewise gifted more than most cKeynoo carvers, but his son Floyd (Klumbo) didn't carve. (Pain from massive wounds suffered in World War 2 at Anzio [while invading Italy] may have been his wall...he never was without pain again).

At first the hollowing out process was akin to chop, splinter, burn, but once the hollowing progressed to areas below the sheer line, careful wood removal by small axes and d'adzes making diagonal cuts was the labor intensive process cKeynoo demanded of its builder. Burning out the inside was also done. The rarely built cKeynoo of today is made using carpenter tools I never saw used sixty years ago. As a learner I helped in those days, but had/have no 'Power' for cKeynoo building. It was always a great feat in my mind but was not my 'Power'.

When the outside had been brought to the desired form, in general, then 'dowels' of Cedar about three-quarters of an inch in diameter, (the length being the desired thickness of the hull), were inserted at various places so that when the inside end of the dowel appeared the thickness of the cKeynoo body at that place was achieved. The hand d'adze *roughed* the inside artistically, so that the eventual slickness of gathered grasses or slime from fish, or Seal blood wouldn't create a skating rink. The outside was eventually sand rubbed and Esau Penn said, "In the old days, shark-skin was used. Fire scorched and then rubbed with shark-skin. Fire scorchin' made 'em black. That way cKeynoo went in the water "slick, silent like fish, movin' to'rds the hunters' prey."

LANGUAGE DIFFERENCE
CONFUSIONS

Retrospect shows the influx of English and its interpretations as funny. Interpreting Quileute into English without the needed guidance brought forth some expressions of meaning which in Quileute were sound and rational but when converted led listeners not somewhat understanding of both languages to bewilderment. (An example is 'the best of Her or His 'profession", translated to 'chief'...'chief' [best] of that or those skills, what-ever they may have been. There were no *political* chiefs. When Whites said 'chief' it had a different meaning than in Quileute. To *Po-oke* 'journey-man or woman', professional, expert at something were all held by one word in Quileuete: Chief. Billy Hudson was *a chief* in cKeynoo carving. Morton Penn and Grant Eastman were Chiefs as *Tssy-uck*. Tyler Hobucket and Little Bill Penn, Chiefs in Quileute/*Hoquat* thinking ways.

A sentence in Quileute meant something different than English because each word was a living thing and the living things were mated to create 'artistically composed' meanings in Quileute. Much of conversation in Quileute was to make other people laugh. Because 'comprehension' was different the comprehension of sentences had to be different.

One such structure is in "...'less'...'less less'...'more less!' 'Less more now.'"

The rational interpretation requires explanation about an activity. For example, to several people working together on a task such as lifting a weight requiring different degrees of effort, a person in charge might say in English, "pull harder!" meaning "more!". Needing even more effort it becomes, "more more". Then it would develop into "less more!" when 'ease up' was the result. As even less effort was required this would finalize into 'less!'; 'more less'; 'Even more less!'; 'More more less'; 'None'; (slack off). The meanings in Quileute interpret to 'pull harder' 'pull easier'; 'still easier'; 'ease off'; 'easier'; 'slack off'; 'that's all'.

Who, in the English speaking world, could understand a directive such as "more less!" or "less more"?

'cKola ahlash' is another as explained previously. We thought two different ways and the languages as used brought confusion and laughter to us at the same time.

GOD'S BIRTHDAY

Chester Johnson was *Tloquali*. He spoke in a high pitched voice, a strained voice, which was called 'whiskey tenor', although Chester didn't drink alcohol. Nor did he smoke. I remember his open, friendly smile as greeting whenever we met. When I was fourteen he still called me '*Chutsk*', a name most 'growed up boys' found offensive but which I found endearing...he meant it in fondness, I recognized that.

One day as I walked toward Ryan's post office/store we met in front of Esau Penn's house and stopped to talk. The memory of the recent Christian epic of Christmas was still fresh. He laughed, asked what I thought of Rex Ward in white wrappings laying in a big hay rack as the infant Jesus. Rex was larger than the sheep borrowed from HobbiesMitt which lent realism to the Nativity scene. After a fashion.

Many in Village had been to the gathering in the meeting hall beside Shaker Church and even after two or three weeks it was still a conversation piece. Kenny and his sister Vera Ward, related to Rex, perhaps his children, played the parts of Joseph and Mary. Chris Penn, (Big Jiggs), Chris Morganroth, and Uncle Yum (Little Bill Penn) played the parts of the three wise men and the *Hoquat* brother and sister from the Maxfield farm, whose names I never knew, were 'sometimes-advisors' as to how the scenario should progress. Brian Cole (Bly) was one of the angels (and tomorrow, would '*kill*' anyone who joshed him about being 'an angel').

Chester said, "Jesus (Rex) had a coupla drinks before he got borned, 'at's w'y he belcht," and we laughed, remembering the fun the whole pageant had produced. After a while I asked him about how 'god' could be born after he was supposed to have made everything first. He stopped walking and asked, "Them min'sters talk to you yet 'bout Jesus?"

"Started to," I answered.

" 'S go talk 'bout 'god' now," he said and we went to Beach. There we stood looking South-west, (our most consistent wind source), watching huge breakers crash against Sand, throwing spray high above Surf, ducking as it reached us. After four or five minutes of being rejuvenated by the glory of *cKwahleh* filling the air with purity, I remembered why we'd come to Beach today.

Again I asked, "How'd 'god' get borned first?" A curiosity for me. (For whatever interpretive reason much of what we said, in using English, [which Chester knew well, he'd been a 'boarding school inmate'], ended with the word 'first'. 'Where you been first'.(Or, 'ain't it'. 'You goin' to P.A. ain't it.)' 'Take me Forks first.' Or, 'Lovey Jackson got into a movie as a crowd member ain't it').

So I asked, "How'd 'god' get borned first? If 'god' made everything then got borned wasn't his Mother and father ahead of him? What they have in the house if he made everythin' after he got here?"

"What can exist before it exist?" he asked me.

"What's 'exist' first?"

"Means *be*, same thin' like *'be alive'*," Chester answered.

"Nothing I guess," answering 'what can exist before it exist?'

"That's right answer. Nothing can give Birth to Great Spirit. *That's all there is. One Life.* Ev'r'thin' depend on *that*. We ain't separate from that one Life. Law for 'how to be blade of Grass' depend on Great Spirit. Law for 'how to be *Po-oke; cKa ayo; cKwalla;'* all depend on Great Spirit. Same Law giver for ev'r'thin'. For our People there's one Law Giver, one Life power, and ev'r'thin' share it and ev'r'thin' which is prove it. *Evvv'r'thin'* belong to one maker. So ev'r'thin' is equal."

"What's 'Law'?" I asked.

"Same thin' as 'blueprint', recipe or rule for what s'pose to be. *cKwyeh-Tee* rules."

"What's *cKwyeh-Tee* first."

"Arranger. Some understand Laws of Great Spirit better than some others, use them. Maybe Jesus was one. Maybe *cKwyeh-Tee* was one. Got to be lots who understands Laws better than others. Talkin' 'bout Boodah (Buddha) likely same thing. Wise."

"*cKwyeh-Tee* was a arranger, made first human people on Earth out of different color Salmons. Caused all Rivers on Coast by his tricks on *Hib Hib waysotsopot* (ol' Grouse Woman). He was father of *Hoo-Day Hoo-Day* girls. He went an' done somethin' made ol' Grouse Woman mad. She chased on his trail to catch him, all up the Coast from cKlumbyuh River. He tripped her up several times as they headin' North an' she flopped down, so mad she wet herself an' cause a river to form at that point. She caused Quinault, Queets, Hoh, Quillayute, Ozette, Clearwater, all them Rivers he cause her to make. Never caught him neither.

"He made Cedar to be great blessing for the People because of its honor. From a man of treachery at Ozette Beach he made *Hawayishka* People. He knew how to use Laws. Plains Indian People have arranger like *cKwyeh-Tee* they call 'Coyote'. Sound pretty much alike ain't it?

"Them talkin' 'bout 'Jesus' says he made blind people see, raised dead ones, walked on water. Knowin' to do them things he was a arranger like *cKwyeh-Tee*."

"How they do that stuff?" Me.

"They understand better than others about all Laws of Nature, how it work."

"But if Great Spirit made stuff to be like it is, how come they changed it? How could they change it?"

"To be of use. Because ever'thin' is from one beginnin', stuff can 'blend'. Look at soap. Take fat an' ashes an' mix 'em an' they come out altogether differnt, what wasn't before but now is. Soap. Stuff changes by itself anyway. Look at seasons. They change. Change is natural. Only thing permanent is Change, even 'bout stars. Look at Moon.

"So if you know how to bring Change, you are arranger. Like electric. Even in Cave times electric was there but nobody knowed it, nobody discovered it. Died from lightnin' which is electric. Electric laws been there for lon-n-ng time. Part of *All Stuff*. Always been there. Like gas engine. Nobody invented them. Only figured out Laws. Who figured out them Laws was arranger. Henry Ford was arranger."

"What they done was not invent something but arrange it?"

"Ayy. Ha-atch brains. (Yes. Good brains).

"But where is Great Spirit then? What it looks like?"

He pointed to *cKwahleh* and breakers. At Ahkalut. Over there flew *cKa'a'yo*, Crow. "Them's all part of Great Spirit. Nothing can be outside powers of Great Spirit. Seein' stuff, hearin' stuff, you experiencin'

God. Even *'nothin'* is part of Great Spirit Laws. If Great Spirit was there, beginnin' of time, makes ever'thin' out of Itself, then Great Spirit Power is in ev'rythin' so then ev'rythin' is Sacred . That's why ev'rythin' should have respect from us. 'f *we* don't make what there is then we got to respect what *does* make ev'rythin', respect ev'rythin' it make. If Great Spirit, what *Hoquat* calls 'god', make it, I respect it, protect it."

"*Hoquat* minister said Indians goin' to a big fire forever if we don't believe him. That's pretty mean ain't it." I looked to Chester for a *good* answer.

"Boardin' school preachers said so too. Tokkt (talked) 'bout 'free will'. If that 'god' s'posed to know ev'rythin' about ev'rythin' at begin-ning of Time, knows ahead how I'm gonna be why wait to now to send us to some big Fire? Who knows? *We* don't. *It* does. How come it's gonna put Spirit in fire for all Time if it knows ev'rythin' and we don't know nothing? Don't worry. It knows all. We know nothing. We don't pick what we gonna be, Man or Woman, *Po-oke* or *Hoquat*; when we to get borned; how big we gonna be; what we lookin' like; if we gonna be sick or nothing. Free will? I don't think so. Don't understand that myself. But them guys do if you pay 'em a little to tell you about how to Live. They talk big about 'doin' bad', but likes our Girls pretty good. Don't worry about Great Spirit. Nobody knows about It. If you believe who says they do, you deserve getting' mixed up like them. Forget it." I smiled. One whom I trusted because he was Village-important had assured me. All which he did showed Wisdom else he would not be so important to Tribal security. I forgot it, as he advised.

Chester and I went to Lonesome Creek for rocks to skip at *Ta-boke* then went home. I never worried about 'god wrath' again. Later, when I talked to Tyler Hobucket about it he added some words to what Chester had said.

I have to tell what Esau Penn, Uncle Yum's father, told us in the lodge which was on River-side of Charlie and Mary Howeattle's store. He spoke of what Spirit said to him about Life being one and all things shared it, Tree; Rock; River; Animal.... Great Spirit is the *only* Life. All things, sharing It, are one in Great Spirit. Because there could be no end to the LAWS of Great Spirit, everything which exists were proofs of It. All which exists *prove* that *Life-LAW by Great Spirit*; prove *IT* by being. How can anything exist outside them LAWS? Cannot.

"There's Laws for to become alive. To become. There's Laws for how to stay alive an' healthy. You don't need somebody to tell you about healthy Living, it's already in you to know. Built in, same like blood. It ain't from no fac'tree.

"Eat the plain stuff what Great Spirit makes, rest good, be honest to everything, don't drink no hootch, don't suck tobacco, don't eat too much. All these is Laws from Great Spirit on bein' healthy. When you *pass* water, drink same amount for replacement, add a little more. Obey them Laws an' you obeyin' Great Spirit. Word 'obey' means same thin' like 'worship'. Obey Great Spirit like what's built in you to know how, you doin' what Great Spirit feel good about. Laws for healthy Life is Laws from God, from Great Spirit. 'Worship' is same thing as 'obey'. 'Obey' same thing as 'worship'.

"Obey them Laws and you worship God. Don't fail to respect ever'thin' God makes. Waste nothin', harm nothin', protect what God made. Protect other kinds than us from us, *(all God's creatures)*. Creatures what need help, help them. That's worship. When you protect what Great Spirit caused you doin' the work of Great Spirit."

That I understood. That I do. But still in mind is 'celebrating God's birthday'.

Taxilit

(and Tomanamus, not a Quileute word)

Symbolic of 'the Power' is awareness of *awareness*. Being 'aware' of *being aware* is speculative capacity maybe unknown to most of Mother Earth's other Children. Albert Einstein felt his *'Tomanamus'* and 'knew' the unseen unknown *existed*. He not only knew 'that', he knew 'how': His *Taxilit* at work found 'E=mc2'.

A highly complex ability to understand *cause and effect* is not too likely in Angle Worm, in fact, as Tyler Hobucket told me in earlier days, it's probable that *human thought processes* are our survival because *we aren't the physical equal to most of Mother Earth's other Children.* To 'know by thinking, to 'prove by doing' is 'Power', *Taxilit*, likely unknown as such where Survival depends on *other* gifts of Life. Although the inherent of Other Life's ways are *Taxilit*, cougar lives its *Taxilit*.

"We was needin' a physical weapon to help us meet the challenge of survivin', of Survival", he said, "Human Brain has to be cunning beyond all its competitors for Life." Unfortunately Beneficial Morality doesn't come as 'automatic' to anything human.

Insights; realizations; comprehensions; when these come to a point in which they are dependable for Self and Tribe as far as 'beneficially productive' is concerned, the resultant *constant knowledge* of those *mental machinations* is called by *Po-oke* 'Medicine Power'. 'Medicine is Knowledge'. (To repeat: KNOWLEDGE is Power). What it is is *Insightful Knowledge*. Tyler continued, "Bein' weaker than most Animals our size we're vulnerable more than most. Our defense, *Human Surviving*, come from our Brains. Brains got more power than muscle."

'Enlightenment' is a term used by a man I knew in Sausalito, California in the *'fifties*.

His probings into the world of 'spirit' took him into friendship with D.T. Suzuki (Zen Buddhist) which I never understood, although terms he used made sense. One term he used which never penetrated my understanding was "'… still (stop) the conceptual mind'". Although the words seem rational, I never 'got' them. Through what Zen labeled 'Enlightenment', apparently, realizing the 'flowing together' of Self with Universe, (Seeing the Oneness of Life), Enlightenment came to the seeker. Stilling the 'conceptual mind' through exclusionary meditation seemed to be the road to this release from 'the material world'. I never progressed to more than discussion about these processes. I have not learned Zen meditation.

However, when I discussed Tribal ways and told him of *'Taxilit'* (and *'Tomanamus'*) he voiced 'understanding'. I described it to him as the overwhelming comprehension of 'conditions of Life' so powerful as to be as much a part of the person as the flow of Blood. "How do you get it?" he asked, eager for the Western natives' attitude toward Spirit to add to his Eastern insights. I read two books on 'the East' which he had written, but always felt the way of *Po-oke* from which I could gain *Taxilit* was easier for me to pursue. Guardian Animal Spirit as well. *Taxilit* is inate comprehension of the fact that 'What is is what is.' Acceptance of NOW without comparatives, ("If only that hadn't happened you woulda; coulda; shoulda)." *None of which has bearing after the fact.*

The first step in opening *Taxilit* was cleanliness of mind and body. For body, the Elders, *Tss'y'uck, Tloquali, Tss'ay-whutleoke*, bathed in *Ta-boke* every morning. Every morning. They rubbed River Beach Sand over themselves and rinsed, scrubbed and rinsed until for me, who made brave and bold effort to emulate them, pain was the result. Then they toughened their skin with Spruce boughs, similar to Finnish People in Sauna with 'wiita'. *But with Spruce boughs!* Spruce needles *are* needles.

However painful to others it may have been, *they* were unaware of pain and cold. 'Where there is no attention there is no sensation.' When accustomed to toughness of body and mind the male (even if a juvenile) is considered ready to become a *Man*; that toughness of body and mind are the Power Tools used to hold control *of Self*, in service to Family, Tribe, Nature.

Uncle Yum told about a Man who wanted to become a great ("a gra a a ate) Seal hunter". He went to where Seal-Ions ("big Sea Lions") live to live with them. They are like Seals, only bigger, an' some live near La Push all year. Easy to study. Sea Lion Rocks.

"He rolled in Surf an' Sand, an' becomes marvelous (mar-r-r-veluss) swimmer, finally become so much like Seal-Ion People that he swum after Herrings and captured them, to eat them as Seal-Ion People do. He learned craftiness for seeking Salmon People, to be able to capture them to eat.

"Sometimes he returned to Village, behaving more and more like Seal-Ion.

"Knowledgeable Elders warned him he had to stop where he was in his development because now he could talk with Seal-Ion People in their language, swim with them, live with them. He rolled in Surf and Sand to clean himself as they did, so "don't go any farther in obeying you *Taxilit* powers," he was told.

But his ambition drove him further and further after that Power and what the Elders knew would happen came to pass. One day, someone in cKeynoo by Sea-Lion Rocks saw him amongst those People, he waved in greeting and when the Person who saw him turned away for a moment then looked again, he was gone...all there was on the Rocks were Sea-Lion People and the man was never seen again. His ambition for change was limitless and he over-rode his Human-ness and lost it. His 'worth' to Tribe was gone...he'd gone too far.

Advice: to understand the goal but not become absorbed in it. Who finds a goal of such magnetic power that it consumes them has lost the purpose of *Tomanamus, Taxilit*. Its purpose is to be a tool for Survival, not an addiction which over-rides its value.

Cleanliness of body and mind led him to fulfillment of ambition. ("What he desired most he become." It should be the way to realization, to learning to 'read' Life. Who lives controlled by Fear-imposed 'Reality' cannot get past the fence of Fear and spends Life defending *self*. One can 'read' the relationships of Life conditions without becoming the conditions themselves).

Cleanliness of body is not mere skin-scrubbing. Internal cleanliness is the first importance. Leads to the near automatic cleansing of the exterior. First of *Interior* things of which to be cleansed is Harmful Thinking. Whose mind dwells on revenge and holds anger as habit must be cleansed of these illnesses or not get into the world of Etherea where all Reality exists...all permanence.

One wisdom is 'resting the body'. (I've related about 'the Animal' we control and letting it rest when it needs rest. Not being forced to 'perform' for Self or Other). Another is eating only foods which don't upset the system causing it discomfort, "...don't eat nothin' if you belch an' taste it later...you body don't like it it get sick." "Avoid them poisons outside world sending us, alcohol an' tobacco an' factory foods pushed on us. They stopped our wanderings for natural food as it come, so we work *keepin' our system washed with Living Water* taken lots, these are forms of cleanliness".

Habits which avoid the wastefulness of lethargy are beneficial practices, such as arising when *cKa ayo* calls to awaken a new day: dawn hours. Copying the natural world keeps us natural and as Charley Howeattle told me, "It's natural to be natural...like Sa-ats is natural."

ADVENTURES

Adventures pursued in the 'old ways' were educations into Knowledge Power. One 'adventure' was a 'trip' with parents to Lonesome Creek where pebbles for Living Water were found. Living Water is made by using pebbles about the size of peas, in various shapes, (on the 'delta' for Lonesome Creek). While there we were educated about Life through discussions about what was going on around us. And elsewhere as well.

Where Surf washes at higher tides and bares pebbles as gold-panning bares gold, these pebbles were washed down by the fresh water of Lonesome Creek and pushed back by the action of breakers. They wash forth and back and stay in an area about half-way between Surf and high-tide line. We put the pebbles into non-metallic containers (such as Kerr Mason jars) and the jars were put onto jar lids in a pot of water. This was put onto the stove and the whole boiled, including the water in the Mason jars. Cooled, this water was used for drinking.

Because of the position of the pebbles as found, 'between land and sea', they are vitalized, 'charged', by the interaction (we thought). As the boiling water swirls around them they interact with the water, 'charging' it with energy, (we thought), to become *Living Water*. It was imperative for taking when going to seek *Taxilit* enlightenment. (We thought). All Elders drank it; all Children; the sick; pets.

We used this water on house-plants, cooked with it, drank it…it was Living Water. It seems to me that it was moderately purified by the process and was at least healthier than straight from the communal spigot told about earlier. I make and use it today trying to offset fluoride and chlorine.

Ocean water in a bucket on the living room heater was left until only Salt crystals were left. This Salt was sewed into bags the size and shape of 'bean bags', as was River Beach Sand into same sized bags. I explained this earlier. A practice against pain was the Sand and Salt bags. Sprains or aches and pains or 'rheum' were all treated with these moderately flexible 'medicine bags'. The Salt bag was kept as cold as possible. The Sand bag was put into 'Mr. Majestic's' oven prior to use, heated to about 200 degrees. (Obviously the range was a 'Majestic'. When Clyde Majestic came to La Push in later years to operate his charter-boat 'Linda Ray' he became 'Stove Man' to older *Po-oke*. They saw it as humorous that a man's name would be like the steam-ship Majestic on the stove.

The way of usage was to put one bag on a sore place and the other opposite it…as, if on elbow, warm on one side, cold on other. When the cold/hot difference was undetectable the bags were switched, hot onto cold spot, cold onto hot. When there was no detectable difference either way the bags were replaced with 'active' ones and the used ones put into cold and heat again, to recharge. This might be done all day if the need was great enough.

I've seen severely wrenched joints, wrists, ankles, etc., brought to normal in as little as six or eight hours when the 'norm' might be days or even weeks for relief. 'Mink' Black, (Roland) played football at Quillayute Union High School, (the Spartans) and got hurt when his knee was twisted. Grace Jackson and others worked on his knee for a week-end and Monday he went to school repaired. It works. Also they used medicine bags on 'croupy' young. Used the same way, opposite to opposite. The care would be ongoing, several Women working together to aid a sick Child. It worked for many. These trainings were part of *Tomanamus* gains. As well as other gains..

The standard remedy for relief of infection was a poultice made of Living Water, Peets, Ive'ree or Fel-snaptha's 'oap, and sugar. Water mixed with soap and sugar until cream-like in consistency was covered with a damp, hot wash-cloth and applied over and over. I remember it because I had a boil, miserable and ugly and the poultice was the relief.

ETHEREA

There were various ways of preparation for 'Quest', the away-from-Village sojourn of the youthful *Taxilit/Tomanamus* seeker. They involved lectures from Elders in Lodge; working with them at their tasks; getting explanations about the 'why' of methods used in the daily routines. How to enter the world of Etherea was repeated over and over. It was practiced to be gained as Power and was related to trance. This was the Ghost World, the Spirit World, 'tssicK ate yala': 'ETHEREA'.

'Etherea'. Where is that place? It's between 'asleep' and 'awake'. Who hasn't experienced the 'JOLT' reaction/response to that point between awake and asleep wherein the *'dream-state'* 'feels' the dreamer falling perhaps, or moving as if to leap. Under any circumstance the reaction is moderately violent response by the body. A physical reaction from the 'near-sleeping' 'victim', legs thrash or feet rebound....

At that 'jolt' we back away from Etherea, from 'between the norms'.

It takes practice of near impossible concentration to enter Etherea, *SPIRIT WORLD*. They told that once inside that 'room' would be walls of doors, figuratively.. A door opened slightly is start of *Tomanamus* power. That is the Power of The Knowledge that a Power Potential exists, which Power Potential is insight into the FACT of the existence of a (perhaps) hitherto unknown and/or unsuspected fact of Life.

However, that doesn't 'give' one the *ability* to *Utilize* the knowledge of insight/aware-ness, one trains for that, to be given in Quest: *Taxilit*: The ability to use what the insight portends. The 'door', now fully opened permits entry into another room of doors, in which the same process is repeated. One door here is chosen, partly opened and a new awareness *Tomanamus* potential is 'whiffed', the door is opened for entry into another Benefitting Power, *Taxilit* again: cKeynoo builder of merit: Knows How, Does. Same person has great success as Seal Hunter: Knows How, Does: *Taxilit*.

Knowing of the existence of the state of mind into which knowledge flows, awareness, the process was same: Leave the body to enter Etherea without jumping back out because 'the Animal 'me' feels the Spiritual 'me" leaving and is frightened: 'What if s/he doesn't come back'. 'Animal' hasn't been able to express more than a few animal emotions in its Lifetime under our dominance of Mind. 'Animal' doesn't know how to survive without 'us'. Therefore as we enter into that state 'Animal' must be conditioned by awareness that Spirit may wander to learn answers to questions of importance for Survival for both. It takes time but is gainable. When Animal is assured we will not leave it to be unguided, that 'we'll be back', the Power to 'see' increases increasingly. Because Great Spirit/GOD! *IS* all knowledge, all ability, all harmony, all perfection as *Constant,* it can be learned. The only way to go to that Constant is to unsaddle 'Animal' of Spirit Being for the time to enter Etherea to find answers. It happens. Rules for gaining ever increasing strength of Spirit Power usage were constant: Harmony with Nature, Fasting, Drumming and Singing to Spirit World that you need Its help to get into that world. You need to sing the problem to Spirit World with drumming.

Fears and doubts will enter the head of the Seeker because that's a 'fence' put between awake and asleep that can't be entered easily. But as in other Spiritual pursuits, Faith in the existence directs process of achieving. It takes sure knowledge of the Reality of a 'World of Real Existence (but unseen)' to pursue the dedication to Mind Power. Energy was one of the specific requirements because of the strenuousness of the Pursuit.

We were told that the ejaculation of sperm (not taking place for 28 days) re-entered its Life's vitality back into the 'host' and added 'Power' to both Mind and Body. The 'nocturnal emission' was the natural path to 'Animal's' processes being satisfied and that 'Power' *built* (enlarged) in who practiced Fasting; Chastity; Body cleanliness (to abandon human-smell). Hard exercise; industriousness, (supplying Village and Family with help as needed), periods of Isolation for analyzing our own 'dramas' and eliminating them (as they are learned conditions), and if negative, can be dropped. (To 'see' our own 'drama' it was directed that by Mind we move back a couple of arm spans, then up the same distance, then to one side, the same, so that 'we' are watching our 'act' over our own right or left shoulder. From a mental 'six feet away' If we are honest we see the drama.

To fast was imperative, mind-stillness and fasting while drumming and singing. The Song came as if it was the 'Music of Revelations'. Mind-stillness-control came from looking at a 'greyed' surface with the eyes out of focus. Seeing nothing in focus presented a 'nothingness' of attention/interpretation and who practiced regularly was able to stop 'thinking' and just 'be'. (Is that what Alan Watts meant: Still the Conceptual Mind)?

'Listening' to Spirit song, Drumming and Singing it while fasting were basic to gaining one's *Taxilit*. Over-riding one's hunger until hunger itself was a pleasant experience was imperative. We practiced it. People of Power took thirst and hunger and cold as pleasant experiences and looked forward to them as *test*. Who couldn't control thirst and hunger and tiredness and lust and IMPULSE had trouble finding Power.

During 'Quest' one was to 'think out' the emotions of *anger* and *lust* and *greed* to see their bases in Fear. To examine their products. To see it all as useless. To see Fear as the engine driving our *defense response* to other people's actions and to control that response, (to see by our reactions if their emotions are in charge of us) was to work toward our personal *Self Control*. "None are free who do not live Self Controlled", I was told frequently. To see our uncontrolled reaction to others was to see *anchors* in operation on ourselves. I was told that these were stimulated to Being by someone agitating for our *Emotions-without-Sense* to arise, when our need is to control them and thus be ahead of the appearances of irrational response in us by us. This was the way to exercise and strengthen control over our 'dumb falling into someone's pit of foolishness'. "Don't play somebody else's game. You follow them by behavin' like they're aimin' for, they want that they be leadin' you. *No*."

Otherwise outside forces controlled ones reactions to the circumstances of everyday Life. Then instead of swimming in the direction of desire, as does Sa-ats, one is like a leaf on water, blown here and there and back and forth with the tide as it comes.

Sa-ats is in control of its direction. Likewise must the seeker of *Taxilit* be in control. This builds character and personality Power for later experiences. When adult, one must not let others cause infantile reaction to their activities. As example, toward one's offspring. Anger is an emotion which must be overcome. '*Anger*' is the LARGEST part of *Danger*. We were told that *there is no Anger* that doesn't have *Danger* involved. Who permits another person's emotions to control the *personal* Mind is *infantile in maturity*...(as total an oxymoron as 'Kosher pork'). *The seeker must control personal emotions.*

Additional to fasting (with view in Mind to train 'Animal' that thirst and hunger are controllable sensations) teachers remind one of the *pleasantnesses* of those sensations if seen in controlled 'light'. *Where there is no attention there is no sensation.* I heard that from many. When common sense said 'drink' or 'eat' hunters drank to fulfil two requirements: Sense of wetness, sense of fulness. If these were available for use.

(However, for separate reasons, the water drinking imperative was that as one voids water, an amount equal to the amount released must be consumed to keep Body water balance in harmony. To release water several times without replenishing it means that dehydration is taking place even minimally. The same holds true for the passing of consumed food, the water for processing must be replaced. We are water creatures and that water balance is to be maintained at all cost. (This was a knowledge of Life Imperatives all the Elders preached to the young).

The rhythm of drumming and singing are potent instruments to transcend the 'common mundane' because the imposed information pushed in through song and pulse-beat of Drum suppressed that 'common mundane'. This doesn't leave 'emptiness', rather, it imposes 'differentness'.

Do all Seekers enter into that alterred dimension? I doubt it. Do any Seekers enter into that alterred dimension? Absolutely. Imposed without being sought by the experiencer, the 'hunch' which comes true is part of that world. Knowledge of the existence of ongoing condition is 'sensed' without reason for the sudden 'hunch' which becomes true. Again, does everyone experience that condition? I doubt it. Does Anyone experience that condition? Absolutely. Insight from unsought Hunch or Insight from actively sought ability, Insight is Insight and how is that argued against?

THE DEAD FLY
and LIFE PROTECTION

One day I enterred 'the dirty house' where Jane Hudson was visiting from Neah Bay. Swarms of Fly People were dining on remnants left in Clam shells. These were on a wooden plank that served as 'drain board' beside a round, galvanized wash tub called kitchen sink. Recently emptied Clam shells still holdiing Clam particles were on the kitchen table, in pots on the wood-range, and several on the floor. There were uncountable numbers of Flies zooming from morsel to morsel around us, over us, and occasionally on us.

The owner of the house was a good man who was overwhelmed (by a Woman whose 'stride was broken', [drank heavily]) and a daughter of sixteen or so. *Her* stride was broken by her Mother's problems. Her neglected one year old somehow survived this onslaught of total neglect. She did nothing except on occasion at the pressure of Her father. This alone was when Her *Chutsk* was cared for. Other Village Women were rebuffed by this poor bewildered Girl and so the Child suffered. It was 'the dirty house'. And that it was. But even there I learned a lesson about Life from the owner of the house.

On this day I disobeyed Mother and went to visit because Jane Hudson James, (married to Harvey James from Neah Bay), whom I loved dearly, had come to visit her cousin and his 'family'. Jane was Dema and Billy Hudson's daughter. She and Harvey lived at Neah Bay so I saw Her rarely. I sneaked in and had the exquisite pleasure of being pulled to Jane's lap and rocked forth and back on the rocker while She sang Indian Mother songs to me and cried. This Woman loved me without reservation and I reciprocated, so when I learned She was in LaPush I went to see her..

While I was there the man reported that a Fly had drowned in a bit of water left in a cup. He said, "Let's give it back to Life, *cKulell*, want to help?"

I laughed. Bring a soggy, drowned Fly back to Life? "How you gonna do it?", I asked.

"You help," he answered. "Here", he directed, giving me a spoon, "pour out the water take Mr. Fly out of the cup put it on the drainboard when I say." He shook a teaspoon of salt onto the drainboard. "Put it (the drowned Fly) on the salt". He covered the Fly completely with more salt and I remember snickering. 'Now", he said, "we'll wait see what happen"

We had been told by *Hoquats* about Flies going from dung to our food bringing sickness and death with it so I was careful not to eat although I was given the chance for my addiction, smoke-Salmons. *Tloquali* that I was I gave no voice to hunger but I admit there *was* interest in some of that Salmons. Scientific interest alone of course. The People there ate of the Salmons and finished off the Clams and we talked and laughed and discussed my adventures in school and whatever came to mind.

An hour passed and I had all but forgotten the experiment with Life regenerating when I was reminded, "See if Fly come back" he said and now I was ready again, grin scarcely held in check.

He took a splinter from a piece of kindling and carefully broke away the now encrusted salt from Fly and to my amazement it moved. He broke away encrusted salt from marvelously tiny legs and wings with the splinter and lo! the Fly moved across the drainboard an inch or so and suddenly buzzed its wings, rose to land on his hand. He looked at it and said, "Ayyy, I know, I save you Life but we ain't gonna get married!" When he moved it rose to join its soaring counterparts. I looked at the man who remarked blandly, "Sometime it take coupla hours; coupla tries. Salt pulls out water. You catch 'em *soon* enough back they come. Fun, huh?"

I'd seen the miracle of the day and left. It was impossible for me to tell that I had seen this miracle in the 'dirty house' because my expeditions into the forbidden always saddened 'Mother' and 'Father'. I tried hard to be obedient, but Jane had been there and that was that.

Long months later the man, who seemed filled with these strange processes showed me how he regenerated Bee People. "You gots to take care of Bee People because Life depend on them all the time. Pay attention to them", he told me when he took an apparently dying Bee from our living room window-sill where it had exhausted itself, fighting to pass through the glass to the visible outside.

He requested a tiny amount of sugar, which Mother gave him, and onto a Kerr-Mason jar lid he put a few grains of sugar and perhaps two drops of water, "make sirp" (syrup). Then he took the non-resisting Bee and put it onto the lid beside the syrup. Again using a splinter from kindling he touched it to the syrup and with a drop of the syrup on the end put it under 'the face' of the Bee. Nothing happened except that the Bee turned away slightly. Next he touched its 'face' with the liquid. It responded with a proboscis of surprising length 'flowing out', with its flexible tip beginning to take up the syrup. I was entranced by the speed of its feeding and watched in fascination as another little draft of the food was prepared. At length it stopped and turned again, "Watch it now, it gonna pump up", and the part I'd have called 'belly' began a pulsating action which lasted many seconds, then as Fly had done previously, it rose into the air, circled two or three times and out the open kitchen window.

"You got to take care of all Life, *cKulell*," he said, cleaning up the small mess created, "We got the most Powerful for damage so we got the most Powerful for to protect with. Always protect Life. NEVER HUMILIATE NOTHING AS NOT WORTH LIFE. You humiliate Life you humiliate God."

I felt sad for him after that because I knew he had 'special Power' which wasn't used. Others of Village felt the same but he was like a Person apart. He hunted, but wasn't *Tssay-whutleoke*. He fished but wasn't *Tss'y'uck*. He had insight Powers but avoided *Tloquali*. Later he began drinking Booze heavily. One day, as passenger in a car while he slumped against the passenger's door, in a head-on collision he was killed. To this day I'm bewildered about the pressures of Life which deprive so many of great gifts that they become thrown away. He was one of these.

After I'd been made aware of the 'personhood' of non-Two-Leggeds by Harry and Tyler Hobucket I told about my 'great awareness', as it were. "Ayy-y," he said, " them people make judgment 'bout what we don't know, all the time. Need to."

"How good they have to be?" I asked.

"Good enough to stay Livin'. Way better'n us."

"How you know that?" I asked.

"Show you," he said. Onto my hands he had me rub some Elk blood from a hanging coup. "Smell it." I did. "What you smell?"

"Kind of like wet flour I think."

"OK, wash with soap." I did.

"Rinse real good." I did. "Smell anything now?"

"No."

"Over there is Horace's dog *kadido*, call 'um."

I whistled. "*kadido!*" I shouted and *kadido* came running. "Fold you arms lessee what it does."

I did so and She arrived, tail whirling in joy. 'Somebody wants to pet me, to feed me, to play with me. Here I am!' When She was three or four feet away Her demeanor changed. Her eyes widened and nose moved as in sniffing and She went directly to my hands, trying to lick them.

"You went an' tole Her you touched *cKeecKee* (Elk) ain't it."

"No!" I answered, laughing at the dog, "Smelled it."

"You smell it again, see what you come up with." I did and there was nothing. "What else they do better'n us?" I didn't know and said so. "Then remember what we are ain't always 'best' of Living things. You washed good ain't it. *kadido* went to you hands right off. She smelled what we can't, easy, moved to get some."

Always I found pleasure at being with the man, appreciating his time with me. I wasn't friendly to a relative of his whose mental deformity carried constant violence toward the defenseless, but he was gentleness personified.

INDIAN JOE and BUD

Village had a malevolent citizen named Bud. He was about twenty, strong and dangerous. His eyes projected evil. If he got his hands on a Child he slapped or hit or kicked it with obvious glee. Several times after he had hurt some Child Bud was beaten by relatives who had tried every other recourse, the only violence toward a citizen of Village I ever knew. The next day Bud would beat some Child as though he had no understanding of the relationship between his action and the consequent punishment. In retrospect I see the distorted face, the leering, misaligned eyes, the ugly mouth and think of Charles Laughton's face as the Hunchback of Notre Dame. Poor Bud was totally deformed of body and spirit and often I wonder why that curse was visited on him and Village. ('Did the hand then of the potter shake?' asked Omar Khayyam).

I don't know when Bud died. I'm grateful that I managed to avoid his surging strength and his pleasure at using it against the helpless.

A contrast to Bud was Indian Joe. Joe Willasi. Joe was the Person in Village Bud avoided. If Joe was with the Children, Bud stayed away. Joe would appear almost magically, suddenly 'just with us'. He was simple, kind, almost reverential in his behavior. We welcomed Indian Joe. The mere sight of Bud terrorized us but Joe never contacted any of us in any way. He'd stand watching us at play in great enjoyment, an amused man of at least thirty. Today I wonder, 'was he a guardian angel'?

Joe was large, today I would call him "gentle giant". I see his facial-skin, totally unlined, his broad grin, twinkly eyes and the gentleness of his face as he laughed and applauded and stood by. He watched over us as 'B.K.' did while we were fishing from his scow. Indian Joe was protection. I had no fear of Bud when Joe was present. I heard Joe bellow almost bull-like one day as Bud approached a group of us, where we would have been cornered, some certain to have been victim of his cruelty. Bud heard Joe's bellow, saw him coming like a charging bull, and ran as if panicked, the only sign of fear I ever saw in his eyes, on his face, obvious even to a ' baby'.

At our hollering and squealing, Indian Joe stopped his charge, smiled at our games and for over an hour was appreciative audience to play he never entered. Great Spirit has to have given Indian Joe a special Potlatch when he arrived in Heaven. I would have, were I that Power.

I never saw Joe on Beach, in cKeynoo, anyplace except around the area we played on at the flat (now occupied by the 'gymnasium'). He was a fan of baseball. When the ball-diamond was in front of Howeattle's store, Indian Joe always shouted joyfully at the action of the game as it progressed. None saw Joe play baseball, but he loved the excitement and was as excited as the players. Chris 'Jiggy' Penn said, "He'd like it better if we played all year 'round. Rain or shine he'd be here." A Village *Hoquat* was the father of a boy our age named Carter Warren. He had no arm, shoulder down, on his left side. This was a source of bewilderment for Indian Joe who marvelled at Mr. Warren's ability to hit the ball by holding the bat over his left shoulder and powering it with his right hand. I was fascinated by it but Joe was goggle-eyed when the ball disappeared into the out-field. Baseball was Joe's game.

Three poles were placed to form a triangle and from them hung chicken wire as screen behind the catcher and batters. One day P.P. (Perry Pullen who tried out for pro-ball I heard) was standing beside the pole toward first base when a runner tried to steal home from third. The ball was in the first baseman's hand and he threw it toward the catcher but it was amiss. Joe was standing beside P.P. watching the attempted 'steal' not seeing the ball hurtling toward his head. P.P. reached out barehanded and stopped the ball just before Joe was hit. Joe turned in surprise and spoke the only words I ever heard him say, "*Le-atska lox*" ('thank you' in Quileute). Eveyone there cheered. I didn't know if it was because Indian Joe had spoken or because he'd escaped serious injury. We all loved Indian Joe, except, perhaps, for Bud.

BROOM BUYING

When I see the care people give to the simple straw broom in their homes, I know the degree of poverty they've encountered. Standing a broom in a corner on the whisks, which soon develop an angle, is a sure sign of carelessness. Especially to who bought things based on the *pennies* they cost rather than the *dollars*.

I was acquainted with a male who related the poverty in his life in the '40's, (when a war was on and both parents worked). While living in my house he stood two carefully selected brooms to develop a sway. That isn't the way in which people of limited income treat what is essentially money. Products they buy with money for which they've traded part of their Lives. So broom buying was a big involvement at home…for most Village people.

It took time to buy new Broom. Broom cost eighty-nine pennies. (We didn't buy items by dollars, in Searziz catalog a new bicycle cost two thousand, six hundred and ninety-five pennies). Awesome. Even one hundred pennies made us blink.

Broom buying time meant an adventure of sorts to Forks. The major store at the time belonged to George Krause who sold groceries and sundries. In retrospect I wonder at his thoughts when six or eight jabbering Mothers, Daughters and youngsters from La Push descended on him at 'broom buying time'.

It was no simple process. Broom, to work properly, *had* to be perfect. That took looking. The steps were always the same. Although Broom lasted for two or three years if cared for properly, the daily use took its toll thus '*perfection*' was sought. We bought many things from Mr. Krause but broom buying was a specialty chore which he had to endure fairly regularly. If it troubled him he never showed it, instead helping to pull the brooms from their storage site.

The first consideration was the straightness of the handle. Even a slight warp put that broom out of contention and it was placed away from the considered supply. The handle had to be straight, number one. Likewise the whisks. The stitching through the straw had to be same on both sides. No twisting of the whisks would be tolerated. Then the cut. I see in mind's eye the careful sighting over the 'business end' of the broom to make sure the cut was even, a slight crown from edge to edge (wide way) but a flat and even cut through the narrow direction. Good brooms came from *The Lighthouse for the Blind* in Seattle. "Only ones know how to make Broom."

It took time to go through Mr. Krause's supply. Finally there might be six or eight brooms in the contest for 'chief' broom. The final test was 'the stand'. Each broom would be stood on the floor to see if it 'stood straight'. Having passed this test it would be tapped lightly at the top end of the upright handle to see if it rocked smoothly and evenly. It would come down to two brooms, generally, and Mothers and Girls would test and compare, noting things they liked or disliked about the way the brooms 'behaved'. Looking back on it I see the humor in the situation. Perhaps eight *Po-oke* discussing the merits or lack thereof relative to two or three 'contenders' for becoming BROOM!

When the requirements had been met would come dickering over 'partial money and partial smoked Salmons' exchange. Sometimes Mr. Krause would be lenient and for a pound or so of smoked Salmons and forty or fifty pennies the purchase was made and away we went, victorious.

Toward 'Rez people' Mr. Krause was 'soft-hearted' thus universally respected. He was invited to functions regularly together with his wife and son and thereat profusely gifted. I remember Basket gifting, model cKeynoo, real paddles and bailers (to empty cKeynoo of rainwater). Smoke-Salmons and Elk and Bear roasts, Salmon eggs in Fall for 'Steel-heading. We over-rode their protests with gifts of True Love and appreciation to Mr. and Mrs. Krause.

I don't remember that he ever came back to Village after his beloved wife died. Even we Children could tell they were loving friends because there was affection in their looks at one another, in the way they spoke to one another...they were loving friends. Important to one another. We respected that. It was a *Hoquat* model we respected.

They went together onto Ocean for a ride with John Rudolph on his troller 'Rita' one day and returned shortly with Her so sea-sick She collapsed on Shell Oil float and Coasties had to come there to help care for Her. I guess She was already dying then, but none of us knew it yet. Shortly thereafter She passed and George Krause showed the loss in his eyes the rest of his life.

I knew of one *Chutsk* his son sired in the '30s but no more than that. So he had one grandchild to love. He displayed love and much forbearance to all young. And what of the continuation of that family? That '30's born *Chutsk*?

I couldn't guess how many times we gifted Salmons eggs to George for his beloved Steelhead fishing. The high-school principal was Mr. Kilgore and these two were close friends. To both we gave whole smoked Salmons, Elk roast and back-strap, Bear roasts. To Mr. Krause went gifts of baskets and other artifacts in return for his generosity to Tribe. We thought highly of the man who oftentimes cut the food prices he sold (because we bought with pennies). Sometimes in Winter we didn't have the where-with-all for obviously necessary items, sugar, flour, milk, etc. We got them. That Krause lost more money through *Po-oke* than he gained there can be no doubt. There can be no doubt he was respected and loved by *Po-oke*. He, among Whites, and 'Holly', the deputy sheriff. "Krause is white-skin *Po-oke*" I heard many times. So was 'Holly'. I accept that.

Anyway, remembering forays to George Krause's store and our dedication, I still examine brooms with care and when the person who lived in my house long ago told me at times of his childhood poverty yet showed no concern for the tool we spent hours buying, I knew the extent of the poverty he'd endured.

CONSEQUENCES

Early in training for *Tloquali* it was instilled as Treasure of the Mind that we be able to examine projected actions in order to see and determine consequences to the acts. Doctor Lester and brother Lavan Coe examined me about consequences constantly. What would be the result of doing this, that or the other were posed daily. Who wanted to be Black Face had to know the strict regimen that followed analysis. Black Face could not leave the Human involvements in Life's processes to chance. We must think.

Who would be in control of personal Life activities could not be 'like a drunk, with booze in charge'. That meant that minute by minute the one who is liquor-drunk has no direction but impulse, without consideration for the consequences thereof. Anger, violence, detrimental actions (such as driving while drunk), out of control talk with no basis but booze-spurred imaginings, these are the same in who doesn't think through the processes of daily Life before involvement, as the drunk creates no consequences of value because the thinking is explosive and irrational, and non-existent on sobering. Who doesn't know the consequence of unthought acts which produce nothing but confusion?

What are the *results* of stealing? Who gains by it? What are the consequences of lying; of carrying stories without foundation which may harm someone not deserving of that harm? In a round-about way things said to one person get carried back later by someone else and never in the manner spoken. Rather than saying something negative about others, which will come back to the sayer even as more negative than first spoken, better to expand on the merits of those spoken about so that they have a base of affirmative expansion. "Find something good to say or keep you mouth shut."

It serves *no purpose* to a 'demeaner' to demean others, except to mollify Fear (of personal insignificance). It lowers the teller to being a *negative,* in the opinion of who is victim, as well as who hears. Far better to be viewed in the eyes of all with whom we associate as affirming; positive; complimentary. This shows us as being of benefit to all Tribal activities because we are seen as positive; constructive. *Practicing* affirmation builds it.

Elders gather to admonish those whose activities are destructive to self and others, family as well as acquaintances. This done by 'Walk-On-Beach' with whomsoever is seen as harmful to Tribal 'health', in a way that points out the direction headed and the inevitable destination. Consequences, inevitably, always, the consequences.

No physical harm was ever administered by *Tloquali* to who was not approachable, instead came ostracism. The unrepentant person so judged as to be no longer of communal value saw nothing of former acquaintances except their backs. No salutations, no acknowledgements; *the person was 'dead'.* The sole way of avoiding this treatment was inevitable: Leave the Tribe. Tribal Survival depended upon Beneficial Activities, activities which didn't *threaten* that survival.

One exception to Po oke non-violence rule was toward males who harmed Wife, Child, or Woman. The gatherings of Women (basketweavers) in various parts of Village passed information about relationships and when someone was violent the message was passed to husbands. The miscreant was taken by several of the men to a place in Woods. There, no more physical contact than incessant shoving of the bully from one to another of men in a circle occurred, until total exhaustion overtook the person. While this education in bullying was ongoing the repeated word "*buss-ayy—buss-ayy—buss-ayy*", meaning 'bad' or 'wrong', 'unacceptable', came from each of the men as they shoved the 'student' from one side of the circle to another.

This ended with the exhausted bully being left to recover no matter the weather, but with the final advice to change patterns, "Or go somewheres else to live. We won't need to have you to worry about." I know of two men who underwent this 'schooling' and both were model citizens from then on. There is dynamic instruction inherent in non-violent punishment which impresses who experiences it as well as who witnesses the result.

In the Memory Days one crime resulted in death: Rape. The offender was driven to suicide. I won't relate what led to it; it was harsh and effective. Well, perhaps it was vicious, but effective absolutely. The offender always drowned himself eagerly. Rape destroys minds and cannot be condoned or it expands to become a mental disease. Rapists must die.

The consequence of 'poor citizenship' being ostracism or 'the pushing session', those of us who were impressionable thought deeply about poor behavior. However, after about 1942 things changed and drink and irresponsible behavior became an expected condition over which Elders no longer had powerful influence. 'Drink' producing irresponsible behavior. The conditions were there from *day one contact* with *Hoquat* and his liquor.

The outsiders could get booze and our young were their associates, especially the girls. The results were predictable and inevitable. Charlie Howeatle said 'when the Laws of the People are no longer respected and obeyed by the People, the People are no longer the People'. Now merely 'a bunch of people'. It was in sorrow that the few full bloods remaining to witness the demise of controlling customs watched it all die. Little Bill and Bill Hudson and Mark 'Mock' Williams and those few Women who lived into the demise were saddened at the acts of their own offspring and kin and the sadness was in every act they did. Dejected is the word I hear on 'listening to *the voices*'.

AVERAGE SIZE

In July 1939 Little Bill and Theodore Hudson and I were on north shore of Hoh River waiting for Herb Fisher to come for us from Hoh Village. It was South, on the point between *cKwahleh* and woods, accessible by cKeynoo only, and Herb was poling across to our 'north side' landing beach, (which once was 'Village side').

A small insect was on my arm and I asked Theodore if that was 'the smallest thing in the world'. Uncle Yum (Little Bill) and Theodore laughed and said, almost as one, "There's no smallest thing in the world."

"Well what's smaller'n this bug?" I asked.

"Everything that's smaller," Theodore answered and when I looked puzzled both laughed again. Uncle Yum said, "Ev'rythin' is either bigger or smaller than somethin' else. Blue Whale's bigger than Elephant. Somethin' somewhere bigger'n Blue. Ev'rythin's average size to itself and so somethin's bigger, somethin's smaller. Nothing can be the 'biggest' or the 'smallest'. Somethin's always bigger, somethin's always smaller."

"Well what could be smaller than this Spider?" I asked, which is what it turned out to be.

"Answer that like *I* asked it," Uncle Yum said to me. I looked at him puzzled some more. "I'll ask this," he said, coming to my rescue, "what would be smaller than that Spider?" I thought for a while and just as Herb scraped ashore with cKeynoo conclusion came: What it eats?

Laughter of success again from them. "Ayy-y-y! What it eats is smaller than it is an' so if somethin' is alive and tiny it eats even tinier stuff."

"What's goin' on?" Herb asked because of the laughter.

"I found out there's nothing that's smallest and nothing biggest," I announced, without sure conviction.

"That's right", Herb said. "It's one more thing you learned"

We poled south across Hoh in Herb's cKeynoo to Village and something to eat. On the way across I thought about learning and as we got to Hoh Village I stumbled onto a question of importance to me. "Why you learnin' me all this stuff?"

"So you know what to do when you got to."

"What happens when I know all there is to know?" Again, laughter. But their laughter always was the laughter of delight. They loved teaching and who was curious was their joy to teach.

" 'S go walkin' ", Uncle Yum said, and together we went to Hoh Beach where he and I would stand, almost twenty years later, holding hands, crying together at the loss of our People, places, customs, and saying goodbye for what both denied but both knew was the last time.

But that 'today', Uncle Yum and I crossed the few drift logs at Hoh Beach and went to Sand. The beach is short, steep, by Hoh mouth, and walking is a low tide enterprise where beach is flatter. We had low tide now and walked the wet sand. Sand doesn't dry quickly as at First Beach and walking this beach is automatic shoe wetting so we walked holding our shoes in hand. I walked backwards, ahead of Uncle Yum, eagerly waiting for the lesson to come…automatic thinking: *we were at Beach weren't we?*

"You worried about when you know ev'rythin', what to do with it ain't it."

"Ayy-y".

"How you goin' to know ev'rythin'?"

"Learnin' 'bout stuff. They ain't all that much."

"What you know about of Sand?" He stooped to pinch some sand grains from Beach and flicked away all but one "When you gonna know all about this?" He was pointing at the grain. "An' this is just one thing out of ev'rythin'."

"What's there to know?"

"Where'd it come from?"

I was mystified. Thinking for a bit I answered, "Beach?" Posed as a statement which was question at the same time.

"Oh. How'd it get here?" He stopped walking so we'd have concentration time.

"It's just Beach. It's been here."

"*Wahss* (No). It got here from somewheres. Surf brung it. Before that it was someplace like a lake or crick and a river carried it down to *cKwahleh* an' then Surf moved it here. Tomorrow it might be somewheres else. There is no 'thing' which is *always*. Once, grain of Sand was maybe even part of a mountain. Storms busted it up and it become a Rock then rolled in some River and then come to become part of a beach. Where from? What kind of rock? What formed rocks? What does it take to wear the rock down to grain of Sand? How long? Same thin' for all the kinds of Sand? Is it possible it was always grain of Sand? The more you learn about somethin' you goin' to find out the less you know about it. There ain't no way nobody can know ev'rythin' because as you learn more you *know* you know *less*."

I'm still absorbing that.

One day I mentioned 'heaven' to Hank 'Lankie Hank' Taylor and Billy Hudson. "Where you hear 'bout that one?" Hank asked.

"Scoobus." I answered. "Coastie kids tolding us 'bout it."

Hank Taylor said to think about that stuff. "How they know what Heaven bein' like?"

"Their book" I replied.

Billy said, "Somebody been over there come back an' wrote down for ev'rybody else to learn ain't it."

"I guess so," I answered. Billy Hudson said, "Must be pretty good place you can't get in if you mess around."

"Where's it at?" I asked.

"In their book", Billy said and both he and Lankie Hank laughed at that cunning remark.

"Best thing you could go there now", I said.

"That's big a gamble as bone gamble, maybe more."

"How come?" This all mystified me.

"If there's 'heaven' who gets in?" Hank asked me. I shrugged and he said, "Only *Chutsk*. Ev'rythin' else made mistakes an' get to go to Hell." Both of them laughed again.

"How you keep from goin' to Hell?" I wondered.

Billy put his hand on my shoulder and said, "Doin' stuff to get you into Heaven. There was no laughter at that remark.

We stopped talking for a while.

Then Hank said, " *cKulell*, you goin' drive yourself crazy tryin' to figure it out. If there's 'test' then 'god' *don't* know all things forever. If he don't, he ain't 'god'. Why worry.?"

"Heaven would be that place to be if you don't like it here. But, would you give up bein' alive to 'go' someplace nobody come back from, reporting 'bout it. Not me. This is Heaven you just look at it. Why give up all the wonders of Life as it come to us in order to go someplace nobody knows is real?"

"*Hoquat* kids all swear about it is real."

"Yeah," Billy said, "They swear all right. 'ats where you kids learnin' it from."

"No, Billy", I said and laughed at the remark.

"That's from 'belief', *cKulell*. For ever'body alive there's different belief 'bout what's it all about. Don't worry about it, you can't do nothin' 'bout it. Any of the believers right, you think? Or all? Or any?"

I thought for a while then replied, "There's only one 'right' ain't it?"

"One." Billy Hudson.

'One.' Hank Taylor.

One. For me until this day: LIFE! LAW!

"Most times ev'body fight to stay alive," Hank said. "How come they fight against leavin' this place call 'Life', this misery. How come ev'body fight goin' to Heaven?"

I looked at these two Men and smiled. I had my answers so I said goodbye and ran to River where nets were being repaired. Lots to learn there at *Taboke*.

My hope for chance to learn to mend 'web' was strong in me.

....

On such a day as this 66 years ago today I left House early, to wander Land for the last time. I would be leaving for Butte, Montana, tomorrow morning, there to spend Winter.

Today I would go to Woods along *Taboke*, skirting Hobbies Mitts' land, and Maxfield's, past where Moore family lived (Charley and Marian and their little sister and parents) and upRiver where we young were not to go alone. We were told *Dawskaiyah* lived in Woods by River. She preyed on the vulnerable inexperienced young

But I was *Tloquali*! *Dawskaiyah* would have been in trouble trying to subdue the likes of me!

I recall that every mud-puddle on the wagon trails provided rippling, concentric rings as the branches were busy dripping the endless supply of *cKwia*...Rain.

cKa cK aliyuh, (Alder trees) had shed leaves; Elderberry, (our name for it was Sibuh), tried to maintain Summer by holding on—but the relentless advance of Time took leaves already advanced toward falling first but without replacement back-up, Elderberry gave up to Wind, Rain, Fall.

Even Fall was weakening its hold. Wind was more forceful. Because N.W. gales had hit us in September we saw 1939 giving up to its Fate long before Winter struck. This day, of 66 years ago (in 2005), as is today, is like that one, gloomy; wet; gusty; dim of light, this day has returned in bewilderment over those years with the question: Without having eaten breakfast, without food to take with me for snack, without thought about food: Why was there no need?

Hunger always arrived daily, but that day I recall Hunger stayed Home and let me roam without reminding me about Stomach. And thirst avoided me.

I heard *Cho-Cho* that day, but *cKa ayo*, *Byack*, even *cKulell* were unheard.

Mrs. Owl hid from Rain as well. *Cho-Cho* and *Dawskaiyah* and I owned the Woods.

It didn't take more than seconds to be soaked through by *cKwia*. I can still see the water running from my sleeves and hands in the steady downpour.

But I feel no memorable 'coldness'.

I wonder if the tragedy of killing the Trees and thus Forest was so numbing to my awareness that I had moved away from physical sense attention so that cold and wet seemed to have no effect.

NEAH BAY

William 'Big Bill' Penn was once married to Agnes, (of family name I don't know, maybe Parker. She was a Makah Woman, weaver of gorgeous baskets.), and occasionally I went with them to Makah. We visited Luke Markistum perhaps half a dozen times. Luke Markistum of Neah Bay was a venerated Elder when I was a Child.

(As with us there were many worthy Makah, Soeneke, Peterson, Ides, Parker, etc).

Luke told us the only logical answer to "what does 'Neah Bay' mean?"

"First *Hoquat* boats come from Boston. Folks called them People 'Bostons' because no matter who you'd ask 'where you from' they say 'Boston'. They had different accent in talkin' from what some explorer-traders had. Other ones who come looking for skins didn't have Boston's way of saying '*R*'. Bostons called it '*Ah*'.

"When they spoke about the Bay of our Village (Makah) they said it was the Bay '*ne-ah*' (near) the Cape (Flattery). When they gave guidance to where Makah Village was, they said like, "You know wheh (where) Cape Flattuhry' is? Well, it's the Bay '*neah* (near) to the Cape'…an' it becomes 'Neah (Near) Bay' because of that accent of Bostons," Luke told us. That makes more sense other than any other explanation I've heard. In fact I've heard no other.

WHALE, *cKwyeh-Tee* and *hu P-da-washh*

Because we were at Neah Bay I wondered if they hunted Whale. "Pretty good, better'n most," Big Bill said. "There is this legend about *cKwyeh-Tee* getting' swallowed by *cKwalla* sames (same as) that one in the Bible. How did *Hoquat* know about this happening even before we told them?

"The story I want to tell you is about this man who used to worry about his people you know. He was a...he was the Adjuster...he wasn't the Maker. He came to adjust the Creation that was made before him. So, he...he worried about these people that was swallowed by a huge whale over at the entrance of Cape Flattery...where there was a tribe of Indians. A whole cKeynoo-load of them would go down and the Adjuster was goin' through the place and he heard about it.

"He made himself a little cKeynoo he called...he...he name his cKeynoo '*hu P-da-washh*' which was a name for his little cKeynoo.

"He went out there with his '*hu P-da-washh*' and he was singing, 'Oh where, oh where are you Mr. Whale that can swallow these people...where are you?'." He was paddlin' around, singing that song an' pretty soon his '*hu P-da-washh*' spin around. 'Oh-oh!' he says, 'don't tip over!' he said to his '*hu P-da-washh*'; he talked to his little cKeynoo, he was getting' kind of...worry about his cKeynoo goin' down and then he...then he spin a little faster. Pretty soon he was swallowed and down he went, bubble, bubble, bubble, bubble—down in the stomach.

"And he find himself among great big logs...it was just dark in there. He felt...he couldn't see nothing and he felt around log after log. He was climbin' around and he was feeling around for the vital spot under the backbone of the Whale.

"With him were five bags of Mussel shells…special made bags he's made for the trip. Mussel shells which he had sharpened to a point. So he was prepared for the trip.

"He find for himself what he thought would be the vital spot. He start cuttin'. Three, four cuts his shell would break. He'd get another one from a bag. Three four cuts his shell would break. Pretty soon he was about half-way through his shells. Then! He felt the Whale start to jump and roll aroun'. He knew he was getting to the vital vein.

"He'd…he'd fall off the logs, go right down to the bottom and he'd scramble up again, tryin' to find the spot where he was cuttin'. He start in again on the same spot when he find the spot.

"He was doin' that until he had five shells left. He couldn't stay up there anymore because the Whale was now feeling that wound. She start really jumpin'. He find himself a spot where he wouldn't get crushed in there, among the logs… and he drift around for two-three days. He was prayin' that he would land in front of a village now that the Whale was dead. He was adrift.

"And, ah…it wasn't very long he felt that the Whale was on the beach now, it was rollin' in the breakers. He laid in there, among the crashing logs. Waited.

"Waited. Pretty soon the Whale…stopped rollin', the tide must be out. Then he was just staying there, he couldn't get out no way. He prayed that someone would find the Whale and start cuttin' it.

"Sure enough, he could hear people talkin' outside, and he…when they were gettin' close to him with their cuttin' he could hear them and he would holler to them not to cut him.. They heard the voice inside the Whale. They'd all run away, they'd all run. Then they'd quiet down. Pretty soon they'd come back and they'd start cuttin' again…he could hear them cuttin'. Then they cut the stomach open and he had a chance to crawl out. He was bald now…bald headed, not a siingle hair on his head. He run for the brush for a spot where he used to take a bath. He took a bath and come out with the long hair.

"And that was this Man-God-Adjuster. He was sort of a god… like…but he was also man…a man. Well, he was a god, but he wasn't the Maker, he came to see that original creation was adjusted, you know. He used to go around the country, kind of to help, to be over-seer, inspector, to see that his people was doin' good and bein' treated right. He took care of his people. His name was *cKwyeh-Tee*."

Reviewing this past and contact with the marvel of Primitive Ways while I was a Child awes me today, and puts me into the position of profound gratitude to Chance for the gift bestowed upon me.

It was during those few precious Childhood and early teen years that I held sincere belief in *cKwyeh-Tee*, a myth/legend as profoundly accepted by us as is the sincere beliefs of others in Allah or Jahweh or Odin, by believers of any 'gods'. (All replacements for previously worshipped deities...which 'god' isn't replacement 'god' for one believed about previously? None. Many of which are Oriental 'gods'. See the similar functions of Babylonian, Sumerian, Akkadian, Israeli, Turkish, Hindu, etc., 'gods', and which isn't replacement 'god'?). Who and/or what preceded *cKwyeh-Tee* I can't say. But we believed tales about him as do others about theirs. Big Bill told that one to me.

And true to basic analysis of 'reality' enjoyed by 'Primitive Minds', to this day I see no compensatory explanation for what my beloved Elders spoke to me about when they spoke to demystify what they all called by two names, 'The Great Mystery' and 'The Great Spirit'...one and the same.

So, being unable to cross the Uncrossable River into the Profound, with the limited Minds of the Human Animal, we were advised about a 'helper', 'miracle being' whose name was *cKwyeh-Tee*...(not *'Kwate'* as *Hoquat* Anthropologists unable to say the word said and recorded it, [and 'Indians' who have no knowledge *of the ways* but from what they've read in such works as Ella Clark's, which is valuable in that it *does* record]).

The Great Mystery was and is and will be inexplicable to who is aware enough of Human limitations to recognize that the Profound cannot be ascertained by nearly unfunctional brains. I was told that five limited senses made to receive five kinds of impressions cannot detect anything else of the LIMITLESS impressions going on constantly except by guessing. How determine INFINITY from the platform of nearly inoperative minds? (Not even capable to the degree of many non-Human creatures' senses...who sees in the dark like Cat People? Owl?

The Great Mystery is LIMITLESSLY expansive we knew. Realistically, how could it be other? But human mind is incapable of being *limitless*. We can't hear what Dog hears, smell what they smell, see what Eagle makes judgment about on constant basis (about what we can never know). Cat judges its far more complex world second by second. Complex is what it is. Hearing, tasting, smelling, feeling, *lower* than our abilities to 'receive' *and above*. Non-human People make judgments about sounds and sights and smells, etc., that are unknown to us, unavailable to us. Even by machine. Ever. As do we, they make judgments about the sensorial input they receive. Much more complex than ours is their world and they make conclusions about things *we cannot* know. They are in a richly endowed world we cannot perceive. But 'they're 'dumb' Animals' I've heard it said. I learned differently, thanks to Tyler Hobucket, Harry Hobucket's Greyhounds. And to *Byack*.

There, at La Push, seventy-plus years ago, before it died, were Women and Men who as Children, learned from *Po-oke* who were sixty or thereabouts, fifty, seventy-five years before that. What the People had known about Life and taught before the coming of *Hoquat* and *Hoquat* 'wisdom': Abject materialism. This work is what I remember of what they taught. And what they tried to teach those of us who are now at the doors of Transition, knee-deep in the water of the River we'll cross once, not to return. As they did not. The horror is that The Gun-people refused to let us continue as we were. And so now we're not.

I'd take you to that La Push if I could. I'd have you listen to Drums from various places throughout Village, not as mimic of yesterday, but as continuation of thousands of years. And as you hear Drums hear Songs. Listen also to voice of Surf. There is no La Push without the voices: Drums and Songs and Surf.

Another 'pulse-beat' of La Push to which I'd direct your attention would be laundry. Any day without Rain brought out colorful drying laundry. Table cloths hung side by side with sheets and shirts and dresses, trousers, sweaters, fluttering to show from whence came Wind …every yard had its planted poles with cross-armed tops and courses of clothes-line, with pinned laundry brightening the day.

The wonderful young surrogate Mothers who took so much of the burden of home-making from their Mothers kept watchful eyes for potential weather changes. At indication of Rain or high Wind racing toward the drying clothes, a shout would go out and those living dolls would scurry out with baskets to gather the threatened laundry. It would be taken into the houses, there to hang from drying-lines.

These were strung across rooms near ceiling height in each house, pulling in stove warmth. Before we could push clothing aside in order to pass we had to prove to *those protectors of the laundry* that we wore clean clothing, that our hands were clean.

We laundered on scrub-boards in water carried to the house, heated on the stoves and soaped with *Fell Snapthesope*. For such as 'dainties' and towels: Ivory soap. Sheets, etc., 'bloopbloopblooped' in the copper-tub of water bubbling on the stove. Boiling with fervor to sanitize what couldn't have been that dirty to begin with...at least in my mind. Steam rose and the vapors of boiling water and Fell Snapthesope penetrated to the farthest corners of the house. This was hard work and woe to who dirtied the hard work with carelessness. Our Surrogates were strict...a twisted ear was not readily forgotten so we protected the laundry.

On any visit we could make back to those times I'd have you see the Laundry hanging in such colors as would never leave your mind. I painted a watercolor of such in 1958.

Laundry to see; Drums to hear; Songs. Hear them, heart-beats of Spirit. Of our beloved Parent, Mother Earth, through Her Eldest Child, Surf; of happiness; of sadness; of Life. In your mind's ears, listen to Drums, hear Surf, then follow as I wander the roads of home again to hear dogs; the voices of young at play...Surf Birds; Gulls; Crows; mechanical noises such as outboard motors, generators on scows. The modern world was awakening from the Primitive condition for us. Follow me to La Push.

Smell the wood smoke seeking freedom in the sky, escaping the confines of Stove. And smell Village. It and we had a scent which came from diet. It came from fish and every house and every one presented it. It isn't there anymore. The smell of some smoke-house with *Sa-ats* or Smelts being smoked in their seasons hung in the air; the smell of venison roasting in someone's oven; one would never forget them. Things which gave to us Life. What is La Push without its Life? Those things were part of it.

THE NATURE OF NATURE

One day before leaving for Butte in November 1939, I was walking on Beach in a driving rain-storm and met 'Mock' Williams coming back toward Village. Surf and Wind were nearly deafening. "What you doin' up at noon?" he shouted and we laughed. "You memorizing ev'rythin' ain't it." Statement of fact.

"Ayy-y-y. 'Sides I like watchin' them big breakers throwin' spray an' foam," I shouted back.

"That ain't gonna change," he said and I knew he was referring to the decimation of Forest between La Push and Forks, which was on-going with furious intensity. (Today, 2007, I see that intense destruction as greed decimates lovely but in-expensive old family residences in Ballard, to put up multi-unit, multi-story boxes).

"Pretty hard to stop *cKwahleh* from bein' *cKwahleh*, ain't it." Me. And I add, hard to stop greed from being greed.

"Oshunt (Ocean). Can't change oshunt. What'll change is what's in 'oshunt'. Nothin' on Earth was meant to be challenged for Life by machine. Too much people, too much machine. Machine got no conscience. You gonna see Earth get sick. Maybe you die with it. *cKwahleh*. *cKwahleh* People, all gonna get sick an' many gonna die before *Hoquat* way get stopped."

"How come they allus tearin' away at stuff?"

"Make 'em money. Worships money…'god' for them, give 'em stuff they want. Only problem is, money should be just for 'Need'. (An' we can satisfy that *our* way). But 'want' never stop growin'. Bullies 'em."

I asked, "How much they wantin'?"

"All they can get."

"How come? We don't gotta have all that, we work together so nobody need nothin' ain't it."

"Ayy-y. They don't work together 'cept at War. War an' Money is gods for them." He threw a stick for his dog 'Hoquat' which was almost all white. "Too bad them ordinary Hoquats can't get the greedy one to behave ain't it." Mock.

I remember the day well because, first, we saw Chester Johnson come onto Beach nearly at Coast Guard trail and Mock said, "Here comin' Chester. He get mad when he talkin' about The Change we had to make." Second, Surf was pounding the salvage barge which had beached earlier in Fall, a rare-to-us show of the power-without-limit of cKwahleh.

I thought about 'War an' Money' as we stood watching Surf-power, awaiting Chester. We were nearly to Lonesome Creek so it would take him a while to get to us. To shout was normal conversation while Surf demolished the barge. We stood looking at the raising and dropping of the off-shore part even after Chester had arrived. To me it seemed sad to spend the time and energy and, yes, money, required to build that invulnerable appearing vessel, only to have it shredded as easily as cKwahleh was doing. Obviously, to contest cKwahleh was a losing gamble. Earlier that year the S.S. Temple Bar, useless forevermore; now this huge barge. cKwahleh had no Equal in Power except Great Spirit.

The raising then dropping of the barge was accompanied by a penetrating 'boom' and ringing vibration as the sheer weight of steel fell back to compact Sand, Earth-old. Felt, more than heard in Village, the ceaseless onslaught had already torn away hull-plates, exposing skeletal frame-work and twisting the heavy steel supports as if pieces from tin-cans. As on the Peter Ayrdale on the beach south of Columbia River (cKlummia river).

Mock bobbed his head indicating a desire to leave so we wended our way along the path beside Lonesome Creek and entered the roadway by the 'point' (where one of Tommy Payne's daughters had been buried in cKeynoo. The road had split the cemetary area separating Her grave from the ones Raefield had had bull-dozed behind the 'hotel').

My head was swirling about Life and machinery and I continued the conversation about the hunger for money. "What gonna happen when they own all the money?"

Chester answered, "Won't happen. Make more all the time in 'fac-trees', for people to borrow. It get borrowed they make some more."

"How come?"

"Nobody knows," he said. "Even them. Smart ones allus talkin' about how money is needed for tradin' what I got for what you got when we want to, but then some of 'em get greedy an' money-fat like food-greedy people get body fat so much it make them sick. Money is like that. It look like the more they get the more money hunger it bring. They get sick-for-money brains."

Mock added, "Money is 'god', without end demanding worship... *obey, obey, obey.* That mean *work, work, work.* You know what's god be-cause people kill for the god, die for it, lie for it. They steal an' whore an' make false money to get 'god', remember what Dema (Hudson) said. What people do all that for is *'god'* for them. That's what goes on with them. Look what they done to *Po-oke* to get money...barred from the Sacred Land an' we got home` in the worst Winter place possible. In exchange for promises. Mouth of *Ta-boke.*"

Chester entered the discussion. "Somethin' wrong in the head of somebody can't see troubles comin'. Big mistake to try farmin' the whole world like it's only a place next door. It's Natural for stuff to grow a certain amount, like Salal grows only so much berries, Salmons make only so much young. When there is more an' more demand on stuff it gonna be less an' less of stuff. Nature ain't no machine with gas pedal."

"Mock, you said about war an' money. How *Hoquat* work together then. What that means?" I needed more input.

"During war people work together to defeat who they fightin' against. Other times they *compete* to be best; to get most; to have most power. Anybody can be president even if they don't know horse-apples from fish-heads. Long as they lie an' brag about how good they are people listen and helps them get their hands in the soup.

"Our way was different because what you done was what people paid 'tention to. You didn't brag an' lie about how good you was an' what you done, if you was that good an' done what you said, people saw it an' they done the talkin' for you. Ev'rybody tried to give more an' more of what they could for *Po-oke*, so ev'rybody had what was need-ed. We didn't compete to bring benefit only to ourself, but lived and looked to Live harmony, to build strongest Spirit power for seein' the not-seen. For help to whole Tribe. Greed for more was not our way.

We tried to give away." Mock shrugged and for a brief moment stared at the barge-demolition, then he turned and looked into my eyes as if from ETERNITY, from the most sorrow-filled eyes I've ever seen. He shrugged again and almost whispering said, "...can't be fixed."

How does one 'people' determine their right to determine for others I wondered. Always *'the Winnah!'* has to strut into position to be seen. Then I reheard Mock, "...compete to..."

"What's a 'compete'," I asked.

"'Bone-gamble' is a compete; cKeynoo racin'. Games. What's differnt is when ev'rybody work together to help some one who needed stuff then nobody needed stuff. *Hoquat* way is one person tries to get ever'body to work for him, ever'body takin', takin', allus takin' an' givin' only words about how important he is, an' promises of what's gonna come about for others." He laughed as if apologizing for what he said, as if even though he hadn't designed it he was ashamed to relay it to me.

"Don't nobody see which way works best?" I asked.

Mock said, "Some do, some don't. But it take Lifetime to understand: There ain't no enemy to Nature which can win. The enemy to Nature is the one who keep on takin', takin', never lettin' up. Over the time since the beginnin' of time Nature figgered how to make ever'thin' work in Harmony. You work in Harmony, lettin' Nature do what Nature does an' you Livin' in Harmony with Nature. Then you Nature's partner. You get blessings from unbothered Nature."

Chester had a thought. "Who wins when Nature is you partner? But keep takin' an' demandin' without respect for Nature's Way an' you become Nature's enemy. *Guess who gonna win a fight between Nature an' enemy to Nature.* The way of Nature is to be Natural an' mankind keep pushin', pushin', pushin'. This is call' *Ignorance*. To be 'on-purpose enemy' to Nature. Who's gonna win between *Hoquat* ways an' Nature, cKulell?"

I nodded my understanding.

Chester said, "Human and all other People gonna pay the price. The Nature of Nature is be Natural and Natural is its pace. We ain't gonna set no pace for Nature to follow. Taking without limit from the abundance of Nature isn't only wrong, it's stupid. She tolerate a little pushin' now an' then, small farmin' shows us 'Nature like to have Her hair combed'. But who think he can force Nature to do his will already lost. Learn to Live in Harmony with Mother Nature an' Her breast will never stop givin' milk. Let Nature do what She does an' help Her a little. But *cKulell*, you gonna live to see mankind suffer for stupid ways. Don't let greed blind *you* to the Nature of Nature."

"Is all this in brains people got?" I asked. "No," both said at once and laughed. "You tell him," they both said again at the same time and we all laughed.

"Tell me what?"

"No," Chester said, answering my question. "Its mind. You can't *change brains. Mind* you can change. So it is just that the way they *see* is set. Could that be changed then ever'thin' would be O.K. People change their mind all the time but not the brain, so it can be fixed. It's seein'. You got to look an' see at the same time. You see nothin' if all you do is look".

"That's right," said Mock. "If you change you thinkin' three times about religion as it come to us, that's only three ways of seein', of mind changin', but still the same brain doin' 'the seein'. It's lookin' *without* seein' what works wrong."

OUR WOMEN

When *Village* comes to mind, through the vast, undefinable Mist of Time, I recall another 'Life-spark' Village had. That was the result of Matriarchal involvement. When I spoke about the gatherings of Women to weave baskets, (which gatherings were in various locations, weather dependent), it was to involve with explanation of the role these gatherings had in the evolvement of Village 'ethic'. We had an ethic of role to be obeyed. That 'ethic' was carried throughout Village by Women, the Mothers, who were in greatest position of influence on Babies. When these family influencing People carried the ethic of Honor, as defined by the Women who sat together frequently, they discussed the ways of Merit for the happiness, health, benefit, of the People, who were, in fact, Families comprising Quileute *Po-oke*.'

They oversaw 'our Nation'.

They who gathered at various advantageous places were such as Mrs. Grant (Clara) Eastman, Mrs. Billy (Dema) Hudson, Mrs. Walter (Grace) Jackson, Mrs. Thomas (Elsa) Payne, Nina Bright, Sarah Woodruff (Mrs. Fred); *Se-ic-tiss* Ward's Mary; Cleveland, Grey; White; Black; Bright; George; Williams; Penn; Fisher; Coe; Cole, and on and on.

No facet of Village, no needs within Village were not carried to the sites whereat baskets were created. The weaving of baskets and the few pennies returned for the hours of tedious gathering and preparation were not allied. Basket weaving gave the Women chances to be together to over-see 'affairs of state': Which Children in the days of Depression were in need of what clothing, or who was coughing TB cough, or which couple had sparked new *Chutsk* and what they'd need, where they'd stay, how to help them cope with the problems ahead: Basket weavers at work with baskets, the largest 'basket' being Village itself. Our Women *weaved* La Push; our WOMEN!

Men didn't involve with the health and ongoing family Life of Village except in whatever ancillary way Women saw need for their contributions. Hunting and fishing and the heavy needs imposed by these tasks took men away from Village Life, removing them from the thoroughly demanding manner it took in Women.

Men learned of Village need for male assistance from their wives and female relatives. Machinery; house repairs, such as roof work, etc. Men saw to cKeynoo work, net 'repair and making/building', part-time (or full-time if possible) jobs, frequently at a distance from Village presence, these the circumstances which made Female activity in Village politics essential for the maintaining of anything like *Po-oke* Life-style.

No Children of seventy years ago and more were not overseen by some Village Woman as the play passed from roadway to Beach or ball-park to *Ta-boke*.

I recall no drownings from my Childhood days, but with the loss of Woman's importance and their traditional role of keeping one finger on the pulse-beat of our way of Life, some Child would disappear, only to have drowned. I believe that 'modern times' took away the treasure of Female importance to the well-being of Village.

During the gatherings, knowledge of which medicinals for which Childhood problems was passed; what to do for a newly pregnant young Woman; what to do to help during a tough pregnancy; which plants were medicine; used for poultices; 'the itch'; hurting teeth...our Women were they who kept Village functional. But the conquest subjugated the Queens of Village who lost their importance to Village.

When the inherent wisdom of concerned Women has been relegated to the role of commodity for the illusionary superiority of the stud animal, the society is doomed. I've lived in the society which sees Women's importance and the one which exalts the male. In the one we knew Peace. Since then I've watched our young, our beautiful young, be pulverized and/or killed in at least six wars...to accommodate Gross National Product.

Too bad *Hoquat* wasn't defeated, to live *Po-oke* way.

CAKE ROCK and
SEA GULL EGGS

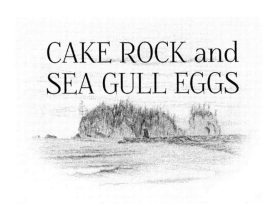

One day after I had run an errand and was savoring the 'errand reward', a Hershey's almond bar, I heard the aggravating sound of cranking, over and over and over, of a balky outboard motor, near the old (two-track) Coast Guard boat-house. The noise was attractive to youngsters. We learned some *remarkably* effective *Hoquat* words as used by the motor owners. Whether or not to define the *actuality* of the motor, not the least of which we learned was the name *Salmon labeech.* Salmon labeech was an extremely malevolent Power-spirit because it was *his* fault motors balked. It turned out nearly every motor on *Ta-boke* harbored this *Salmon labeech.* "Get *going* you Salmon Labeech!" He could be in several motors at a time because he was shouted at and told to 'Get going' by several would-be operators at once. Sometimes he'd leave and the motor would operate. For some, no.

There were *other 'brand names'*, (many of which got a tongue lashing for me when I used them where there were other than outboard motors present). But I won't reveal my arsenal of 'secret words' to use on those machines. Or on other obstacles. The magic words would spread Wild-fire like and the magic would be gone. Learned a lot of magic words from commercial fishermen talking to one another all right.

Anyway, after the errand I was at *Ta-boke* Beach between C.G. Boathouse and Shell Oil dock talking to operator Dan Wilson (who had a shack on Shell Oil dock tank pad)(and who would create a couple of 'red-lead' sandwiches for us, pumpernickel bread and cat-sup, (excuse…'ketchup'). Watching a drifting cKeynoo and struggling boatman we were both 'pulling' for his success. His momentary enemy had pistons and propellor and a liking for gasoline, but no prospect of co-operating by functioning, whether Evinrude or Johnson or Searzez or air-cooled Lawson.

It was Morton Penn and I knew immediately I wouldn't be learning any of those Magic Words which sometimes made machinery operate. He didn't know any, was my interpretation. But he knew almost everything else. I yelled to him that he had to call it 'Salmon labeech' and it would start and immediately I said that it fired and kept operating. I knew that I had had nothing to do with the function but we laughed about it. *"cKola* (come)", Morton said, and he eased his *cKwahleh* cKeynoo (ocean/sealing canoe [now hanging at the North end of Lake Union in Seattle in Ivar's Salmon House]) to Beach and I jumped in.

I was nearly beyond the age of permission-asking for several things but not yet where I was going. Thus going with Morton without permission from Mother was *'bussayy'*, *bad*.

"Where we goin'?" I asked.

"Cake Rock for startin' get eggs," he said. *He was goin' on cKwahleh' to Cake Rock!* This was awareness about my doings which my parents had to judge as all right, so I raced home, shouted through the doorway toward the kitchen, "Me'nMortonsgoanovahtheregeteggs!"

"You siddown in cKeynoo do what Morton says."

"I get you some big ones Mama."

"O.K. You siddown in cKeynoo do what Morton says."

"I will. I love you Mama."

"You better or I'll give away all the smoke *'a-lita'*."

She wouldn't do that I knew, smoke fish was my reason for Life.

Pete Clark was standing on the north 'balcony' of the Coast Guard look-out tower as we raced toward *Ta-boke* mouth beside *Ahkalut*, and waved at us then went into the enclosure to note our departure in the 'log book': 'Indian canoe out, two aboard."

There's a small wash-rock...small compared to *Ahkalut* but solidly attached to MOTHER EARTH...at *Ta-boke* mouth. Small vessels, even small commercial trollers could pass between it and Island at higher tides and through that opening we shot, full speed, and into the long, smooth swells coming from 'over there', Asia, or wherever, swells that were oil-like, glazed, non-breaking. Huge. Then we were zooming along-side 'J.I.' with the shelf beside Island visible beneath us as we passed toward Cake Rock.

This was *cKwahleh* unlike what I'd seen before. Lazy, greasy-surfaced 'napping' waves: 'ground swells'. From crest to crest was at least three cKeynoo lengths.

I sat as far forward as possible to cut the cool breath of *cKwahleh* now increased by cKeynoo speed. I looked aft toward Morton and he smiled and waved, then pointed at the myriad numbers and varieties of Sea Birds already showing up along our coast. They seemed mindless in their frantic wing flapping onto Ocean when they surfaced. Surfacing from a dive only to face this roaring monster which was our cKeynoo caused Bird adrenaline to soar..."squack", flap, and away.

Especially attractive to me were Sea Parrots because of their bright colors, red, white, black, heads unmistakably theirs alone, with the fascinating eye-surround they sported. Soon I would be introduced to the voices of Mothers and their Young to learn about other kinds of People and their languages, but for today I watched ahead.

Morton whistled and I looked to where he pointed: Two Sea-Lions from Sea-Lion Rocks...Jagged Island...floated easily to one side of us, heads out of the water and watching us skim by. They sank out of sight without a ripple and Morton whistled again, indicated that they would reappear ahead of us; he said they were curious as Cats.

I doubted they'd catch us as I watched the, to me 'hurtling', rate we were experiencing, but half a mile beyond sighting them he shouted and pointed to our left...two Sea-Lions with heads out of the water, watching our progress: The white scar-patch on the neck and head of one verified Morton's prediction, they were the same ones. And they had out-run us. I had looked at the wake we were leaving and thought we were the fastest things on *cKwahleh* but they had to be faster, to dive, out-run us under-water to such degree they could surface and watch us coming toward them from a near quarter-mile.

That brought speculation that made me miss something important; suddenly I was aware of the slowing speed of cKeynoo coupled with the lessening of the motor's roar...as Mock would have said, "more less", which is to say, 'slow even more'.

I looked toward Morton in cKeynoo stern. He was watching me, a bemused look on his face. I could raise my voice slightly and be heard, "How come we to stop?"

"You been watchin' ain't it."

"Sometimes."

"Always watch."

Something 'was up' about watching so I looked around. I'd brought my gaze from ahead, over the Wolf-ears of Morton's *Ta-bil cKwahleh* (Ocean Keynoo; actually, cKeynoo ocean), to the right, ten-feet or so from us, where languished two strange, to me mysterious creatures, circular and flat, as a fat pan-cake would be. These two sea-beasties swam almost vertically and sported a strange fin on top and bottom. We were close enough that I could see the eyes and gills and strange, rubbery looking 'lips'.

These were about two feet I imagined (from today's perspective), the diameter difficult to gauge because of the slight 'list to starboard' they presented. If an auto tire of milky-grey color was 'tire to the center' (i.e., no rim nor wheel, rounded at the circumference) I believe that would approximate both size and shape. And color. I remember wondering what the devil those things were and hearing Morton Penn laugh. "What's them folks?" he shouted just above the idling outboard motor.

"What *are* they?" I countered, watching fascinated as the slow, partial flip-flop of their fins seemed to stabilize them. The two were not bothered by us. Did their languid move-ments indicate disdain or such? I wondered how they could escape becoming Shark or Orca food, they appeared ponderously slow.

"What are they?" I hollered again.

"Sunfish. Ain't them odd lookin' 'ducks'?", Morton's way of saying 'creatures'. My response to this was, "They're crazy lookin'. How come Shark don't get 'em, Sea-Lions? They're so slow!"

"Slow huh? Watch slow," he said taking up a paddle from near his feet. With the silence of long-tradition long-practiced, this Hunter-on-the-sea moved the paddle so cKeynoo bow pointed toward the Sunfish, then paddled so we moved toward them to within three or four feet. I sat unblinking as I looked eyes-to-eyes into the personalities of other Life-beings, and I recall even now that I saw two different 'people'. Because of inexperience I was unprepared for the surprise of seeing 'individual personalities' in fish. But I did.

Apparently we got too close and they moved their spiky top and bottom fins almost invisibly. Re-acting at the same time as if by signal, they made one fast move of their fins. Gone. In pristine clear water, they were there and then simply disappeared. There was no sign of them streaking away, into the depths. They were then they were not.

"Pretty slow ain't it" said Morton. With that came the intrusion of the out-board's roar as we picked up speed again toward Cake Rock. I found myself searching the waters ahead and one side to the other to spot as had Morton. But then Morton Penn was *Tloquali* and *Tss'y'uck*. Without peer it was said.

From looking I began to see *'Hoquat'*: *unknown things drifting on the water*, which would resolve into Kelp clusters or pieces of broken Tree branches or floating tin-cans. Or Sea Bird popping to Surface suddenly, rearranging the position of a captive little fish until its head-end was where it could be chuggalugged. Then Bird would raise itself almost vertically for a brief second, tail feathers would snap one side to the other. Then Bird would pay attention to us, swimming directly away while looking back and squacking, then becoming a rounded mound whose head dipped beneath the waves followed by a body-dive without splash and POOF, it would be gone.

I began to see this was not an empty wasteland, a Life-less wasteland, and to feel, to suck in every smell; the feel and smell of the chill breeze our speed created, increased by speeding into an existing breeze; I marvelled at the sight of a *big* Spring-Salmon (*Tyee*) leaving *cKwahleh* in a long, silvery arc, then splashing with glittering spray back into its home. "You know why that one jumped?" Morton asked me later. "No." "Somebody kept a nose bone after eatin' an' threw away the rest. They lookin' for the nose bone when they jump like that." Just past *Ahkalut* and beneath us was at least *one* big Sa-ats!

More Sea-Lions appeared as we approached Cake Rock, and now Bird People of various sizes, shapes and colors, like the melting-pot of humans in America, left the water; dived into the water; tried frantically and desparately to fly away from us and the water; to get no further above the water than might a lead-balloon. Fed to capacity with the now-blooming food supplies of Spring, they couldn't lift their swollen stomachs into the air. And how they protested our intrusion. While through it all the 'barking' of Sea-lions at Jagged Island. I'd not been so close before.

Closer to Cake Rock, Birds calling became a babble I heard as shrieks; moans; bellowings; Gull calls. They could be heard above the Sea-Horse propelling us. We slowed to paddle speed as Morton stopped the engine and proceeded to the landing shelf. Here a 'safe' mooring. That place is unknown by nearly all now I guess.

"Jump out with anchor line," Morton commanded and I was out of cKeynoo onto the 'shelf', holding fast as Morton raised and tied the motor into place so it wouldn't drop and damage the prop blades. He came forward and lifted a partly filled gunny-sack of what I learned were stones. These to separate new eggs from old. He began the climb on the narrow and nearly unseen ledge/path with about a milk-pail of pebbles to carry to the top…thirty or so pounds.

It was cold in the shade of the rock-island. At the top Wind was *stiff*, cold and constant. I'd had no idea of the discomfort of Life experienced at the top of Cake Rock and realized that where there were no trees to break the force of the wind the air moving over *cKwahleh* would be chilly at best across *barren rock*. I pitied the Birds which had to sleep on that place. But of course I had no feathers.

Cake Rock is much larger than view from Village or Rialto Beach showed and much different in shape, it's long and narrow. I'd judge it as less than two acres.

The top was a startling surprise to me. I suppose the mile-plus view from Village indicated a sterile, scrubbed clean top, but what a place in fact. Scrawny tufts of tough 'grasses' poked through cracks in the rock. Feathers lay in caked guano, lay tangled in the grasses, or blew about as if trying to find a place to become planted. Mussel shells shattered to almost sand-grain size, together with Clam shells, were inches deep in places so they hid the surface of the rock. Star-fish pieces appeared to move when the congregated flies flowed over them. Egg-shells from countless years of nesting were pulverized everywhere but still recognizable as Sea-Gulls' because of the speckled shell remnants.

Twigs from wherever lay in profusion and abandon. Some were part of nests. Feathers were intertwined with the twigs in many of the nests and seemed able to withstand both the high winds of deep Winter and the mountainous seas which, when *cKwahleh* was raging, scoured the island, top included. We could see during Winter storms that spray made Cake Rock almost disappear, so these nests which appeared to be old and abandoned but still in place had to have some sturdy construction. The nearly powdered condition of the shells was mysterious to me then, and is today. If a malleable surface was required to produce nests, they provided it. Why didn't that shell-powder blow away in Wind, or be scoured away in Winter. I don't know.

There were hundreds of nesting holes 'wiggled' into the sparse covering; into survival-determined grasses; in pockets worn into the rock itself after thousands of years of feather abrasion from nesting Birds; into the crushed shells. And at this season of the year all of them contained eggs.

Morton took a handful of pebbles from the gunny-sack and gave some to me. "Make a circle with them rocks 'bout same size I do. Now watch." He let the small rocks dribble like water-drops from his hand and created enclosures around several nests of eggs, some with one or two eggs and several with three. His enclosures were from five or six feet to as much as ten feet in diameter. Now I made my 'rock fence' and we put ten or so of the 'circles of rocks' into place. Then Morton said, "Put eggs out like this," and took the eggs from inside the circles methodically then put them outside so no eggs remained within.

Meanwhile, I had had no previous knowledge of the things which occur above islands used by Birds for nests and rookeries. Birds shrieked at us and flew close-by our heads and protested our presence with bombardments of guano. Little on either of us, rain clothes Morton brought, hands, hats, that was not the chalk-like white of the top of the island. We were guano-ed with a vengeance

The circular enclosures of pebbles emptied of the eggs Morton said, "Going time. Days like this offshore wind comes up strong late afternoon an' ev'nin'. Back home now."

Arriving at cKeynoo I slipped and fell into *cKwahleh*. I drew myself out of the water as if leviated and dropped into cKeynoo, actually, I was wet from the hips down but I felt as if I'd been held underwater. "Salmon labeech that's cold!" Scrawny eight-year old legs banged one another in the frantic effort of Body to get warm.

"Don't use them *Hoquat* words when you come with me, an' work this into you head, you pay attention to cold you gonna feel it. Rem'ber, where you don't put no attention you don't get no sensation. Cold is sensation you got to forget about. Same as hungry; thirsty; tired. *Tloquali* don't feel nothing they don't need to. *Tloquali* don't need to feel cold or hunger or nothing. If you ain't got the stuff there to satisfy the need don't think about it, it'll go away," Morton said as he reached into another gunny-sack, ('Indian luggage' same as cardboard or apple boxes). He tossed dry clothes to me and said, "You don't haff to put it on if you don't wanna."

We laughed at that inanity and I stripped and redressed as if by magic. Then he tossed a blanket and I surrounded myself with it. I was shivering almost out of control, especially my legs, which hammered one another at the knees. Strange white 'squares' covered my thighs. 'Salmon Labeech it's cold I thought'. The blanket cut the cold wind but didn't stop the shivering. I hunkered down in the bow as close to the wood as I could get and tried to reduce my size to a ball-shape as legs and arms seemed to withdraw from the outside world and find shelter inside my body. I was cold but not repelled by it. I told myself that it wasn't cold, it wasn't any way, (thinking *Tloquali*).

I remember that we moved away from Cake Rock but that was the last thing I remembered of our homeward trip. The drone of the Sea-Horse motor and the long, gentle rise and fall of cKeynoo as we glided over surface of *cKwahleh* put me away until Morton shook me and said, "Hey, *Tloquali*, we back now. Go home. *Ahlash*. We go out day after tomorrow the mornin', get some eggs. I'll come by get you. Listen for *cKa'a'yo* wakin' the day. I'll be there."

"Thanks, Morton," I answered, feeling a pride previously unfelt. I had slept like the dead apparently, and I was much warmer now. "That was fun!"

"Think you can do it again, cold water and all?"

"Got to", I said. He smiled.

I moved toward home a few steps then turned to him and said "*cKola ahlash.*"

Morton answered, "O.K. For coffee." And here went 'two' *Tloquali* (and one *Tss'y'uck*), his hand over the top of my head patting gently. "You done good *cKulell.*"

Home again I was eager to report about the adventure. I realize now that I babbled when I told of what we'd seen and done. But we enjoyed the report, both they and I. Father had been to the top of Cake Rock over forty or more years, countless times I knew, but in case he'd missed something, I knew I hadn't, so I told him and Mother all about it, but kept to myself about getting wet. I was tough. '*Tloquali*'.

I felt tough. Not 'tough-guy tough'; capable. Strong. And proud of a strength previously unknown. I anticipated the return to Cake Rock eagerly, gathering eggs for all Village, putting them into baskets held in cKeynoo. And I knew the Men of Village would hear of our adventure.

I'd gone to Cake Rock with Morton Penn. Before I'd gone to bed however, Mother had me in the galvanized laundry-tub scrubbing away anything *cKwahleh* hadn't removed. I don't remember climbing the stairs to bed, but I awoke when *cKa'a'yo* woke the dawn, a proud boy different than yesterday morning's unaware Child had been. *I'd been atop Cake Rock.*

Later I learned that water by islands is noticably colder than water at a distance. Sun can't heat islands and thus a zone of colder water surrounds them. Offshore in dense fog *Tss'y'uck* would feel the water of *cKwahleh* to find when slight differences in temperature occurred and if colder they'd know they were close to island(s). Because *Tss'y'uck* Men had every island and its position relative to Village and *Ta-boke* branded into Brain, simple temperature sampling told them 'close-by island' and when they saw it they knew which it was and soon were home. To learn of such changes as 'colder near islands' was a determining factor in my dedication to 'tough it out' with the Men no matter the next test: They had done it. I would.

QUEST

I heard about Quest early in Life, from no less than Charlie Howe-attle. When the occasional nickel came to hand I would go to Mary's and Charlie's store (to buy 'Green Rivers soda pop' or Juicy Fruit gum). They were dedicated to guide youngsters toward beneficial Life-long behavior. Charlie was Shaker minister. The times I saw him and others of Village in old Shaker Church worshipping began early I suppose… when it began for me I have no idea but until many years later I knew only that Mary and Charlie had Shaker 'Power'. One day in the store, looking out the windows at the near night-time gloom of a day of coastal Rain, Charlie and I talked about SPIRIT and duty to that world. "You gone (for) you Quest yet?" he asked knowing I hadn't. I remember looking at him and asking, "What's 'Quest'?"

" 'at's when you get growed up an' start looking for you own answers 'bout you own Life. What's Great Spirit got ready an' holdin' for you to discover wot (what) you want to be. That's Quest. Your duty to how to help the Tribe."

"That like tryin' find a job?"

Charlie smiled and answered, "Kinda. But with 'job' you learn how you gonna do, like *Hoquat* job-stuff, doctor, or policeman like Holly, or get a troller an' start fishin' like you dad doin'…."

"Like you an' Mary's store, ain't it."

"Ayy-y. But this is a 'made up'. Quest is looking to the big question ' bout you Life. Quest is opposite that job stuff first. With us it's allus been, 'somebody don't Create what they gonna be, they discover' it through fastin' an' bein' alone with what they been trained to do to find the Power, *Tomanamus* Power. Work to get their *Taxilit*."

"You mean 'have I found out what my 'help' gonna be?'"

"Ayy-y."

"Not yet."

When I was ten or so, *Tomanamus* practice/guidance came from the Men Elders increasingly. I noticed the intensity when 'never getting lost' education began at about five years; more and more practical guidance followed as the 'game of observing' commenced.

Uncle Yum was always concerned about Children getting 'grone-up to growed-up'. First on his list for the young was with 'not getting-lost training'. First came "lookin' backwards when you goin' 'Over There'. Go ahead lily-ways, 'en turn 'roun' an' go back, 'bout cKeynoo length. You lookin' at stuff on you path an' what it's lookin' like. Branches? Forked? Alder? Hemlock? Ferns there? How tall? Trees? Alders? Big? Small? Is Brook hollerin' 'I'm over here?' What shape Rocks you seein', how big? You walkin' up or down slope? You walkin' around on side-hill? See stuff so you can tell somebody else where you was an' they know they found where you was. What does stuff soun' like where you been goin'? Remember the sound about stuff you ain't used to hearin'. When you listen for somethin' over there turn you head tilted to right, then to left, keep goin' until you got the source of the sound. Same like seein' an' winkin' one eye then other one."

"Go some more...fifteen cKeynoo long. Turn aroun' again. Memorize stuff on Path, memorize Path both ways so comin' back is easy as goin' out. Then you ain't goin' get lost."

The first day this process was introduced to *my* 'World' (and how to expand that) was the day Mock Williams and a younger relative of his, Archie Williams, (close friend to Verne Black, second son of Rosie and Roy) and I went to drift logs looking to find a Cedar log *Se-ic-tiss* Ward could use for carving.

Village children ranged the drift-log pile for usable wood, be it Cedar or Fir or Yew...whatever...when we went to Beach. Our parents encouraged us to run as fast as possible on the incredible jumble Drift logs made, at the same time recording the sizes, types, degree of being buried in Sand, 'what's in them Drift logs'? A Life-style based on Fish and Wood educated us all to seek practical materials for Village, being aware of who would need what and why. Thus we three roamed across the logs sometimes taking a chip from a log with a hand-axe or hatchet, whichever.

Now I recognize the ritual involvement not known about then: We of Village knew every log and its content, where it was, the entire length of Beach, so 'lookin' for logs' had a separate purpose, a togetherness involvement: A time for guidance and trust building: Dependability, relating. 'Baby sitting' of the impressionable young.

Walter Payne (brother to Rosie Black (Mrs. Roy), son of Elsie and 'Tommy' Payne) was on Beach using his drag-saw (Eureka Pony) as we searched the log pile. "Good log for *Se-ic-tiss* over there," he told us, waving toward Bluff, shouting above the popping voice of the gas-engined saw, 'kuhbunggkuhbunggkuhbungg'. He was just South of Lonesome Crick and had been for some time, the blue-grey plume of drag-saw smoke rose almost vertically then spread, as it rose toward the South, eventually passing over the Trees along the top of Bluff. He set his saw-blade to a new position and engaged it. I saw the 'Pony' as the same thing as 'lots of work'.

"*cKola*." He'd take us to the log. A short walk away we came to it, Sand-buried about half way and under a couple of small logs. "Got to take it out by hand," Walter said, "Too much sand for my saw. Get somebody dig sand then I'll help."

"Me!" I shouted, eager to involve. Even at my age I'd had experience with shoveling sand, chopping branches, cross-cut saws, one and two-man ('man') both. Already I knew why cross-cuts were called 'misery whips'. The three men laughed in satisfaction at my offer. But we learned by doing, in Village, so I'd get to try my hand, as it were. First was to dig sand. Later, to be pulling saw opposite Walter Payne would be a lesson in energy...he was a fully grown man with children my age and I'd be trying to keep with him. The confidence of the inexperienced. Walter returned to his saw-work to adjust the cut then came back.

While we were waiting for him, Mock Williams asked me about the drift logs we'd been over, looking for Cedar. "Seen any Snake People?"

"Wahss." Snakes on Beach sand?

"*Byack?*"

"Ayyy y. Three, above Bluff."

"*Ha-atch* you was lookin'. But you din't see the ball of Snake People around the one what was shedding, ain't it." I hadn't.

"They was way up in log's root-system first. Over there." He motioned toward a root-system *cKwahleh* had left beside 'the Crick'. "In Sunshine," he continued. "*cKola*, let me show you." We marched toward Lonesome Creek as he continued his lesson. "You was allus lookin' at ground. Walkin', you got to keep your eyes ev'r'where. Tell me about all around you after we crossed Lonesome Crick, what you heard, what you smelt besides drag-saw stink; what you seen."

Mock, as did most *Po-oke*, especially the Elders, hated the smells from gasoline machinery. They had come from a time *before* stinking air and never passed the chance to condemn it. Yet all owned some form of outboard motor to push their cKeynoos. Salmon Labeech's spirit notwithstanding.

We arrived at the huge root-system. Now Ocean and Beach diminished as he pointed to the still-present 'ball' of Snakes, and I saw at once there was one which seemed to be blind...eyes covered with the dull skin. "Tell me what you seen," he repeated.

I saw 'serious' on his face so in memory I raced back over the last half-hour, since Lonesome *Crick*. 'What did we pass', 'what happened with Bird or Squirrel or Mouse as we walked toward Walter Payne'. 'What did you hear?' I was stumped.

"Eh-y! Lemme skim your memory. First, them snakes. One gettin' out of it's skin. Allus look like them ones sheddin' their eyes gone blind. Normal, clear skin over their eyes has turn to be like milk color like Foster Jackson's eye, *Byack's* eye. When that happen others come from someplace an' hang around it until skin splits an' Snake can see again, has new skin, then go someplace. They was up where roots was, on a drift log an' around the one getting' new skin. Way I seen it was they was shiny against the scrubbed wood of the log an' I wondered, I looked an' they was there."

"How many Gulls was at Surf by Lonesome Crick an' why an' what?"

Mentally I tried to 'back up' half an hour until we had a distance yet to go to the Crick. Today Surf was moderate to occasional 'boomer'. I had noticed that!

Clear sky and hot Sun created diamond-color hot-spots in Surf-spray. I sensed that I had sensed a family of *Hoquat* tourists behind me. Thrilled, shrieking, a boy and girl with parents, likely, and Dog, insane in the Surf-air, alive, vital, exhuberant. I noticed that because of action, excitement. Dog was chasing Gulls which merely glided a hundred feet or so and settled again, to let the air-drunk Dog pound the wet Beach-sand as if a race-horse reaching for the end of the race. I recalled that.

Sea Gulls standing on Beach behind jetty rocks would lift and glide (on an avenue of Wind which seemed to be there) when chased, then, chased again, fly another hundred feet or so and settle, watching the inevitable ensuing chase Dog(s) which enjoyed it all.

Mental 'vision' (memory), saw one Gull wading in Crick, one on either side of Crick, all watching the Dog-chase spectacular further toward *Ta-boke*. Elated at discovering that recall 'picture' I began looking for other 'since Lonesome Crick events' in my memory.... I told him about the Gulls but could remember nothing further.

"What did you hear?"

"Can't 'member."

"*Tloquali* remember. Make your head listen to what I'm going to remember for you. "You heard Ravens talkin' over there?" (High on the Bluff).

"Ayy-y."

"*Byack* could tell us what they was sayin' over there. Was they words like *cKa-a'yo* make, 'cKah...cKah...cKah?'."

"They was garble-talkin', same's them at garbage dump, *Byacks*, talkin' to each other about stuff." Me.

"*Ha-atch*. Which done the most talkin' an' why?"

"Don't know."

"Maybe they was talkin' about Hawk gettin' Sparrow, at the Crick. You din't see that either, ain't it." He laughed. "*Be ready* to 'see' more of what you lookin' at first, an' hearin'. Don't just look, *see*. You done good goin' back to before we come to Crick. We're lookin' for you to do that. Look 'roun' you, 'f a branch on one of them Trees over there (he waved an arm in the direction of stubby Tree growth just beyond the drift logs) move by itself without no wind, why its doin' it? What kind of thing makin' it do that way?"

It excited me to think about recalling events...I had a good memory for what caught my attention...all I had to do was to *see* what I was looking at and put it to memory. I looked forward to this challenge eagerly. I recall well to this day. What good fortune to do so.

"*Eh-y* (pronounced eh-ee), *cKulell*, this shovel needs a driver. Let's get the log out for *Se-ic-tiss*," Walter called, holding up a shovel and I went to help dig a trench so an axe could be put to work cutting away stubs of branches, branches now acting as log's anchors in Sand.

Archie and I dug in the sand trying to keep ahead of it sifting into the holes. This far up from Surf and into Beach six inches produced drier sand. "Hey Wallie," Archie said, "this like trying to dig *water*, come show me how." "Practice, just like me," Walter said, laughing. "How else I got Perfect?" When Walter was sober he was funny and pleasant. Drinking he was, as Mock said, "*Bussay.*"

Dry sand above Surf line seemed to pour like Water, but wet Sand compacted. We managed to remove enough of the dry stuff at last, then Archie and Walter took axes to the branches. Soon Log could be retrieved. I thought about this a week or so later and wondered, with the largest body of water on Earth less than a hundred feet away why hadn't we bucketed up water to pour onto the dry Sand to compact it. Water can be carried. En route his barn Harvey Smith bucketed ten gallons twice a day for half a mile, washing cows' milk bags. I thought it a good idea and decided to experiment a wetting system. I did and it worked beautifully.

But now I wondered about the work being done to get the log for *Se-ic-tiss*. Respectfully but somewhat bewildered I asked, "How come we doin' this to get it for a ol' man? *Se-ic-tiss* must be hunnert. He can't do nothin' with it. He ain't got no time."

Mock kept watching the axe-men as he answered, "He need it to carve." Then, "He gots the same 'mount of time all of us got, 'cluding you."

I laughed. "But he's real old an' I'm a kid. Someday he'll be up On The Hill an' I'll be here."

"Nobody know who's gonna get crost River first ain't it. He got the same time in Living what we all got, includes you" he repeated. That bewildered me.

"How can that be if I'm a kid an' he's a old man?"

"When you gonna die?"

I shrugged. I didn't like that thought very much. Looking at the dead in coffins presented something bewildering. I remembered the drowned Dale Brumble, the strange blue hue around his mouth. "How does somebody know?"

"Don't."

"How come he got the same time left as me?"

"He got the rest of his Life, same as you; same as me. Same's all of us. That's what time we got to do stuff in, the rest of our Life."

That relieved me and I laughed because I understood immediately what he meant. It's been a motto worth-while to me ever since: Do what you want to do, you've the rest of your life to do it. You run out of time doing it you're doing what you want to do when you die.

I said, "Ayy-y-y! I'm young and he's old but I could get drownded today an' he still got time to do stuff."

"Ayy-y."

That advice rings like a bell to this day.

GO DO IT!

Billy Hudson had a *Hudson* car (before he bought the *new '39 Chevrolet*). It was a work-horse for the community. 'Hudson' had been a sedan, straight up and down ultra-moderne, 1920's style. Billy and Theodore (his eldest son) left the roof in place to cover the driver/passenger, then removed the rest down to frame and axle over which they built a wooden platform with removable side and end stakes. They had a nifty home-made flatbed, stake-side, pick-up truck. Of course the Hudson's built it for fun and Community Service. They were like that. None were faster to find ways to help than they. So, now, Village had a nice manageable vehicle Theodore or Billy alone would drive, that was their rule. Until 'cKlumbo' could drive...(Floyd Hudson). More about the truck later when I tell about the two-wheel brakes it had...both on the left side. It was fun. Harrowing is more the term but I wouldn't have missed it.

Anyway, today again. How Billy knew to drive to Beach today, to carry the log to Willie's yard I knew not; I know not. The process of retrieval was engineering to match temple-building of long ago. Rope was wound around the log with ends wound under the succeeding wraps. Finally the loop, which is what remained, was laid over a bolt in the front part of the car's frame.

Loop in place Billy eased the rope to tension in reverse-gear ("reverse, it's more slower an' powerfuller" Billy said, "won't spin the wheels"). The rest of us with pry-poles on the side opposite the tow-truck strained mightily but still buried in sand were branches we couldn't reach to chop. The shaking together with the nearly snail-crawl of the truck, axes to branches worked, and wham! in minutes the log rolled out of the hole and onto Beach. The men made short work of the rest of the branches. Now to deliver to *Se-ic-tiss*'s house.

HobbiesMitt had a 'field-sled', a sort of Summer-harvest 'field-taxi. Ten-foot long Alder tree trunks (runners) had been rounded up, sled-like, at the 'front end', overlaid with a deck of small poles to haul cargo. His draught-horses (one or both) pulled it. HobbiesMitt brought that to Beach that evening and helped by a crowd of musclers, including a few of the commercial Salmon fishers, the three-foot Cedar log, at least fifteen feet long, was set in place on the sled, lengthwise, and as easy as blinking the eyes, Hudson's Hudson, pulling the sled along the Surf-wet Sand, (front-wards now), had outrun the chasing Children and gone to *Se-ic-tiss*'s to off-load the log.

From this retrieved log *Se-ic-tiss* worked with Ada Black's husband in carving the Quileute 'logo', Thunder-bird and Whale. It stands sentinel in La Push today. Ada's husband was large among Indian People at La Push. Horace Bright was bigger than the average Village man, (yet he was not in the six-foot one or so range of Ada's Man, like Fred 'Sonny' Woodruff today). Ada's Man did all the muscle work for *Se-ic-tiss*. I spent a lot of time at the carving-site watching the release of the subject: It's in there, *Se-ic-tiss* would repeat, "Got to help it out." Little else occupied my attention while the 'release' was ongoing. And ah! the smell of freshly cut Cedar!

I stood on one foot, balancing, then the other, offering to sweep chips into bags for fire-starting; run errands; whatever *Se-ic-tiss* might want. I hoped against hope to be involved, not realizing that what I was doing was involvement. I was learning by watching, first, later would come hatchet and d'adze experience.

MORE LESSONS

Before fall hunting-season *Se-ic-tiss* Ward and Joe Pullen took me to Beach. 'Lessons' were due. I see now that my incessant babbling (involving carving, and Cake Rock, and Jackson Creek, and the wrecked ship Temple Bar, and Life exhuberance in general) was to them as *cKa'a'yo* calling out to others would be to me. Today, listening to memory, I guess I never stopped talking about *Po-oke* Life; about anything. Yet I believe they welcomed it because exhuberant reaction to *Po-oke* ways was declining among our young as car and airplane and other *Hoquat* intrusion diminished the Old Ways. Newness.

This day we arrived at Beach near Lonesome Crick and sat on a log in such way as to look away from Surf, facing almost North.

"We'll find out what you see, *cKulell*." We sat facing Trees and Joe said, "Tell us ev'rythin' you see goin' on."

I looked at anything and everything of interest to me. The usual Drift-log activities were obvious. There was Wren and what we called Chipmunk and *cKa'a'yo* and Sparrow, and I reported them.

"*Hoquat* sees them things. What you see others don't?" *Se-ic-tiss*.

"Just what I seen." Me.

He laughed lightly and said, "Too bad you dint see nothin'. You got to learn how seeing gets done first. If you keep movin' you head an' eyes you can't let nothing '*signal*' you…ev'rythings moving, you an' game. Right now while you was lookin' your eyes was moving a-a-all the time, here an' there, you head was movin'."

Joe Pullen said, "What you got to do is *SEE*, like *Tss'ay-whutleokes* do

When you out huntin' you need to let stuff come to you eyes. What you do, pick a place to look at. Fix you sight there, don't change that

234

spot while you wait for stuff to happen over there. While you lookin', 'stead of you moving head and eyes finding stuff, you let you eyes pick motion in many places, signaling you, around your picked spot. After while, nothings happen, move you gaze. But understand, what you lookin' to see if you do *still-gazing*, it's gonna happen."

Both looked at me to see if I was paying attention or understanding them. *Se-ic-tiss* said, "You lookin' at no motion an' so motion signals you to see! Don't blink both eyes same time. Let things move into you vision first." *Se-ic-tiss* elbowed Joe Pullen and said, "Tell him some more." Joe remained silent.

I was confused by the 'don't blink' instruction and asked about it. "Eyes gonna get dry an' burn," I said. "How can somebody not blink?"

Se-ic-tiss said, "Easy. Don't blink both eyes same time. When both eyes blink at same time you ain't seein' nothin for 'the while' they're shut. Might be just then something you should know about happen an' you miss it."

"Eyes blink together by their self."

"Control that. Blink one eye when you need to blink, open it, then blink other one. That way, you watchin' a place, something happen around there then you see it, *you allus got one eye open*, watchin'. You got to 'see' same way as Owl does, blinks one eye then other, allus seein', seein', turnin' its head, one eye allus open. Do it now an' see what happen."

I tried and found it a clumsy practice at best. We laughed because of the confusion of both eyes staring until hot, then blinking one, the other, both at once…but they did it. I'd do it. I don't remember what success I had that day. But I learned that action and, observings that came of themselves, without being sought after, were easier to develop than I would have believed. I was elated…here was *Po-oke* way of doing not known to many hunters. Stanley Grey *hunted this way*! I wanted to go to Hoh River and scan for Elk; China Pheasant (called 'Ring Necks), *Hoo-Day Hoo-Day* Girls (daughters of *cKwyeh-Tee*), *Waysotsopot Hib Hib*…Grouse Woman). Even to watch here in Village as Crows or Gulls sailed the Wind, with eyes fixed at a distant and perhaps non-object spot, (as, in a cloud), and to practice the 'Seeing' skill was so rewarding that I still 'see' that way.

The eyes were likewise involved in 'clearing the mind of actions'. One stares at a neutral place, neither dark nor light, (medium grey is best) and lets the eyes go out of focus, so nothing registers specifically.

In the state of mind when the eyes are unfocused there is nothing to interfere with losing random, unnecessary thought (which draws energy from the body of the mind-clearing person. Removed that waste energy is there to go into the 'Spirit' realm).

The ability to be 'natural' about individual eye-blinking, the 'recallability' of seeing 'motion out there' registering itself rather than to be looked for as I would have done, these practices (of letting things reveal themselves rather than to try to find them, and more) were easy to develop. Soon I could see more 'as a 'statue" than my head and eye motion might find. Soon *Hib Hib*, moving one foot, then the other, carefully, revealed itself by even the slow movement. I *saw* when my vision was unwaveringly fixed at one place. Then I was seeing inclusively.

Then Joe Pullen said, "You learn to hear same way. Somethin's out there movin' an' you can't locate it exactly, close you eyes and point you nose where you think the sound come from. Tilt you head side to side an' up an' down, pin-pointin' the spot. Then open you eyes an' see with one eye allus open. That way you find stuff easy. Same thing with smell. Sniff toward where it gets strongest an' when sound and smell comin' together you startin' to be *Tss'ay-whutleoke*." I nodded understanding. *Se-ic-tiss* laughed a laugh impossible to describe. I loved to hear him laugh. Then I thought of Stanley Grey. No wonder Stanley was respected for Elk hunting power…he knew how to be successful.

I began to isolate certain stimulations and found that mice and bugs and other sounds began to be easier to locate; to be commonplace observations. Even though they might have been under some cover… when I was *silent,* they revealed themselves.

BURYING *Chutsk*

Robert Taylor was a Forks undertaker who prepared and oversaw *Po-oke* burials for many years. In mind's eye I see his hearse, a full coffin inside, backing to the old Shaker Church to begin another final ceremony.

Recalling funerals I see bleak, Coastal days (evening-dark at noon), little light from Sky and that all but shut out by a dark, grey, Rain laden cloud. Horizon to Tree, one cloud. And Rain pounding Earth as if angry. In 'those days recalled', I see folded news-papers held over head and shoulders; coats pulled high enough so collar was on forehead; hats held to block Rain from the face; any and all ways to 'beat Rain' were tried but Rain always won as we raced to get into Church even moderately dry. I never saw an umbrella at La Push.

Misty time-visions see *Po-oke* sloshing through Church-yard mud-holes made where cars had parked for hours on previous visits. It was funny to watch because trying to leap past water to hit occasional 'dry places' made the 'dodger' into a dancer. It was a dance they did, not for humor, but 'funny' because each person did a personal dance learned as 'best for me' in getting to Church. Some were beautiful to see. Sometimes even in uninvited pratfall. Mostly these were Children feeling the urge to jump, run, slide, etc., so they did. Challenging, challenging, challenging Life, to see the limit of Life's control over 'me'. Where are Children different?

However I may recall those somber days, the sadnesses felt by all of Village remains in me vividly as physical ache for what we were; how we felt. Our sadness as well as our joys.

Coffin-making always saddened us. We made coffins for *Chutsk* of wood salvaged from new packing boxes in which Salmons might be iced and sent to Seattle. And painted them if we had paint. The 'Coasties' always seemed to be able to drop off paint for us.

Especially I remember the burial of Nellie Williams' Girl-Child, which I attended during a return from California to Village in 1958. Wind drove Rain at us relentlessly. A typical funeral day. In Church Charlie Howeattle officiated as Shaker Minister, with whatever 'civilized world's burial contribution' was filled by Robert Taylor. (His sincerity in sorrow with us over our losses was real. We all liked Taylor. As we had liked deputy sheriff 'Holly' [Hollingsworth?] assigned to the Forks area. And George Krause. Understanding of *Po-oke*).

Charlie drummed and sang some 'strangely worded song' (which I learned later was once-upon-a-time from Russia). Then Chris Morganroth began to drum and sing with Charlie. Neither of them could sing Russian songs with knowledge other than mimicry but the sincerity was there. Lavan Coe knew several of the Russ songs. One Russian had been here in the early to middle 1800's and the last Quileute to sing Russian songs knowing what they meant was Lavan Coe, according to Uncle Yum. (I heard that the Russian was a survivor of the wreck of the ship San Nicholas from Sitka)

This song Chris and Charlie were singing was a heavily corrupted imitation of Russian but we all knew it was what they did in Russia. Maybe. And we clapped our hands together with the rhythm set by the drumming and shaking rattles and clack-clack of Cedar sticks. Then, by the candle-lighted altar someone began to ring Shaker bells.

Rhythm keeping with bells and drums and Cedar-sticks built to a crescendo which was augmented by rhythmic stomping of feet. We mourned with an almost middle-Eastern wailing. From someone, 'tremelo'. The saddest part of these ceremonies was that our sorrows were for ourselves: we knew that the Quileute, people who called themselves *Po-oke*...the People...were soon to be dead.

Mourners/worshippers followed a path well known to each participant. Some then entered another dimension of cognition. Transcending the mundane of Life *outside* Church was transition to '*inattention to 'normalcy*'' and to the presence of ubiquitous Spirit feeling and power.

Doors away from Church the encompassing vitality of rejection of the mundane world filled the area with penetrating rhythmic sound as less and less restraint robed the participants and as one, all sang and kept military-like rhythm with bells, drums, sticks, stomping and prayer; *with whatever kept the rhythm.*

There in Church we brought back to ourselves the Spirit of 'the River Crosser' and sent our Spirits with that one recently departed. In those days we lived Life seeing no 'separation' of 'things' and saw all elements of living as having to obey Laws set by Great Spirit. Laws which, creating all, encompassed all and therefore All (encompassment of what is) puts *everything together* dependent on what it is itself: Life. The same Spirit presence that visits who seek Quest, the entry of '*Taxilit*' into the seeker.

The body is less involved with mobile Life now than then, but is still involved with the processes of Life, Body being obedient to Laws for what it is; Spirit obedient to its Laws. Absolutely unavoidable. Unavoidably absolute. It's hard to rationalize that away.

So we continued the bond with the one mourned, in Spirit if not in flesh. In Church we separated ourselves from 'out there', our minds focused on a common goal (continuation of attachment to the departed) and concentrated on transcending to more in-depth awareness of the non-ending of ongoing Life. The overwhelming thrill of completion, by way of realization is attainable and powerful. We knew the endlessness of Spirit involvement with all Life's processes. Now our recognition of the departed's presence in Spirit is as if our response to the Spirit is no less than were the person/condition to have been present. As if behind us. As the silent person behind and not seeing nor seen by another is felt, it is felt by Spirit. There is no physical contact, but awareness *is.*

By rejecting more and more of *the conceit of the consciousness* (the 'I' aware and *enacting* person) as secondary in importance to palpable communion with the Universal Life Spirit, spiritual identity with All which is, the 'River Crosser' remained with The People. And we remained with that Person in Spirit.

Was and is any of that correct? Our experience said 'yes'. I think so now. In our way of Religion we cut off no hands; burned none at stakes; imprisoned none in dungeons; wiped out no hamlets nor villages; we salted no farm-lands, thereby destroying Life sustaining Earth as if it were our property to corrupt and ruin. We tried to pass through Life in beneficial relationships with all Life and spent much of our Lives in effort to attain that experience of actuality: True HARMONY with Great Spirit.

So, in Shaker Church we concentrated our minds onto the Harmony Great Spirit developed, and worked to Live according to those dictates. And once imbued as much as possible with the Oneness with Life (which *death* forced us to see), we left Church and went with our now Eternal relative to *The Hill* to put constancy into the 'newly', (totally), Spiritual being. The sorrow was largely that we wouldn't be able to associate with the departed 'Tribal relative' in 'physical person' again. We got lonesome for friends and relatives and that in Life or death.

On The Hill we were confronted with a Reality of Life: Unhindered Change And realization of the quickness with which Life alters to 'something else'. We *imagine* an 'after-Life as being, though un'seen' by any but rarely gifted 'seekers', [they who've given a Life-time of study to the unapparent of Life]).

At the open Earth where our mourned departee would be placed forever-more, we waited action by someone who understood our sorrow in depth.

Then Chris and Little Bill Penn (Uncle Yum) and Johnny Jackson and Robert Taylor lowered the smaller, home-made Coffin as the rest waited for this scene to end, as do movies, so we could leave with our lost one fully restored and, outrun the sorrow. But how outrun Reality?

Cold, wet, surrounded by bleakness like dead Winter, hearing 'muffled-by-Trees' Surf, caught up in the sorrowing relatives' anguish, hearing the drum(s) begin as a (or several-together) mourner(s) put drum-beats to song; it was possible to feel the oppressive pressure of anguish as one feels Wind; Heat. As wetness from *cKwia* spread over the Group, supportive relatives…at La Push everyone is related… cried with the grieving parents as family. The tears were for the unspeculatable unknown to which we must bow. We could feel Spirit; all Life Creatures 'feel' Spirit. It's what they are.

Then came the inimitable *drum-beat sound* of dirt shoveled onto the waiting casket. It is hollow, a booming, attention grabbing sound; penetrating; unique. No sound resembles that of dirt falling onto a casket just beginning to be covered. That sound rings in memory. Heard once, unforgotten. It rings through the woods surrounding the little cemetary; it echos in the resemblance to slammed smoke-house-door sound, in a shoe dropped to floor; in a 'push-pole' or paddle dropped into cKeynoo, yet these are but reminders of the one specific sound: The first shovel load of dirt onto Baby's coffin. In fact any coffin.

Rain, *cKwia*, pours over all. Streams of muddy water rise over the rim of the grave-site and into the hole. Around the lowered coffin dirt dropped into the grave splashes as thick mud-soup while we work to cover *Chutsk* then go ourselves to dryness and warmth. Misery in the form of Wind forced the cold, wet Rain into our anguish making it more depressing. Every seam on clothing let in water.

Chutsk's coffin was dirt-covered and the casket-drumming sound was now changed to sloshing wet-dirt sound. Heavy breathing sound came as diggers worked to the pulse of singing and drumming. This continued until three or four drummers were singing. And the DRUM. Two pulse-beats a second while Singers sang to EARTH, to GOD therefore, the Ultimate Powers upon which our Lives are based.

When tremolo (not frequent at La Push) came into the songs the surprise brought tears to me...the heart-break throb was not for the Child alone. Unconscious to us all *but known*: Each dead child brought *Po-oke* that much closer to forevermore. Every Child dead was a good-bye to Quileute ways. Every half-breed Child born put a Full-blood in the ground. The sadness was for our own demise.

Suddenly Rain and Wind stopped, clouds thinned then parted and Sun shined onto Bay and Beach and Village.

And Hill. In moments the beaming Sun-heat caused a steamy vapor to rise from any bush or blade of Grass and we saw this vapor as rising to take *Chutsk* Spirit with it. We took this as a sign from Great Spirit that Nellie's Child was now "...crost *Taboke* and home'.

The feeling of elation which accompanied this swept over us as an instantaneous transition of mood. Cheers and approval and assurance to Nellie of the meaning and importance of Weather change energized us and the burial progressed to the placement of symbols and totems and flowers...always the flowers. Even if they were sometimes fake; *Po-oke* love color. We drummed and sang with Hope now! With fire and passion: the sense of *Surety!* Great Spirit, Great Mystery, Our source of Life, had touched us with Hope. Great Spirit had taken one of us home and given a message about it.

Then we returned to Meeting Hall beside Shaker Church where we ate and told about our good fortune in having the food and care which Great Spirit provided. A cash collection and parcels of remembrance were passed around, then we drifted slowly out onto our own Rivers of action, having expressed our love and hope to Nellie.

And to one another.

CEDAR

No more could the word 'Air' be said than we smelled Cedar. We Lived in Cedar scent. Kindling for fire-starting; paddles a-forming for who made paddles from Cedar; Cedar strips pulled from trees for the creation of baskets and mats; capes…Cedar-smell, and Fish, perfumed *Po-oke* homes. Bundles of Cedar strips for basket-weaving hung from hooks or nails in ceilings, walls; dried bundles were piled in boxes, stuffed under beds.

How could *Po-oke* live without the fragrance of what provided for us: Cedar, which was always near enough to stoves to dry and send the fragrance throughout House. Cedar shingles roofed our houses; Cedar logs were being formed into cKeynoo. We were never away from Cedar-smell in Village. We didn't talk about the importance of Cedar to our Lives anymore than we talked of finger nails growing. We couldn't have Lived without Cedar. Cedar became important to us as gift from *cKwyeh-Tee*.

cKwyeh-Tee AND SOME OF HIS 'DEEDS'

In reply to my question about 'origins' Uncle Yum recorded the following Legends for me in 1958:

"They a...there's a...there is a lot of things that comes to me that the people explain in legend that goes back to...to a time where it was true...it was true.

It was true. Like this ah...the Indian live here long ago, an' there was a man that was formin' animals or fish or somethin' into human bein'. They call him '*cKwyeh-Tee*'. He turn to other form of ...well, he turns things to other form...maybe Animal; maybe Human.

"Come(s) to Hoh River. That's before there was any White-man or Indians or any Human bein' a tall. He went over there an' he make a fish trap an' he place a Cottonwood...a Cottonwood stick right there on the bank. He said, 'If there is any red-skinned fish comin' down an' get into trap, you holler...wake me up.' To the Stick. He went to bed there.

"He hollered, 'Hey! He-y-y-y, fish comin' down went in the trap'.

"*cKwyeh-Tee* come up there an' he pull up the trap an' no fish. He get this...this Cotton-wood stick, he says, 'Why you lie to me like that? You will not be used by the Indians or the people that's goin' to inhabit here, because you good for nothin'. You will be no good for fire-wood, 'cause you will be wet all the time.' That was the punishment for lyin'...useless to the People.

"So he went over there and place a...a Spruce...Spruce, put it there, an' Spruce done the same thing—he lied to him. He woke him up there was the red-skinned fish comin' down. No fish. He said 'You lie to me again.' He throw it away. 'You will burn, when they use you for fire-wood but when they begin to stir you 'round, to poke you, you gonna go out...you turn black.' That was the punishment. Useless.

"So he come...he come to Knot. He find Knot in the river. Place it in there. He hollered, 'Well,' he hollered, 'there is a fish in there!'" Well, right enough there was a fish. Red-skinned. A male fish...male fish there.

"An' he said, 'You tell the truth to me. You gonna be useful to people that's gonna in-habit this place. You will be more useful than anything to burn, even if they get it from...in the water, you will burn as if you was dried in the Woods. Even Cedar ain't gonna be as useful in the people's fires as you gonna be.'

"That's what...that was his reward. That's why the Indians use that, even if it's in the water they take it up...up there to use for fire. That was Knot's reward for tellin' the truth. He was always useful to the people. The greatest reward. Even today...even a thousand years from now...his reward for truth stand as from the beginning of time. This is always the reward for truth.

"So *cKwyeh-Tee* went up an' cut the fish up...cut the inside. There was two size of milt bag there——the large size, see, they have that, you know...the milt bag of the male fish. There is two...two of them...one on each side an' one is bigger. It was Salmons, a red-skin Silversides, goin' up the river. So there was this small size milt, it was kind of dis-color, not exact white, an' there was this liver, an' somethin' else...he picked five kinds from that fish; five parts of its body, an' he put that away an' it turn to Human form.

"One was the extra white; one was this kind of yellowish like; one the brown, an' red an' black."

Uncle Yum pounded his forefinger on the table. "How did the Indians know at that time there was five kind of people in the face of the earth? That was before the White-man come to this side...long ago.

"It could be...you could...you could ask what was the parts used—what part did he use for different color of people. What part did he use for the black...Negro people? How did the Indians know there was Negro people? Well, anyway, I think they...they use the back, you know, the backbone...that is, the ah, well, you know the inside the fish backbone is your blood. Blood. He use that. It turn black when the fish is dead. He use it inside along the backbone. It's black like Negro people.

"They use the one white milt for White-man. The one just lily-bit off white, he use it for the ah...the Japanese—for the Yellow man, Chinee.. They use the one for the Brown race of man, that is, the liver...an' the Red-skin on outside he's makin' up the Indian people... Indian race with it. He use it...ev'rythin'.

"He put it all aside an' it come to take on Human form.

"Anyway it turn out to be all girls, all the part. All girls. So...cKwyeh-Tee was the only man, an' he was oldish man...ugly lookin' man. He was a man—he was a...he was a man that can turn ev'eythin' into different forms, you know.

"He wasn't the Creator...well, in one way he was, in one way he wasn't. He wasn't recognized as a big man like that. But he can do lo-o-o-ots a tricks, he...his tricks was above ev'rybody else...do lots of forms of work.

"An' ah...well. Well. Well, you know. Him alone with all them girls. Well, he ah...he try to get...try to get with the girls, you know. Can't do it because they know him, it was him.

"So he goes over there an' turn himself into a little baby. Cryin' an' the girls found him. Well, they took him home...a little boy. Well, he cried an' cried an' cried until the best lookin' girl get him—take it to bed for warm an' comfort an' now he stop cryin', see, an' begin...he begin to turn into a big human man, you know, an' they know him. Throw him out.

"So that...one day, they left. They come to be full grown Girls now. Full grown. They left. They was goin' to look for...for mate. They walked and walked. Finally they come to a...to a...to a *Hib Hib*... Grouse. Spring of the year. An' there was the Mother, drummin', out in the Woods an' a old lady was...a little lady was pullin' the spring-pole on this little baby. Old Lady was blind. She was blind. An' here the Girls was an' they find it was a male...so...they took it, they took this babe, stoled it from the old Woman, an' She know, She sensed it; it was them Girls.

"She said—she hollered to this Grouse Woman, 'Here? You still drummin'? This ah...*Hoo-Day Hoo-Day* Girls took you Child away... they stoled it.' (*Hoo-Day Hoo-Day*, that means *cKwyeh-Tee*'s children). So She...Grouse Woman, look up an' notice, doin' that, you know, (twisted Her head sideways to listen), with the head you know, try to listen some more. An' finally She find out what She wants; here She comes, you know, goin' back an' forth on the ground an' She find that the Baby was gone, right enough.

"She took this Old Lady on Her back an' track them from Sky, down the Beach, up the Beach, goin'…goin'…once in a while She'd throw this Old Lady on the ground, like that, an' She discharge lo-o-o-o-ots a water, an' sometimes cause a river. Every once in a while She done that as She fly up the Beach. Throw the Old Lady down. The object was, to try an' get the Girls this side of the river so She can catch them, so they won't have a chance to go across. Sometimes She make a lake, She discharge so much water, turn it into a lake. Goin'.

"Finally they saw a little track; Boy is walkin' now. So. They give up. She give up when She saw the Boy is getting' big, walkin'. He was big enough to walk. That…they give up when they know the Boy can take care of the Girls. He is big enough now to take care of them when they have needs.

"So the races of man is started by *cKwyeh-Tee*'s daughters, *Hoo-Day Hoo-Day* Girls an' the son of Grouse Woman. He (*cKwyeh-Tee*) make it all from Fish.

"That's how come the races of man-kind, how come rivers an' lakes an' how it come to be that certain things has more value for the Indian people than other things when it come to be makin' fires." He drummed and sang and I drove him to his nieces house.

I don't know much about Fir or Yew from the standpoint of legend but both plants were used by ancestors 'until the Thirties'. Strong, straight and powerful, as, bows from Yew for hunting. I don't know how and why *cKwyeh-Tee* arranged for their appearance and why they were so highly respected. Some test by *cKwyeh-Tee* I know nothing about.

Among Northwest Native Peoples, Makah knew of *cKwyeh-Tee*; Ozette; S'cKlallam; Chimacum; Hoh. He was involved with the Lives of most around the Olympic Peninsula so there is no mystery to the manner of his existence except to those outside the area.

VILLAGE'S BRAIN

With a friend Uncle Yum and I drove to Lake Ozette in August 1958. We hiked through Ahlstrom's Prairie to Cape Alava (I wish others could have tried to keep up with 65 year old Uncle Yum on that three mile hike), then back to Ozette. Later, beside Lake we ate a picnic lunch. While we were eating he told us of several *Po-oke* characteristics and knowledges.

Among these was about Village Brain; about Thunderbird and Whale and another was about the round rocks of Beaver Prairie. He had pointed to these that day, having spotted some of the few remaining 'Thunderbird eggs', (occasional rocks on that Prairie's several fields. While the town of Sappho *was*, these round rocks were frequently used by the inhabitants to line their auto driveways. A few years ago I tried to find even one to show to Joanne but in vain: none were to be found).

Uncle Yum was thoughtful, "Village is a 'result' you can't describe... you feel it. Can't be described, Village." He continued, "Village has its own Life. Which is its location first. Being it's someplace it's something. It's not like no place else on Earth. Two places can't be on the same spot so each is different.

"Any place Life is concentrated there's Action. Rock pile has 'action' only if something moves it, otherwise always same. *Life* in action makes changes to 'always different': Altered from being always unchanged. Village, (Life concentrations, like Humans, *kadido* (dog), *po-osh* (cat), *cKa'a'yo* crow,, Houses, Cooking Fires, etc.,) has result that's Total Interaction. Result is Village Life; Life of Village.

"No 'good' or 'bad' results from ongoing Life of Village. Excitement caused by Fear, or Panic, or Joy, cause 'big activity'. Fighting away invading neighbors making sneak attack on us cause big activity. Often from *Ahkalut* we fought Makahs when they come warrin'. Elders claimed it was from *Ahkalut* top. Makah, they got poured over by hot water, left.

"Mostly, Village Life is from human behavior, what caused Village in the first place. Whoever is the population of Village at any time is what cause its 'personality'.

"Ev'ry thin', Robin, Snake, ev'ry Living thing Living under some influence of Village, gives Life back to Village. All Life things 'think' (what they need to survive: Survival Need). It comes there's one great over-ridin' Thought. Results from the combined thoughts of all. Total of all is *One* an' the One is Village Thought. From Village 'Brain'.

"One way or other ev'rythin' in Village behaves as Village Life dictate. Village Brain in charge. Village behavior is result. You see this workin' when you watch flocks of flying Snipes. Or any Birds what Live grouped. They fly along, swerve, all goin' the new way, now, all of a sudden they change again, goin', an' another direction. Evasion? Seen food on Beach? Heh, that way! Heh, this way! Heh, settle an' eat! Heh! Go again. All at same time in same direction. Some kind of chance? Nope. Flock Brain. All of 'em tuned to it. Same as us, *Po-oke*: Village Brain. All of us tuned to it.

"They do what they do different than as if they was lone, like Eagle. Like Meadowlark. These act by the lone Brain they got. For 'swarmers' seem like it work like radio does, somethin' send out music or news an' all (he said 'a-a-a-a-l-ll') the radios 'play' the music they been told to play.

"Watchin' flocks of flyin' Birds, you figger how they all move same way same time? Watch Smelts. They swirl 'round each other, dartin', flashin', divin', allus movin' same way toward same place together. Herrings. Pilchards. Can't deny Naturalness. Natural to be Natural.

"Village Brain is combined from each Creature of Village so then each Creature of Village receives in-put. Result is How To Behave. Mouse in house live different when Cat move in. Village Brain got more power over Villagers than anybody know. When you do stuff, figure out if Village Brain is in charge or if you doin' what you're doin' without control from all the things makin' up Village Brain."

(As an observation about flock-Birds wheeling and darting and swooping with common but bewildering unpredictability, downtown

Seattle in the Yesler vicinity several flocks of Starlings perform some amazing precision flying. Watch at dusk).

"Remember, what you think and do give Power and Control to Village Brain. Look how good to have Village Brain giving out what it get shown: received an' sent Harmony."

Uncle Yum looked out toward the South end of Lake Ozette, silent now. Sometimes I think about his birth-place down by *Bo-ckWa cheel* (near the end of the Forks airport runway) in a Smokehouse, in 1893. He spoke of boy-hood there at times. Now, was he musing about a vast 'homeland on which to live directed by Tribal custom' (rather than by made up laws in books which few seemed to obey, gov'mint or religion-talkers)? Or, simply, was he enjoying the view on this lovely August day?

After a short while he observed to 'Universal understanding' (as much as to me), "But Harmony don't come from booze."

That sad commentary was followed by silence as each of us thought over the implications of people where booze is concerned and the havoc wrought at the "breath' of' booze'. The silence was also because now that we'd eaten we became lethargic in the noon-day Sun.

We enjoyed a brief siesta before we drove back to Ozette store for dessert. Ice-cream cones in hand we stood against the north-side railing for the bridge over Ozette River and as I looked at the water and rocks I saw the outline of Thunderbird as plainly designed as if done on purpose. I pointed it out to Uncle Yum. He almost choked he became so excited on seeing the image, "*That's you Tomanamus, cKulell,* that's you *Power!* You got *Thunderbird* Power! Take the picture! You got to keep the image of Thunderbird!"

He was still elated over the discovery as we pulled up to Phil Riebe's house in La Push where Uncle Yum was staying temporarily. (Riebe married one of Uncle Yum's nieces, Vi, then a lovely young Woman, now a widow and 'still good lookit' Uncle would say).

My remaining visit time was melting as ice melts. Henceforth was a burst of 'speed-up' in order to get into my La Push visit everything possible. In early August Chris Morganroth Sr.; Uncle Yum; my wife and I drove to the Huelsdonk farm on Hoh River to visit Elizabeth 'Betten' (Huelsdonk) Fletcher and Her husband John.

We had no more than departed Riebe's house where Uncle Yum and Chris had waited for me than Uncle Yum spoke of the Thunderbird photo. He'd told Chris about it earlier. Uncle Yum wanted me to send a copy of the photo to him. Alex Camera Exchange in San Diego made a beautiful enlargement of it and I guessed he got it, I never heard again.

BROKEN STRIDE

I'm to tell you about 'broken stride'. One Woman took Her husband's Eagle feather, doe-skin, beaded, dentalium rain-cape to Tacoma to pawn. For ten-dollars. The last one known. When he discovered the loss (his son told him what had happened) five days after the loss/ theft, (that's what it became), he went to Tacoma to claim it. Had to file a police report. They went to the pawn-shop to retrieve it but for whatever mysterious reason it couldn't be located and nevermore was found. Priceless. I saw the cape myself and can draw a picture of it but that's only a picture. The Woman knew She must not return to La Push and didn't.

He was heartbroken and really never recovered from the shock of losing the most ancient and irreplaceable of Village artifacts left after the Village was fired in the late 1800's..

I asked Charlie Howeattle how come she'd done this. " ' get booze, *cKulell*."

"What's so good 'bout booze?" My vision of booze was the disgusting conditions displayed by drunks stinking of beer, white flecks at the mouth corners, eyes wallowing as if a sledged steer; not in control of body functions…disgusting.

"Booze takes away smart mind and practically everything done is thoughtless. *Thought* hurts them what gots to booze-up. Many booze-up because their 'stride' got broke."

"Nobody knows why *Her* stride got broke. She never found it again. Same thin' with him but he din't take to boozin'-up. His treasure from his family was gone it broke his stride. Pretty hard to recatch you stride when it get broke. Got to try keepin' you stride. Don't give up. Don't give up never. Keep you own stride. That's you *Life's rhythm*; music of you Soul. Don't let nothin' break you stride." He was right. Booze has no power to improve Human thought; behavior or intellect that I've seen.

MARY and
Se-ic-tiss WARD

S tanley Gray met me as I left Skoobuss one late afternoon in winter. *"cKola.* 'Sco-over there." I ran home to tell where I'd be. "Heard drummin' when I left Skoobuss so goin' to be with Stanley an' them ones."

"Don't forget *ahlash.*"

"Won't." I ran toward Howeattle's corner Lodge-hall and burst onto the porch as one possessed, then walked lightly, one foot ahead of the other, Indian style, so as to roll my weight, 'to be lighter'. I'm sure the crash on the porch wasn't noticed. Inside all eyes were locked on Door to see what danger caused that huge thump. I looked down, moderately subdued by the 'frowns', then looked up, lip popping drew my attention and *Se-ic-tiss* was wiggling a finger, 'come here' it said.

I moved to kneel by *Se-ic-tiss* Ward, *Eldest of the Elders!* Imagine the thrill of being seating-partner with *THE ELDER?* For a ten-year old? In Quileute he said, "We hearin' 'bout Jesus an' them." That meant all that pertained to the many 'gods' various preachers kept bringing to Village to sell. Immediately I thought about the things I'd heard about Jesus and *cKwyeh-Tee* and the varied 'power people' who were with us even unto this day, as it were.

I blurted a question: "How come he to walk on water? I can't do it no matter how hard I try. Washes over my feet gets 'em wet." Today I imagine the humor the Elders saw in that but I was serious.

Also: How come like Billy Hudson says, he can't talk *Po-oke* to tell *us* 'bout hisself? The *then* 'presently-preached' story about 'Miracle-Men'.

Mock Williams said, "That's their business. That's the way them folks make a living. Why I don't believe in what they say is same like Billy. Same like Grant Eastman. Same like Lavan Coe. Same like 'em all."

"What's that?" I asked.

"How you gonna start believin' 'bout some god who let their 'believers' kill an' steal an' isolate somebody else who don't deserve being butchered? Good 'god' got good followers ain't it. Ain't gonna believe about no 'creating 'god'' with Love an' understandin' what lets one part of what it made destroy a other part of what it made like one is important an' one ain't. Can't believe in something ain't got 'sacredness', perfect Balance. I listened to what was said by one and other, taking in the smart-talk words about 'all perfect all knowing God' who sent them to wreck us. But their 'god' couldn't talk Quileute to us."

Drumming and singing, which informed about us, continued until no one put more wood into Stove, then, out into the dark with *Se-ic-tiss*. This was about 1941, late Fall, early winter. We walked past Howeattles's store and house and up a slight rise of the road past Joe Pullen's house on the left and Black's on the right. We were going to his home. In a move so surprising that I feel the sensation as I write, he put his hand on my shoulder and said, "*Hotch all*" (walk slower). I asked if he was OK and he replied, "Ayy- but '*ibbPo-oke*' (Old Indian.)"

He motioned me to follow him into the house and sit. In the old rocker-chair (HobbiesMitt and WesleesMitt had given him for his 80th birthday) he sat facing me. (Remember, my language skills were 10 years experienced and his were over 80). He presented a new view of Life to me. This is the 'feel' of his words, the sequence, etc., are not likely to be as they occurred 70 years ago, but what I carried away is this:

"I been seeing through clear air lately, on down-hill trail, easy to follow. *Every* day I see last Horizon of Life now. I'm packing away stuff in my head and heart. Looking over memories. In my head I had to stop walking for a while so I could look back at the trail I been on and see all that I seen, walking. Then I went by myself on 'old Person quest.' Remember everybody looking for me? I'd took old trail to Hoh so I could look back without problem, best to be alone ' you trying to remember. Way down the trail (memory) I see when first *Hoquats* moved to the territory we once used for keeping alive. Some liked *Hoquat*, some didn't. Mostly it was curious: new ways.

"Some of them who came to Mora and Quillayute I knew to talk to but not as friend, Taylor; James; Anderson; Sprowel; Smitt (Smith). Looking back from this little ridge I'm on I see Mary and me. Family come from Her. She knew (how) to build good *Chutsk*. She was the best Woman.

"Also I see other stuff going on, on the trail I been on from my Mother. Misery been big for us since *Hoquat* come with guns, moved us. But they don't know the happiness we (them near my time) seen on the trail. *Happiness don't work for them.* Always been mystery for us. Always wants something else; different; better. Like killing Elks. They want biggest, strongest, smartest one dead, on the wall. Think about killing best and leaving less good for making next generations. Hunting you always leave biggest and best to breed better stock all the time coming up. Funny how they don't care about Living things except to kill and eat. Don't see *other things* as People like us, just looking different; different costumes on. Like them shows *Hoquat*s put together Chrissmuss, ev'rybody in different costume, but all alive as People.

"Trail ahead is smooth now, all down-hill no boulders. Now Horizon I been trying to see for 20, 25 years I can see it, real close. Hope I get to be awake when I get there so I can enjoy starting the new trip." His laugh at this was contagious. A fun-filled, exhuberant, contagious laugh. "I hope some of them is waiting for me to get there, not gone too far ahead. When I was a boy I had a *kadido*, gone there before me. Her name was in Russia language, 'SoocKa', from the Old Russian guy who lived with Howeattle family when his ship beached. Where I was was SoocKa. Licked my hand when She was dyin'. *Chicko'sido....* Died." He felt pain even today about her.

"She's waiting. All of 'em I know over there waitin'. I stand 'here' on this little rise and I see Horizon best of all. Looking back I see why we get born first place: Like a wheel, rolling all the time. One part on the ground when we get born and starts rolling. Stops rolling the trip is done. Some gets big wheel, some small one. Too much it happens Babies don't get any wheel of Life. You feel it when the wheel starts slowing, slows so much you feel like getting off the trip. Now it's close to time for my wheel to stop.

"You will know them of me and Mary who will be coming along. Tell them about La Push. About us. About tonight."

I looked at *Se-ic-tiss* unbelieving, did he mean he was dying?

"Ayy-y."

"Ain't you scared?" I asked.

"'Bout what?"

"Dying". What lay within coffins, inanimate and firm and snake-cool didn't appeal to me as the way I wanted to be.

"You ever died?" he asked.

I looked at him in bewilderment. "*Wahss!*" I answered firmly.

"How do you know that?" he asked.

"Know what?"

"You know you never die before ain't it." His face appeared soft and wise as he looked at me to attend my answer.

"I'm alive."

"What started you up?"

"Somethin'", I said.

"Spirit. Power of *Spirit*. Never go away. Animal (body) wear out pretty fast, one Lifetime then let Spirit loose. Gonna go somewhere, maybe beginning as Animal again. Who know about tomorrow? But *we know when the trail gettin' short*. That's where I am. Want you to remember it ain't the Animal I'm in that's the Power. The Power is what you know. When you need to talk to me, to any of them already gone Over There, talk to us, tell us you problem. Sit down where we got buried, tell us. It let our Spirit tell your Spirit the answer. From the beginning of when you come to be known to me it's been my Spirit talking to your Spirit, learning you about Life. Why should that stop because my Animal died? Animal only talk what Spirit tells it to say. Your ears hear it today, Spirit will talk to Spirit tomorrow. We been training you to hear it, Spirit. Keep listening.

"Going to stand on Horizon real soon. I been proud for how you want to be, told you stuff to help you get 'over there' (wise in our ways). You be a good *Tloquali* when you grow up I see." Then in soft sadness, "*Tloquali* getting to be less all the time you're getting older. Important strength for Life, *Tloquali*, don't forget it."

He stopped talking but rocked forth and back gently for several minutes. "OK, sing, drum for me now. You sing, drum for others when their spirit is tryna get outa body shell, then you helping to make it happen. Closer them get to crossin' the River, more they need drummin' to give help. Take Drum off hook over there. Sing me about *Sa-ats* coming home Fall of year."

His wife of an eternity came to the room and fed the heater. Her name was Mary. I don't know from which family She came, born before *Hoquat* arrival. She could have come from any Upriver family, or maybe Strawberry Point; Jackson Creek; Goodman Creek; Hoh River. She said, "Sing so he don't go until *cKwo-od* (Salal-berry) times," and She giggled. "He likes them *cKwo-od*, let's get him one more time with them." We laughed because we all saw *Se-ic-tiss* dropping into some berry patch and gorging on *Salal*. I drummed and sang about *Big* Salmon return, all *Sa-ats*, fat, ready for smoking, eggs perfect for eating, big heads for Salmon-head soup. Then about 'China Hats' out on *cKwalleh* rocks, including *Ahkalut*. Where the name 'China Hats' came from for Limpets I don't know, *Hoquat* word for their shape.

It was a kind of funeral song, more funereal, telling how China Hats hold to Rock with tenacity when *cKwalleh* left with Tide, all squeezing hard to Life support. Common around the world to Ocean creatures, Rock. No specific independence, like swimming Fish, for any until Tide comes in and the nourishing, flooding arrival of Ocean allows them the limited freedom of relaxing their stressed hold onto Mother Earth. It's about Living and dying in whatever way, a daily 'death' for them when tide is in and out, desparately tenacious every few hours, totally relaxed and getting nourishment every few hours. An important song from Uncle Yum who gave it to me when he gave blessing. *Se-ic-tiss* liked the drumming and singing. "He said, "*Leots-kal*," (thanks). "I felt Spirit" he said.

Weeks passed. The more feeble he became the happier he looked. "Got to leave. Only way I get to see them offspring what will be coming after I die", he said. "In Spirit world all is known, ain't no yesterday, today or tomorrow; just 'all'. Everything is known to Spirit World, that's where design for everything come from." It was said he had told someone on the day he left, "This is a good day to die".

Here sat *La wotsa kil* (Wolf) (in the blood line of 'Round', whose heart was covered with Wolf hair). When I'd asked Lavan Cole why *Se-ic-tiss* was called *La wotsa kil* he said it was because he was better at finding young Elk calves through their scent than even Wolves. "He find them an' talk to them about hiding out. Use to talk to Elk calves to 'obey your mother'." We saw the humor in that and laughed with the truth, realizing outsiders couldn't understand that we were proud of La wotsa kil's Power and knew it as fact. 'Ridiculous' to *Hoquat* but not to us.

Soon War came to fill the national cash-register again, our young men left to fight and die for their conqueror's success and *Se-ic-tiss* crossed the River.

I went to the drift-logs and cried racking sobs: I didn't want *Se-ic-tiss* to be hurt by Death, he was an Angel to me, to Village: Guide; advisor; encourager; friend: *Tloquali* Medicine Man, *CHAMPION!*

While I cried a sudden calm enveloped me and came the idea: *I* had had *Se-ic-tiss* for '*ho-cK tee*' (Friend), while I was a little boy. He never called me *Chutsk*, always '*ho-cK tee*'. *How lucky that I hadn't been born* after *he'd passed away!* I couldn't cry anymore because he was where he wanted to be. If I needed him all I had to do was talk to his Spirit and he'd answer mine. I knew it would be so, everything he'd ever told me had been true, why not this too?

Then an imperative of thought which Mary once told me, revisited. "Where ever someone of Blood-line is, Family Spirit remain. Like it says in Christian book, 'the Life is in the Blood'. Because the Life is in the Spirit from which it comes, then while that Blood remains the Spirit of the Family is ongoing. While you pass the Life of your Family you also passin' the Spirit. Life an' Spirit are in the Blood. Long from now you will know me an' *Se-ic-tiss* when you be together with our Family. Remember, when you talkin' to them you talkin' to us." That made me cry but it also pleased me: At this late date in my Life I still associate with Mary and *Se-ic-tiss* when I associate with their Family. Very deep satisfaction.

I accepted that Spirit talks to Spirit because I had seen the FACT. Separation wasn't any different than if he had gone to P.A. where I knew he was, and we had to communicate by Spirit. *Easy to understand.*

Now, however, I looked at the Elder men to see if I could see Death stalking them. I'd had enough of Mystery for a while. The Elder Women seemed *Eternal* so I didn't worry about them. Angels 'just transform' is what I concluded about *Women*.

The sorrow, I concluded, is over 'mystery', without explanation. (Billions of guesses, but no explanations). We equate our '*Animal*' with and as *Self*, and, where is Self without Animal? Not seeing the melding of the two to near-oneness wherein each depends upon other for 'animation' is fearsome. But to who sees Body as mortal and Spirit as immortal fear is not existent.

The sorrow, I concluded, also is from the realization that something, in the form of someone, will not be available to 'my' physical contact. It is like who goes to Beach expecting *Ahkalut* to be there. Suddenly a 'rock' one has come to depend upon for stability and balance is gone. *Where did Ahkalut go?* A stable point upon which to stand was taken away. Body, visibly gone or not, *Spirit continues.*

Trained that Spirit is all we've ever known of anyone/anything, any way, is to accept presence or absence with equal calm. 'Design' and 'object' are inseparable. The design exists in order to create 'the thing', whether the 'thing' *is* or not. To know the 'design' is to know the Spirit and to know the Spirit is to relate to the 'thing'. I learned this from *Se–ic–tiss* as I saw him begin to shrink in his form readying to '*cross Taboke*'.

Drumming came from everywhere in Village for the days it took to put him on the hill. To say his name no more for a year.

Today, meaning '*these* times', I know what he meant by 'seeing glimpses' of Horizon. When I was younger I'd thought I saw it occasionally but after having 'come over a rise' (open heart surgery) recently and caught a slight glimpse of *real* end Horizon, I know where *Se–ic–tiss* stood. This I've not seen before.

JAMES' LAKE and BIRDS

Old Man made a 'popping' sound to get ones attention. This was by way of opening the teeth behind closed lips and with sudden opening the sound made is somewhat like a 'popping' noise. I heard him in the back yard while it was still five a/m dark; *very* early for a boy under ten. I looked out into the dark back-yard and saw a form, darker than Earth Herself: Dr. Lester, (Old Man, *Byack*...truly my first authenticated Shaman acquaintance). I made the popping sound in answer. "*cKola*", he said in a hoarse whisper, and walked around the house to the front. Stealthier than a raiding mouse I was down the stairs and close to the door when *cKa* (Mother) whispered, "You goin' out with *Byack* get on warm coat chill out you get TB". I laughed quietly as She hugged me and kissed my forehead.

"Don't worry *cKa*', I said, "Won't get cold...I'm *Tloquali*".

"Ayy y", She whispered, "an' still a little boy too. Obey him so you be safe," She said.

Where do Mothers come from? I *KNOW* I was *mouse quiet...kadido was dog-asleepin'*, on his rug, unmoved. House was 'house asleep quiet'. My stockinged feet were unheard by me and, for whatever cause, I heard well. cKa must have heard beyond hearing.

Where do Mothers come from? Old Man's call was unnoticeable because it was 'just another Night sound', so how was She there to bless me? Later She said to me about that 'sense', "Mamas hear it in our Spirit." O.K. Mama, that 's good enough for me. I believe it.

We pushed his cKeynoo away from Mud-flats and started the up-River paddling to James' Mora Park. True to the Spirit wisdom of

Woman-kind it was indeed chill on this big-feeling but small eight or nine year old, but as *Byack* instructed, "Paddle hard you gonna get warm." Before we got to HobbiesMitt slough in fact, the coat.came off. We passed Rialto Beach bluff, rounded the turn and paddled on, past Sprowel's and Taylor's at Dicky River mouth.

As we had 'pushed' up-river, from across *Taboke* we could hear 'Old Al' (Hobbies Mitt hired man) calling to 'Silver', the Smith family Collie, as they drove cows to barn for milking. *cKa ayo* and *cKulell* and waking Birds now commanded Day, "Awaken!". They never stopped talking.

Seagulls followed cKeynoo upriver. They wheeled around, voices demanding from cKeynoo what they knew it oftentimes carried: Fish. Diving birds appeared on the shinny skin which was River-surface then dived quickly to escape whatever we were. The splendor of a new Day wakening to its Life thrilled me but by now my arms had tired. I was glad to get to James' place where we beached cKeynoo.

Here were cawing Crow flocks both up and down River. I watched Old Man as he listened to *cKa ayo*, cousin to *Byack*, Raven (whose language he understood).

"What they sayin'?" I asked.

"Got to be quite (quiet) lots of Birds over there." Meaning, 'we have to be quiet goin' t' James' lake because talk would frighten away many birds now at the lake'.

Bill and Dick James were feeding horses as we went by and together we walked a ways on the trail until they returned to the horses. From their house Stove smoke climbed a few feet into the air, then cooled, fell toward Earth and hung above ground eight or ten feet, wafting through trees and down River-bank to float as a mist six feet or so above River. Then, drifting toward La Push, it gradually dissolved. The smell was soft, 'homey', and I sucked it into my lungs relishing the feeling of 'security' it gave.

Now Dawn, on this Spring day, was chasing Night to China, which was 'over there'; daylight began to fill the holes Night tried to hide in and the day was now 'on'. Sun comes up, 'over there'.

We trudged along an open path-way past stumps now rotting into red-brown flesh; heard Grouse thumping; *T'dayokes* drilling holes into old wood; ahead of us at Lake, Duck and Geese talked incessantly, flew away, circled back, talking to friend and foe alike: 'It's me! Let's eat!'

All preparing for their journey North. Kingfisher called from branch to branch, privately discussing the invasion by these 'others'.

One purposely made human path led a quarter-mile through Ferns, Devils Club, green-budding Alder, forty-year old stumps, all shielding us nearly to the lake. A downed tree, one end on the bank, the other in the lake hosting Ducks which had 'hopped' onto it, off of it, swimming around near-submerged branches and when we entered their awareness 'so brazenly', they jumped to Lake tails twitching, they scolded us, then, in their fashion, they stood on their 'rumps' and left for other 'beach sites', where something new would catch their attention

We were there to learn more Bird talk and *Byack* 'shushed' me, pointed to a place I was to sit, then he became still. Soon he was no more intruder than a stump. I, (*Tloquali* don't forget), emulated this Elder (born before Lincoln was president of those United States).

I watched him as he stared at a place, letting action fill his eye, not moving, seeking action. I did it too.

Then he 'popped' his lips and I looked to him. He was looking toward the end of Lake to our right. For the time we'd been here a 'Canadasonker' (a 'Sonker,[a Canada's Honker]) had been flying; swimming; calling. Periodically it would fly away, "Goin' next pond", *Byack* said. I asked why. It flew toward Prairie.

"Lookin' for it mate", he said. Then, to our left another Goose was talking to everyone, swimming the edges of the lake, into 'coves', (formed by downed trees laying partly in and out of the water), swimming through grasses growing thickly from bank into lake; calling the while as if a name, endlessly repeated. "Somebody got lost", *Byack* said.

We watched this and the Ducks, and watched what they did as they 'said' one thing or other, indeed, I saw, they *were* talking. Definitely. About an hour after we'd arrived the first 'Sonker landed on the end of Lake toward East and continued its honking. From the bird to our left at the opposite end of Lake suddenly its calls were answered and the two began to scream at one another, swimming and half flying and 'honking' wildly. The closer they got to one another the louder, the more frantic their effort to dissolve distance and then they were together. With necks laid onto one another's backs, bills pointed upwards and crying sounds mixed with almost trumpet-like blasts they said all I needed to know about 'simple birds'. Around and around one another they swam, so happy to have found one another that no attention to us or other birds was involved. For eight or ten minutes this joyous reunion went on then away they went, side by side to feed at the 'east' end of Lake, muzzling one another frequently as they began bulk regaining. I grinned until I thought my face would break. So did *Byack*. We were elated to have witnessed a pair which had lost mates, how long ago we couldn't know but *Byack* said, "Probably month or so."

"Mr. and Mrs. Goose," *Byack* continued. "Been looking long time. See how they both look skinny, not like other ones? Dull? Ain't been eatin'. Them get married Life time. Nobody or nothin' else make no difference. They gonna be OK now. When I heard first one callin' mates name I know it got apart somehow, maybe in storm or somethin'. How many of 'em dies of broke heart nobody knows, but they need one another same like us, like me an' Molly." Then, as we watched, they stopped eating simultaneously and moved to stand, one legged, on a water-held log. Finally, their heads were under wing and joyous exhaustion took over, the long, tiring search, the anguish, gone. *Byack* popped his lips and indicated a direction for us to go to leave the pair and the other Birds to themselves.

As we walked back toward James' Mora Park Old Man said, "Learn from them two. When you Animal (Body) tell you it need rest, Mind and Body, REST IT. That's what they done. What do non-Two-leggeds got (have) to teach us? The way which ain't been planned. Do what other kinds do and learn."

I learned to pay attention to all the sounds from Woods and Lake. Same way as what I learned with Morton Penn along Surf when I went to learn how Baby Surf birds are called by their Mothers.

"Everything has some kinda talk (language) to let other ones know what they think. Same thing like us. *cKa-ayo* says stuff other ones hear, act how the one's words tell about."

How sad is the loss of the knowledge of Life's *own*, *un*human-ized realities. '*Civili*zed man' will never know the Truth of how 'lesser' creatures live.

MORE LODGE MEETING
and TALK

Again I asked why I was met at 'Skoobus' by one of the Elders so often. Charlie Howeattle who had just met me at Rosy Black's corner cupped his hand over his ear, (his *ahlecsat*), and said, "*cKokalli*," (listen).

From Baseball-corner Lodge the throb of drums, singing. A 'meeting!' I was on my way. As I tugged at Charlie's hand for speed he said, "Talkin' will be TommyPayne. *cKokalli* (listen hard) tonight. Wants you to hear about some other time comin'. You'll see it. *We* (Elders) won't see it."

Laughter in Lodge meant TommyPayne had said something they inside had reacted to. TommyPayne had a wondrous sense of humor and just now he had used it I guessed.

I had no idea of the life-long impression this evening's Lodge meeting would become. I looked at the circle of Elders. This was important. Lavan Coe; Old Man (*Byack*); Mock Williams; Esau Penn; Jack and Eli Ward; Tyler Hobucket; Charlie; Grant Eastman; *Se–ic-tiss* Ward; Joe Pullen, Willi Wilasie...I was shocked by this impressive group...Major Men of Village. I remember at least a dozen Men gathered. I can't remember whether Fred Woodruff and Daniel White were there. Stanley Gray began drumming and singing and the rest joined in. I joined with rhythm sticks...I had no drum yet.

When drumming stopped Mock Williams stood and said to me, "You got to carry this (information) with you rest of you Life. This is about after *Hoquat*s get gone and *Po–oke* way of Life get to be brought back. We telling you so you understand when the time comes for *Ho-*

quat disaster. We telling you tonight 'what and why' 'bout *Hoquat* failure."

I stared at him: *What? Hoquat* owned the lands from side to side and top to bottom. I said, "They got army full of airplanes; thousand soldiers...what's gonna beat *Hoquat?*" I was dubious.

Charlie Howeattle beat his drum and sang a 'vision' song...what he 'saw'. As answer to my question, ('What can beat *Hoquat*') Charlie sang, "Theirself. Greedy without end gonna destroy their world." He stopped drumming and said, "Got to be ready, let who come after us to this place know there's difference between *Greed* and *Generous*. What we goan (going) tell you here tonight about laws Nature put there for food an' stuff to be for all time. *Hoquat way comin' to end, (in) you lifetime.*"

"How *that* comes out?" 'Tell me' eagerness shook me. Both eager and anxious, I awaited this teaching-to-come ...how could the Commercial World on which we were *dependent absolutely* come to grief and not include us?

"Great Spirit put all together, then comes *cKwyeh-Tee* rearranged it for the People who were to come to Earth, Bird People; Snake People; Fish (*ahleetah*) People; *Yoksi* (rock); *cKwia; cKwyeh-Tee* fixed it up to Balance up for us. Us all," he said sweeping his arm to indicate 'for all things', "Life's like cKeynoo: Ev'rythin' balanced no problem. Get it out of balance it get to be dangerous for who ridin' it. More out of balance less it can do its job. Finally it capsize and what it carried, protected, supported ain't got no cKeynoo, safe like it was. Now you become you own cKeynoo."

I caught a picture of the problem with cKeynoo but how did that apply to *Hoquat* world I asked.

"Great Spirit", (that's God). " Ev'rythin' exist because God gived rules for how to be., what to be. (If 'it') ain't one of God's rules, 'it' ain't there. All which is come because of law for 'being', same like recipe for cake or bread or stink-eggs. What to be, how to be, all come from Great Spirit. *It can't be separate* from anything which is. Nothing can't be apart from Law for 'how to be'."

Mock Williams put up both hands to say something. "Problem is *money*." He spat out the word. It surprised me because he wasn't the kind to be negative. Like Chester Johnson, I never saw an unsmiling 'Mock'. "We seen it from when it got brought here first...*kill* stuff an' sell it. Killin' *Hawayishka* (deer) to sell to fancy-hotel cafe, don't need the meat need money and lots. Otters. Destroy stuff God made an' fixed up for Earth to live in balance. In order to get money, to get more an' more, nobody need that much.

"When *Habit* come, makin' money to buy stuff get to be growing *Habit*. Then caution for Life things goes. *Any*thing is victim of Money. More an' more *Hoquat* world converts living stuff into dollars more an' more problems developin'. All them things which lives grow only so fast. (The) more human people convert Life-stuff to dollars the more problem comin'. Goin' to see even *cKwalleh* (Ocean) getting' sick. Ev'rything out there belong to *cKwalleh*: *cKwalla* (whale); *Ahleetah*; Cedar Tree; Snow…all depend on *cKwalleh*. When *cKwalleh* getting sick Whales ain't got no food. Stuff eatin' other stuff all the time in Ocean. Somebody ain't got no food what happenin'? Start breakin' up The Chain. Turnin' Ocean stuff into *Money*, alla time *more* Money, more Money. Too many links comin' out. Them workin' the Woods, towin' out logs, know what happen when a link come out of the chain."

Grant said, "Our kind (human) is enemy to ev'rythin' else. We don't have a mind's-eye to see the damage because *'what's out there'* is natural for who is here now. We grow up into a way of being without bein' able to compare what's goin' on now with what it should be to be healthy. If you ain't seen the huge forest you can't know what Nature lost. Way trees look they don't look like living People but they breath in and out too. Go past Neah Bay on Straits, towards PA (Port Angeles), see Mist hangin' around through Trees…*that's their breath*! They're living People of *their* kind."

I wondered. 'Breath?' I wondered. "They ain't got no lungs have they?"

"Ayy-y. (They) Look like animal lungs turned inside out. Air goin' *into* us breathin', but Air breathin' *through* leaves of their kind. All them leaves stretchin' for air. (You turn all that *inside* it get to be lungs. Same stretchin' for air). Tree ain't got no muscles so air blows around their 'lungs', muscles pumps it in for us." I wondered, "How are they People? They don't got no brains have they?"

"Ay-y-y. You feel heat too much what do you do?"

"Pull away."

"Ay-y-y. Same with Tree. Fire come they feel it and shrivel leaves for protection. Like with no water. They start reachin' for it, roots deeper, leaves open waitin'. Ain't inventin' nothin' but they got to 'know' 'bout survivin', they doin' that stuff. They're people of their kind, same as all things. Survival 'thinkin'' built in.

"Things all depend on each other an' somethin' depend on Tree breath. Gone, Tree breath ain't there for what need it, an' *that* croak. Remember what we tell you about *Balance*. Long before human-kind come to this place (Earth) only Mother Earth got rid of stuff, earthquick (earthquake), flood, no rain, things like that. Forest fires eatin' Trees. Exactly what was needed for to keep up *The Balance*. Balance wasn't monkeyed with like from humans. Now we figure we're smarter'n Her an' don't have to obey Her rules for how to keep Life strong. Including us. What you gonna see is *way too many humans*, eatin' like Rats all which come before them or 'choppin' it down' to sell for money. Money can't cure the problem of hungry people because of too many an' too greedy. More you take of Earth's garden less there's goin' to be of it. Sometime soon it's gone.

"Then there come war like you never figured, more an' more humans. Less an' less their God money an' what to convert to money. *They gonna be eatin' each other*! That's why *you* got to know how to survive, let them who's comin' next know about *balanced way to live*, obeyin' laws for the *plenty* Mother Earth figured out. You change the way She operates you goin' to get different stuff to face. You won't like it. Her way made food and what all need to exist. Men turnin' the ground to brass like *Hoquat* book tells about.

"Them old bible people who wrote that could see Reason bein' balanced with Life. What learns (teaches) you 'bout Balance? Yourself. All you got to do to find the Life's way is ask, 'Is what I'm gonna do something Great Spirit needs done, or *cKwyeh-Tee*, or what my greed wants me to do'. If you are honest you can tell the answer right now, livin' in Balance, if you know between what we all Need for Living or what we Want."

" *cKulell*, you 'bout twelve now ain't it. You goin' to see more people on Earth than She need. You goin' to see less Trees, less Iron from the ground, less gas for automobiles to drink to move. Pay attention to how you been living at this place and remember it all. DON'T NEVER FORGET HOW YOU LIVED AS CHILD, SIMPLE, HELPFUL, *STURDY, FOR THE PEOPLE TO COME*, of ev'ry kind."

TommyPayne was like Little Bill (Uncle Yum) Penn, he could think in English and *Po-oke* languages, also Chinok, apparently equally. One Fourth of July I saw him talking in Chinook to Wesley Smith.

Probably 1936. Blew me away to see them understand that strange sounding talk. This night when he raised his hands we all turned to him to listen.

He said, "We see results of *Hoquat* ways, reckless with Life. Arrogant towards *Great Spirit's* laws same time they pray for plenty more money. You got to remember *cKwyeh-Tee's* laws for plenty are obeyed only with the work-help of who needs what's provided. You don't waste Life for fun or profit. Life ain't *ours* to play with. When our reckless thinking destroys homes and Life places of creatures besides two-leggeds ev'rybody is put in danger. Remember you heard Danger is of Anger. *They* don't know it maybe, but *we* can *think* about what happen when the Live Things start to diminish in number. Less of Life means less Life. Diminishing Life. That won't come along for us as long as all the other things are there for us, us for them, to Live by/ according to *cKwyeh-Tee's* laws. You waste, you die. When Life things can't reproduce enough to keep up with what we kill and destroy for Money then suddenly there be less of them, dyin' from bein' sick like *Small-pox* come, silent; deadly. Life gets to be more, or less, it don't stay same ever.

"Small-pox of Mother Earth. Us.

"They gonna run around with guns, gangs is, all rangin' like Cougar, to find what can be made into food, even other Two Leggeds. Robbin' the home of weaker Two Leggeds. You got problems ahead. So, you be hid where those who ain't self-sufficient can't Live. That's the safe place to be. Hidin' out on Coast someplace. Nobody know you're there nobody come for what you got."

"Keepin' 'love' for Life (respect for it, protection of it, dependence on it without question, so as to nurture it), this is what you got to learn. You got to learn about plants an' what's safe or not. For instance remember where is the Halibuts hole to bring fish from if any are left (an' they volunteer to help you). 'f you got a message to carry to tomorrow; it's comin' from yesterday." We drummed and sang and went our ways.

WALTER PAYNE

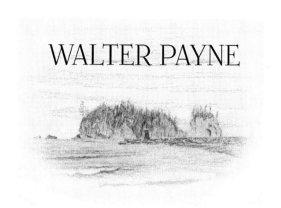

One August I came into possession of a 'Street and Smith's Western' magazine…which I was not encouraged to read because it showed 'gun' as way to justice. I went to Drift Logs to find a hidden, sun-warmed hide-away to read when I came across Walter Payne pouring gas into his drag-saw tank.

"Goin' to be readin' 'bout how come the good guys won an' bad Indians lost ain't it," he said and laughed. "Lots action in them 'venture magazines ain't it."

So far I hadn't read one but the temptation of the forbidden beckoned. I answered that I didn't know yet, "…never read one."

Walter capped the gas tank and can and said, "Easy readin'. Guy allus gets justice pullin' his gun from his pocket an' '*shootin' to kill*". At which he laughed. "Easy readin' *cKulell*, biggest words there no bigger than 'hungry', or '*fast-on-the-draw*'. Maybe you read it easy your age. When I was twelve I could."

Somehow it all surprised me because I hadn't thought of Wally as a'reader'. He was husband and father and son and brother, and fisherman, log-cutter, fish-smoking expert, (as was his sister Rosy [Mrs. Roy] Black), cKeynoo builder. Why would a Child think of someone not seen performing some act as capable of performing the act? I'd not thought about it and here was Wally telling me about his knowledge of cowboy-magazines.

Not thinking about the question my statement would bring I said, "Dint know you could read." He looked at me quizzically, scowled almost imperceptibly, then stood from the kneeling position he'd been in. Suddenly he laughed. He gave his head a 'direction' nod and said, "*Dehocks*", (sit). I sat on the log he'd indicated and looked at him.

"You ever seen hand-writing by Tyler? (Hobucket). Most beautiful hand they ever seen, they said at school."

This was Walter Payne. Son of Elsa and Thomas Payne, (some of the '*biggest*' *Po-oke* of Village). Walter's children were as I, just starting in Life. As with all adults (always bossing kids around) I'd not thought of Walter as a conversant for a kid. He sat on another drift-log and continued. "Any Indian born after Smith got here, (A. Wesley and kin), knows how to read and write a little bit. We was more interested in huntin' and fishin' and doin' Village work than to get schooling." I understood that urge very well. "Them 'parents' of ours was the first Quileutes ever to learn readin' an' writin'. Tyler lived with Ollie (Oliver) Smith an' learned to be office worker. I got educated to do carpenter work, same like Gideon Bright who was teachin' me. He was taught by WesleesMitts (A. Wesley) an' them. Rex (Ward) learned to read an' write like *Hoquats*, him an' Jack an' Eli. Wards was good with education. Look at Kenneth and Vera. Sick as kids but they learn anyways. Rex yoos to (used to) write for Hudson's La Push newspaper. We *all* got educated to do 'white' stuff."

I must have jerked around to hear about 'La Push newspaper'. "Newspaper?" What I thought of as newspapers were Forks Forum; P.A. Paper; P.I.

"I'll give you a old one, from early 1900 for you to read about. Story there by Rex Ward."

I absorbed this while thinking about what a difference booze makes in a person. Sober, Wally was a *very likeable man*, I could see, but he drank booze. (I had asked Billy Hudson why Wally boozed and he said, [as he did about many people], "That's his habit).") I analyzed this interesting man's features and had to agree with people, he was nice looking. He had no scars nor broken nose nor tooth-less grin to offer. Smiling, he was a nice man to talk to. Thus purveying I was brought to the reality of our moment when he said, as if reading my mind, "How come we don't do nothin' with the education what's s'posta make us more 'civilized' come to your mind ain't it."

I said, "Only *Po-oke* workin' *Hoquat* jobs is loggers, fishermen, stuff like that. How come Tyler ain't workin' in a office or something?" I hadn't yet seen the ongoing job prejudices.

Wally laughed, as at a Laurel and Hardy movie, belly laughs of amusement. "Ayy-y-y! How come?" A pause, then, "They took away our own way of living an' trained us their way so we could be equal. When 'we got equal' nobody would hire us. Daniel (White) an' Mrs. would get hired *to do labor*! DANIEL an' MRS. WHITE! Servants to *Hoquats* to do laundry, stack firewood, 'gut' salmons, *the Whites*! Same thing Mars sends folks down an' king of inglun (England) washes their laundry, cooks. In Indian culture the Whites was like royal people for what they did, but they didn't know the *Hoquat* way as good as we who was born *after Hoquats* got here. Hired our Mothers and Fathers for what yoos (used) to be slaves' work. At 'boarding school' first they beat on 'em. Then on us to learn."

True to temptation, Wally could no longer tolerate merely looking at some inviting round, flat rocks. He stood and began gathering 'skimmers' and said, "*Taboke Keedack-sadlo*, (let's go to River) skim rocks. I joined in the gathering, a dozen or so nice 'skimmers' and we headed for River side of jetty.

Wally continued talk/muse as we walked. Almost to himself he muttered his thoughts. "How come we don't do nothing with the learning'? Me, I tried to start house jobs, here to Forks, down to Bogachiel Park, up to Beaver. Spent Tommy's (Dad's) money to get ad in Forks Forum. Cost too. Cost about $1.75 for the month." He shook his head. "He worked for fish buyers two dollars a day. They'd load fall fish into cKeynoo, run'em out through Surf at Rialto Beach to some fish-tender. I was tryin' to get business goin' so I couldn't do fish-work. Tommy done that an' used half day wages for ad."

"What happen?" I asked. He turned and looked at me quizzically. I saw that he was being saddened by his memory and I was about to change the subject when he said, "Ayy-y. What happen?" As we walked he scribed some meaningless lines into Sand with a stick, and said again, "What happen." After a while, as he was looking over *Taboke* his back straightened and he pulled a deep breath. Then, back from wherever he'd been he turned toward me again. " *cKulell*, what happen was we got beat." That dealt with our land-loss. "What about you?" I asked.

"Me? *Nobody* answer the ad. Then I tried bein' fish-dealer but them in Hokyum, 'Berdine, the 'Sound' cities (Seattle, Tacoma, Evert) wouldn't discuss how we could work together; Indian don't know business they said. Tried to get advice from 'Aunt BIA' (Bureau of Indian Affairs), 'We'll see what we can do.' Long about then I got drunk one time an' ev'rything what was happening only made me mad and I got to be mean, same's you gettin' now. Took to boozin'. Stay away from booze.

"No, none of us successful 'cept as *drunk* Indians. Succeeded at that. I'd allus hoped I'd have good business, buy good car, good house, good clothes for Mrs. an' them kids, good school so's my kids would get respect in their Life path. Nothin' worked. Aunt Bia did nothing. But suppress us. Their job by design: No help." He stopped and put his hand on my shoulder to stop me. "Look. Down at Timber claim (Indian Quinault Timber allotment) we get $4.00 for stumpage, RIGHT NEXT TO US, SAME TREES, *Hoquat* owner gets $13.00. Ain't honest but it's legal. Hey! How they get the Olympic Peninsula without they stealin' it? No surprises. Treacherous is treacherous. So when *'Allotment'* comes we stan' there drunk hands out. 'We got pride too you know' we wanted to say but *had to take the allotment.* What else give us some money? *Hoquat* jobs?"

We stopped at *Taboke* to skim rocks. Wally wasn't as good as Tyler but was far better than I. "Lots of big talk, *cKulell, 'look what we're doin' for 'the Indian'* they keep sayin' in their church an' places. Listen to the Smiths. "We makin' *Humans* out of 'em they say." Then, "So's they can get to Heaven from 'bein' godly." The same bitter laugh.

"Wally," I said, "How come this happens?"

"They compete for getting the most. We don't understand *that,* way they do. Except where nobody get hurt like cKeynoo racin' compete. We help ev'rybody so's all gain. We don't know how to do it that way like them. That's their Life-style an' we ain't learned' it. Once after another of *failing* whatever you do make you sad. Can't Live their way, can't Live ours."

I had a question. "What's 'Life-style'?"

"Nothing alive ain't got 'Life-style'. That's the way they are; behaves.

'*WiedocKt-sie*' got Life-style different from *Hawayishka* (doe-deer)."

"What 's '*wiedocKt-sie*'?"

He laughed. "You don't know word for Cougars?" Then, "Too much of words, with lots of languages." He paused to think, as was his way. From his wood cutting he'd taken a long sliver of word and chewed on it, put it between his teeth. He scanned Sky, Surf, Bluff where Raven soared. Then, "Life style means what *cKwyeh-Tee* put into stuff for how it's gonna behave. *Hoquat* got different stuff put in, ain't in us. 'S why we're different from them way we behave. When your own 'behave' get took away you come up empty." Then specifically to me, "*You look* like *Hoquat*, who knows if their way an' our way ain't both of 'em in you. Maybe you be happy, livin' like them I don't think so. We Live to Live, they Live to gain. That's 'Life-Style'. You already learned 'helpin'"

Thinking about this I recalled 'broken stride'. I blurted "Stride gets broke, ain't it." I thought of Billy Hudson. He'd talked about the Woman who pawned the Eagle Feather Rain cape for booze money. Short days later they couldn't find it in the shop. Priceless treasure for Quileute…the only treasure left after first houses in front of the 'bluff' got burned out. On 'flat' below Coast Guards. Gone.

He smiled at me. "Ayy-y-y", almost a sigh, a long drawn-out 'ayy'. Then, "*cKulell*, you gonna have problems. White skin, red-hair like that you look *Hoquat* so they (*Hoquat*) think you are one but they never goin' to accept you account of your *invisible* person. You are *Indian in white cover*. *Hoquat*s won't none understand why you so different and Indians won't understand 'cause you don't act '*Hoquat*'. *Between* the two skins *you* are invisible, *nobody won't* ever see *you*. Either way you marry, *Po-oke* or *Hoquat*, trouble for you ahead. Only kind what can understand is them like you, full nothin' and half somethin'. Problem. Porky he's same way. Beans. (Porky's brother). You. Look how many we got now half an' half.

"I had to give up tryna be 'big business man' an' work some times like at *harvest* with farmers, or fish with *Hoquat* fishermen if fishin's good. Come into our land, make living, an' maybe give us few cents work for them. I made 'habit of *loser*' into way of Life. All over the world many people do that." He waved his 'all over the world' arm. "I done good at failin' an' that become my excuse for boozin'. Kills my whole family w'en I get drunk but pain of *sober* is more pain than I can stand most of the time." Clouds came.

We skipped rocks a while, then, no longer warm from unclouded Sky the chill came which said Rain was moving toward us. I never learned which cowboy out shot his enemy and the magazine was lost to my attention and memory.

Years later I was thinking about Walter's sorrow and anger. I realized it was a condition for the 'older ones' throughout Village. Doles and handouts and restrictions by way of the unknown condition called 'legal system' had taken the freedom of self-determination from *Po-*

oke…in North and South America both. And where else on Earth? India? China?

Explorers with the Gun, for Go'd (Gold).

TWILIGHT

When Uncle Yum and I roamed the land in 1958 savoring the last of the Elder influences, Charlie Howeattle finishing a cKeynoo; Agnes Penn (Ag-Ag) with Sarah Woodruff crafting baskets; someone cutting wood on Beach; when we roamed from Hoh Village to Neah Bay, Ozette and Cape Alava, trying to 'suck in the Spirit that had caused us', we played an act of happiness. But both of us were sad I realize now.

As was the way in past times, the Elder takes the hand of the learning 'youth' be it male or female, emphasizing important guidance for Life with a squeeze and a statement, and to have the contact of protection for the young hand in the hand of the Elder, Uncle Yum took my hand and we walked Hoh Beach. I was soon to leave for California and we knew we would not meet again. His hand was soft and warm and he pressed to emphasize 'points', the Elder and the Youth. A sadness gripped my heart unknown before or since, (I loved 'true' Elders almost with worship). Uncle Yum and I talked, 'next year I was to return and together we would carve a cKeynoo'. I would work and save money for a Cedar log from some mill, "Maybe four, five hundred dollars, good one," he said.

We stood on Hoh Beach looking north toward Hoh Head and Uncle Yum said that *Po-oke* had had a trail to La Push which few remembered but which had been an Indian 'highway' for years without numbers.

"Always looked out for *Dawskaiyah* when I'd come down the trail with my parents to Hoh."

"*Chi-ila* (Uncle), What about *Dawskaiyah*? I was scared to move most of the time when I was a kid."

He laughed and said, "You an' ev'ry Chu-utsk ever born! She was call Witch Woman in English. Witch Woman of the Hoh. But She comes by any place She wantsta (wants to). Lived far up Hoh River close to Rain Forest. She would swing...swing in there. Little kids would...kids, you know, She would fatten it up to roast it. She would swing an' make them kids get hungry workin' pushin' the swing. People always tried to catch up with Her an' this swing was a lo-o-ong one... they'd follow it...wa-a-a-ay out into Rain Forest an' then She'd get to the end of the swing an' come back...leave it (them) there. They get lost. They get left in there when She head back an' they get left. You can't find you way in there because light cause no shadows...always just like it's glowin'...only glowin'.

"Many of the People died like that. Tryin' to catch the Woman. They was tryin' to kill Her to save their children.

"Once in a while they could see Her runnin'. Runnin'. Just black clothes when She dodges behind a tree. They see Her an' then She just disappear. They would tell the children to look out an' obey or else She'd find it...find them...She always come an' took them children which was bad." ('Bad' was disobeying, roaming to the woods, *Taboke*). "She'll find it an' take it to the Rain Forest an' then roast it on the fire. My Grandparents used to tell me all the time, 'If you don't be good we gonna give you to the Witch Woman.' *Then* you was good. His laughter floated into the little Hoh Village and children giggled.

"So She'd disappear...disappear. Once you'd see it an' then disappear. Well, anyway, She had this cage filled up with this little children...getting it fat. She was doin' this swingin' an' laughin', trying to get more to follow Her into the Rain Forest. If they did follow She'd get them lost, see.

"Well, one time She got...now She's getting' old an' She can't see too good...She got this man who is not too big...an' he had the power to change himself to a young looking person (*cKwyeh-Tee?*). An' he is skinny. So She said, 'You push me...you push me on that swing...I want you to push me. You got to get fat, you too skinny for...roastin'.' She had his arm see, an' it's skinny an' hard. 'You push me easy...not hard...just easy on that swing so you get hungry an' eat an' sleep a lot.'

"That's what this man wanted. He done...he done it on purpose, he let Her catch him on purpose. He knew She'd get him to push

Her. So anyway, he's pushin' Her real easy on that swing...re-e-e-eal e-e-easy. She was laughin' an' shriekin' an' trying to get people to follow Her. She's relaxed, see. Suddenly he makes a big leap an' gives a powerful push an' snaps the swing quick. It goes so fast She loses Her hands on it an' it leaves this Witch Woman behind...She falls out of it, from high up...high up an' She breaks Her head.

"Well, anyway he lets all the children out of the cages an' they come back home to their parents."

"*Chi-ila,* has anyone recorded all the *Po-oke* histories?"

"Some. Not all by no means...hundreds of them was part of the culture for to lay down laws for behavior. I know a lot of stories which was left to me...gifted to me to keep an' pass to tomorrow's people. There is lots of them...I got lots of legends to give you..I'll come down to your home an' give them to you." Uncle Yum smiled as he anticipated going south to California. "At 65 it's still not to late to travel," he said.

It was afternoon now, Fall was sneaking in and we felt it. Behind us Children saved from *Dawskaiyah* shrieked and ran and came by us to see what we might offer for amusement, but left shortly because we were no fun.

A smoke-shed wafted smoke out into the sky as Smelt hung from gills, the youngsters tending the smoke-fire, mentally hurrying the process...they were as much addicted to smoke fish as I...perhaps more.

A cKeynoo resting against a house emptied of children and then refilled and then emptied again, a game of tag of their own making. Uncle Yum and I watched someone in a cKeynoo near the sanded mouth of Hoh River, he perhaps thinking of the centuries of this historical action soon to be no more. I watched, wishing I could be here with these, my people, to be the natural person I'd been guided to be while I was here, on our Coast. Then, as if on cue we stood and looked seaward, hundreds of sea-birds rushed north to south and back, diving, stretching, shaking, then diving again.

I wouldn't see this at Albion, to which I must return soon, so I tried to absorb the day, the time I had spent here among *Po-oke* of passing lives. Then Uncle Yum said, "Remember us Howard, talk to them (outsiders) about what we was. We're almost gone now. Many got the story of *Po-oke* in some form or another but you got born here, learned, then got *Hoquat* education in Seattle. Keep us in your heart an' tell about us. They got us with our backs to *cKwalleh*, we're standin' knee deep in it now, with no further place to go."

We walked to the house he stayed in at Hoh and he got his father's two medicine poles to give to me for safe keeping. "You take care of them until my children ask for them". His children had both died in 1918's flu scourge.

"Take me to La Push now Howard. You goin' to leave tomorrow. You got to go to Richwine's an' pack."

We returned to La Push and Uncle Yum said, "Warmer here ain't it. Go to drift-logs a minute."

The evening was warm and we sat on a drift-log below River mouth looking toward *Ahkalut*. Another beautiful Coastal twilight.

"How many *Po-oke* do you suppose have lived and died here? How many Quileute have known *Ahkalut*?" I asked.

"I don't know," he answered, "many hundreds when we lived on the branches of the Salmon Tree. But I know there won't be many more. You know, there are only a few of us now…let's see…must be less than two dozen…who know the languages good enough to talk both equal."

"Uncle", I said, "what's 'Salmon Tree?"

"Quillayute River. Short river up to Bockaheel, Soulduck, then other rivers are like tree branches…all full of Salmons in their time to travel…Salmon Tree. *Po-oke* lived in the branches of Salmon Tree. *Taboke* is laid out like a tree with branches full of Salmons."

"Salmons maybe come back," I said in hope.

His eyes were moist. "*Wahss* (no)," he whispered sadly, looking seaward.

We watched the outboard motor boats returning from fishing out between the rocks, where for centuries *Po-oke* had fished. There were no cKeynoo now though, only the outboard-boats, aluminum or glass; or plywood.

As is the glory of clear late Summer evenings there, Sun dropped behind *Ahkalut*. In the brilliant yellow-orange sky a cloud shaped like a bird hung, just above the Horizon. "Let's lissen for Music of Sunset Uncle Yum", I said, "Another twilight on *Ahkalut*."

Little Bill, (Uncle Yum, *Chi-ila*), looked toward the bird-shaped cloud, thinking his own private thoughts. Then almost whispering said, "Wahss, I'm afraid it's Twilight on the Thunderbird."

I've done what I can Chi-ila.

HA-ATCH TLAKS ALA, Po-oke. Chi-ila

About the author

HOWARD HANSEN (*cKULELL*) lives in the Ballard neighborhood of Seattle.